Suzanne Lenglen
Tennis Idol of the Twenties

Suzanne Lenglen
Tennis Idol of the Twenties

Alan Little

First published 1988
This revised edition published 2007

Published by
Wimbledon Lawn Tennis Museum,
All England Lawn Tennis Club,
Church Road, Wimbledon,
London, SW19 5AE.

Copyright © Alan Little and Wimbledon Lawn Tennis Museum, 2007

ISBN 0 906741 43 2

Designed by Roger Walker
Typeset in Optima and Electra

Printed and bound in Great Britain by
L&S Printing Company Limited,
Worthing, West Sussex

FRONTISPIECE
Portrait of Suzanne Lenglen (National Portrait Gallery, London)

Contents

Acknowledgements	vi
Introduction	vii
Early Days	1
1919	13
1920	23
1921	31
1922	41
1923	51
1924	59
1925	65
1926	75
A Professional	93
The Quiet Years	117
The Principal Characters	127
Records	131
Index	213

Acknowledgements

Many people in many ways have made a contribution to this book which I wish to acknowledge. General assistance has been given by Manuel Adrio of Madrid, Gianni Clerici of Como, Doris Colley of London, Hermann Fuchs of Vienna, Joe Ledgerton of Dunmow, Savina Lukiardopulo of London, Frank Phelps of Avon, National Film and Television Archive, London, Blackpool Football Club, Manchester United Football Club, Queen's Park Football Club, Glasgow, The Rank Organisation plc, London and Selfridges, London.

The compilation of the records section, listing tournaments and exhibition details, has been a labour of love over untold years, involving scores of friends. The production of the Professional tour results would not have been possible without the tireless enthusiasm of Richard C. Hillway of Colorado Springs, USA who never waned in the year or two he spent enquiring all over North America to complete the task. This really was virgin ground. His co-operation on this project gave me much pleasure and a friend for life. I am also very grateful to others who contributed to the results section – Odanis Calrates Aeosta of Havana, Dominique Arot of Lille, Gill Barton of Cobham, John Beddington of Checkendon, Lorna Cawthorn of Malaga, Jean-Loup Coignard of Paris, Bud Collins of Boston, Alain Delaqueriere of New York, Scott Ehrig-Burgess of San Diego, Geoffrey Felder of New York, Robert Geist of Vienna, David Godfree of Sheen, Pedro Hernandez of Barcelona, Richard Jones of Wimbledon, N Kandelaft of Amiens, Jan Kodes of Prague, Marc Lasry of Paris, Brigitte Lust of the Federation Royale Belge de Tennis, Brussels, Jim McManus of Jacksonville, Michala Rossi of Rome, Michel Sutter of Paris and Regine Tourres of Paris.

Thanks go to the staff at Wimbledon Lawn Tennis Museum who worked so hard on the production – Assistant Librarian Audrey Snell and Rosabel Richards, who both gave continuous support, Kay Crooks, Linda French and Maggie Henderson. I also well recognise the skill of the designer of this book, Roger Walker.

Alan Little

Introduction

Suzanne Lenglen, the legendary French lawn tennis player, died in Paris on 4th July, 1938. For eight years after the First World War she completely dominated the scene with a game that had been tuned to perfection.

Although born in Paris in 1899, Suzanne spent her childhood winters with her parents in Nice, where she made her home for the next fifteen years before settling back in Paris. Suzanne's father was constantly her mentor and trainer and undoubtedly was responsible for her great success. She immediately shot to fame in 1919 when, at Wimbledon, she defeated the seven times champion, Mrs Dorothea Chambers, in an exciting Challenge Round, watched by the King and Queen of England. Remarkably this was the very first tournament she played on grass.

To some she was the greatest lady player ever. Whether this is true is open to conjecture, but what is certain is that during her adult career she towered above all her contemporaries and no one can ask more.

During this period most of Suzanne's opponents measured their success in singles by the number of points they won. If they played extremely well they would count the number of games. Three were able to claim a set, but only one a match. Nine times Suzanne won a singles title at a tournament without dropping a game.

At The Championships at Wimbledon, Suzanne won the Ladies' Singles and Doubles Championships six times and the Mixed Doubles Championship on three occasions. On the Continent she captured hundreds of titles, including 19 at the French Championships, six in the Ladies' Singles and Doubles Championships and seven in the Mixed Doubles Championship. Suzanne also won two gold medals at the Olympic Games.

She withdrew from Wimbledon following a misunderstanding and decided not to grace the courts again. Within a month she had signed a professional contract and relinquished her amateur status.

In the mid-thirties she channelled her expertise into coaching but just after being appointed Director of the new French National Tennis School in 1938, she suddenly died at the age of 39.

This second edition of 'Suzanne Lenglen – Tennis Idol of the Twenties' has been considerably expanded to relate in more detail her life on and off the tennis court, in particular her history-making professional tours to the United States and Great Britain. Also, many hitherto unpublished photographs are included. The book contains records listing every match she played as an amateur and professional, which, collectively, have never been published before.

In 2006 Amélie Mauresmo became only the second Frenchwoman to win the Ladies' Singles Championship at Wimbledon. This is the story of the first.

Early Days

Suzanne Rachel Flore Lenglen was born on 24th May, 1899 at 29, Hameau des Boulainvilliers, off Rue du Ranelagh in the Passy district of Paris, the first child of Charles and Anaise Lenglen.

The Lenglen family, which originated from Lille in Northern France was quite wealthy. Suzanne's grandfather, Charles, owned a horse-bus company in Paris which carried passengers from Gare St Lazare to the Place de la Republique and the Bourse. At one time he maintained 800 horses. Charles married Adolphine Charlton in the mid-1850s and they had two boys, Eugene and Charles, the father of Suzanne.

Neither of the brothers was interested in the transport business, which was eventually sold, and opted to pursue the study of chemistry, with Charles becoming a pharmacist. He was always sport-minded and in his younger days enjoyed cycle racing.

Charles' great friend was Louis d'Hainault who had four sisters, Rachel, Berthe, Eloide and Anaise. Charles married Rachel, but their joy was short lived as she died soon after in August, 1896. Within a couple of years Charles had married Anaise.

Suzanne had a brother, Philippe, born on 26th May, 1901, but he died three years later on 28th August, 1904.

In 1904 the Lenglens moved from Paris to Marest-sur-Matz, a small village five miles north of Compiegne, where Charles Lenglen had purchased a house two

Suzanne had an aptitude for many sports and games as a youngster including tennis, boating, golf, skipping, cycling, jumping, walking on stilts, diabolo and riding.

years earlier. During the winters the family sought the warmer climate of Nice, where they lived at 13 Avenue Auber facing the Place Mozart and the Nice Lawn Tennis Club.

Suzanne had a natural aptitude for sports and games which included swimming, boating, golf, skipping and cycling. She excelled at the game of diabolo, which was very fashionable at the time. Often, as a youngster, she would be seen demonstrating her skills to the crowds of tourists assembled on the Promenade des Anglais in Nice.

In June, 1910, when Suzanne was 11 years old, she received as a present from her parents her first tennis racket. This was little more than a toy and her father felt she would hardly use it other than to hit balls without any definite purpose. At first he paid little attention to Suzanne, although he did allow her to play with her friends on the tennis court he had constructed in the garden. After about a month he was so pleased with Suzanne's progress that he ordered a racket, light and well balanced, especially made for her by Williams and Co of Rue Caumartin in Paris, who became her supplier for life. Charles Lenglen, who often played with Suzanne to test her capabilities, rapidly came to the conclusion that for her age she showed outstanding flair and tactical ability.

During September, three months after she had started playing, Suzanne visited Dr Cizelly, a friend of her father, who lived at Coize, near Chantilly, about 25 miles from Paris. The doctor, who was a great tennis enthusiast, owned a tennis court, which was a rare possession in those days in France. It was here that Suzanne played her first game before a 'gallery', which was spellbound with admiration.

About that time the annual Chantilly tournament was about to begin and knowing that many of the country's leading players would be participating Suzanne entered the singles handicap event. With a handicap of 15.3 (she received a point in each game and two points every other game) she won through four rounds to take the second prize, much to the astonishment of the players.

A few months later when Charles Lenglen returned to Nice he applied to the Nice Lawn Tennis Club for Suzanne to become a member. Normally children were not allowed to play at the Club but he obtained special dispensation for her to play on Thursdays and Sundays, when she was not attending school at the Institut Massena in Nice. At this school she did a course in classic Greek dancing and this enabled her to acquire agility and movement, so useful for her tennis.

Charles Lenglen's ambition was always for Suzanne to be outstanding at a sport and once he realised her potential as a tennis player he sold the family business, which allowed him to retire and fully concentrate his life on the fulfilment of his dream.

At the Nice Lawn Tennis Club he made a profound study of the game, taking every opportunity to examine the strokes and manner of players, with the purpose of teaching Suzanne the best points of each player and so make her the greatest all-round performer.

There was no shortage of top class players for Suzanne to study each year during the period from Christmas to the end of April as a weekly circuit of tournaments was held along the Cote d'Azur, which attracted leading competitors from much of Europe.

British players were the first to discover the possibility of playing lawn tennis in the winter in a mild and dry climate, instead of suffering the cold and damp conditions at home, where outside play was virtually impossible. As early as 1880, the legendary twins, Ernest and William Renshaw, began their regular excursions to the Mediterranean, where they made the courts at the Beau Site Hotel, Cannes famous.

Their successors, the Doherty brothers, also visited the coast each year to compete in the growing number of international tournaments. The Beau Site was first in 1890, followed by Nice in 1895, Monte Carlo in 1897, Menton in 1902 and so on. By the middle of the 1920s tennis had become all the rage on the Riviera with over 100 courts in Cannes alone. Royalty, nobility and their like were eager to participate or give support to the events, where, generally, British players were in abundance and very prominent.

For a year or so Suzanne used every spare moment of her time practising on court, constantly under the watchful eye of her father. Then in March, 1912 she made her debut on the French Riviera when she participated in the South of France Championships staged at her own Club in Nice. In common with most tournaments of the period, several handicap events were held in conjunction with the main events and Suzanne, at 12 years of age, was allowed to compete in the singles handicap. With the aid of a bye and two walkovers she reached the quarter final, where she lost to Mrs Maud Barger-Wallach, the 1908 United States Singles Champion, 6–1 6–3. Later, Suzanne played in the north of France. At Compiegne she astonished all present by her all-round play in pressing Mlle Jeanne Matthey, four times French Champion, 1909–1912, in the semi-final and also winning two

---

Facing page: The Programme for the Ladies' Singles handicap event of the 1912 South of France Championships, played at the Nice Lawn Tennis Club in the Place Mozart. Suzanne making her Riviera debut, lost in the quarter-final to the past American champion, Mrs Maud Barger-Wallach.

37 Entries.

LADIES' SINGLES, HANDICAP.

Best of 3 sets throughout, deuce and advantage games will be played only in the third set.

1st Prize, value 150 frs. — 2nd Prize, value 75 frs. — Two 3rd Prizes, value 40 frs each.

No.	ODDS	1st ROUND	2nd ROUND	3rd ROUND	4th ROUND	PENULTIMATE	FINAL	WINNER
1	+ 30 3/6	......(a bye)...	Mlle Lenglen...	Mlle Lenglen (w.-o.)	Mlle Lenglen (w.-o.)			
2	+ 15 2/6	......»......	Mrs. F. B. Lacy..					
3	+ 5/6	......»......	Miss L. Cadle...	Mrs. Nutcombe-Quicke 6/4 – 2/6 – 6/4				
4	owe 15	......»......	Mrs. Nutcombe-Quicke........			Mrs. Barger-Wallach 6/1 – 6/3 3rd. prize.		
5	+ 30	......»......	Mrs. Cadle......	Mrs. Barger-Wallach (w.-o.)	Mrs. Barger-Wallach 6/2 – 6/4			
6	+ 2/6	......»......	Mrs. Barger-Wallach					
7	+ 4/6	......»......	Mrs. Willford...	Mrs. Willford 6/3 – 6/3			Mme Blatin 6/2 – 5/6 – 6/2	
8	+ 15	......»......	Mrs. E. F. Gibbs.					
9	+ 15	......»......	Miss Wheler.....	Miss Wheler (w.-o.)				
10	+ 2/6	......»......	Mrs. Wheelwright		Mme Decugis 6/2 – 6/5			
11	+ 15	......»......	Miss Hardman...	Mme Decugis (w.-o.)				
12	+ 3/6	......»......	Mme Decugis...			Mme Blatin 6/2 – 6/2		
13	+ 30	......»......	Mme Blatin.....	Mme Blatin 6/0 – 6/0				
14	+ 30 3/6	Miss Grünberg...	Frln Rieck 6/4 - 2/6 - 9/7					
15	+ 15 4/6	Frln. G. Rieck..			Mme Blatin 6/2 – 6/3			
16	owe 15 3/6	Mrs. Perrett...	Mrs. Perrett 6/3 – 6/2	Mrs. V. Cornwall 5/6 – 6/4 – 6/3				
17	+ 15 3/6	Mrs Gwynne-Evans						Mme Blatin 6/4 – 5/6 – 6/0 1st. prize.
18	owe 15 5/6	Miss J. Tripp...	Mrs. V. Cornwall (w.-o.)					
19	+ 15 5/6	Mrs. V. Cornwall						
20	+ 15 2/6	Miss Newberry..	Miss Harper 2/6 – 6/5 – 6/3	Miss O. Ranson 6/1 – 6/3				
21	+ 15	Miss Harper....			Miss O. Ranson 6/1 – 6/3			
22	scr.	Mrs. A Crosfield	Miss O. Ranson (w.-o.)					
23	+ 15 3/6	Miss O Ranson..						
24	+ 30 4/6	......(a bye)...	Miss Hart.......	Miss Hart 4/6 – 6/3 – 6/4		Miss E. M. White 6/2 – 2/6 – 6/1		
25	+ 15	......»......	Miss K. Lillico..					
26	+ 30 2/6	......»......	Mlle Heudebert..	Mlle Heudebert 6/2 – 6/3				
27	+ 15 1/6	......»......	Hon. Mrs Barker-Mill		Miss E. M. White 6/1 – 6/0		Miss E. M. White 6/3 – 6/3 2nd. prize.	
28	+ 30 1/6	......»......	Mlle de Farensbach	Miss E. M. White 6/2 – 6/2				
29	+ 3/6	......»......	Miss E. M. White					
30	+ 4/6	......»......	Miss Hulbert....	Miss Hulbert (w.-o.)				
31	+ 30	......»......	Mrs Weidemann.		Miss M. E. Stuart 6/4 – 6/4			
32	+ 15 4/6	......»......	Miss A. L. Pagdin	Miss M. E. Stuart 6/0 – 6/2				
33	owe 15 1/6	......»......	Miss M. E. Stuart			Miss M. Tripp 6/4 – 6/4 3rd. prize.		
34	owe 15 3/6	......»......	Miss M. Tripp...	Miss M. Tripp 6/0 – 6/2				
35	+ 5/6	......»......	Mlle A. V. de Bocarmé		Miss M. Tripp 6/1 – 6/4			
36	+ 15 4/6	......»......	Miss Street	Miss Street 6/4 – 2/6 – 8/6				
37	+ 30	......»......	Mme Zambaux ..					

handicap events. Three weeks later she reached the final of the doubles handicap at Le Touquet, with Mme S.A. Puget.

Suzanne made enormous progress in 1913, when she started by winning local handicap events and ended by being hailed in the national press as a sensation, after capturing three well established tournaments against tried opponents.

Her year began in January, when she won the singles handicap title at the meeting in Nice by defeating Miss A. Hulbert in the final, 6–5 6–4. Her reward was to be selected, along with Miss Hulbert and two men, to represent Nice in their annual fixture versus Bordighera, just over the border in Italy on the 18th. When Suzanne and her mother arrived for the match the local secretary thought that Mme Lenglen was competing and directed her to the dressing room. Suzanne had no difficulty in winning her match against Miss Dale, 6–1 6–1.

The Monte Carlo tournament, staged towards the end of February, was a memorable occasion for Suzanne as she teamed up with Miss Elizabeth Ryan for the first time. Although they lost in the final of the doubles handicap to Miss O. Ranson and Miss M.E. Stuart after a fierce struggle, 6–3 2–6 7–5, this was the beginning of a partnership which quickly developed into one of the greatest the game has ever known. Elizabeth Ryan, an American born in California, first visited England in 1912 with her sister, Alice, and decided to stay.

Suzanne's initial attempt in the open singles at the South of France Championships at Nice was short lived for after beating Miss D.G. Beckett, 6–1 6–1, she succumbed to Frl Dagmar von Krohn, the eventual winner, 6–1 6–3. In May, the Lenglen family moved to Marest-sur-Matz for the summer and within a week or two Suzanne had won the Picardie Championships, beating Mlle L. Marcot in the final. Further success was gained at Lille during June when Suzanne, with surprising ease, won through five rounds and defeated Miss Beatrice Butler in the final, 6–1 6–1. She also beat Mme Leon Wibaux in the handicap singles final, 6–1 6–2. A month later, Suzanne competed at the Chantilly and Compiegne tournaments and each time lost in the singles final to Jeanne Matthey. In the first she lost after a close first set 7–5 6–1 and in the second gave a walkover, being exhausted after playing a long mixed doubles final. However, as consolation, Suzanne won both handicap events.

Suzanne concluded her season at the Channel resorts of Wimereux and Le Touquet, where she beat Mrs Gladys Colston in both finals. At Wimereux,

Suzanne just managed to survive a very long second set before her opponent eventually retired in the deciding set, 4–6 9–7 3–2. Suzanne was given a great welcome on her return to Le Touquet where she played a very good final set to beat Gladys Colston, 6–0 2–6 6–1. The spectators were quite amazed how her all-round ability and determination had flourished since the year before. The Lenglen family were quite elated by the performance of their 14–year-old daughter.

Suzanne played much more tennis in 1914 when she concentrated her efforts on open events. With the year less than a fortnight old she had captured two singles titles on the French Riviera. In the first final, at the New Year Beau Site tournament at Cannes, victory was achieved with a simple 6–0 6–0 win over Miss M. Ward but a week later, at the new Carlton Club at Cannes, she required much skill and patience to overcome the experienced Mrs Ruth Winch, 7–5 3–6 6–1. This was the inaugural tournament staged at this Club, which a few months earlier had laid down five first class courts in the grounds at the rear of the famous Carlton Hotel. At this meeting great interest was shown in the mixed doubles event, which was won by Suzanne linking up with Anthony Wilding, the four times Wimbledon Singles Champion. The immensely popular and very athletic New Zealander was to become a victim of the First World War, when, as a Captain in the Royal Marines, a shell struck a direct hit on his dug-out at Neuve Chapelle in Northern France on 9th May, 1915.

Suzanne with Anthony Wilding, four times Wimbledon Champion, after their win in the mixed doubles at the Carlton Club, Cannes in 1914.

Suzanne found a tough opponent on her hands when she met Elizabeth Ryan in the quarter-final of the Monte Carlo tournament at the end of February. Although the result was hardly in doubt, the American winning 6–3 6–4, Suzanne played admirably and often had the better of the exchanges. A fortnight later at Nice, Suzanne faced Mrs Dorothea Chambers, the six times Wimbledon Singles Champion from 1903 to 1913, in the semi-final of the South of France Championships. Suzanne, utterly untroubled by nerves of any kind, stood up to the best lady player of the day to win three games in each set and be somewhat unlucky not to get a fourth game in the first. Five years later these two players were to meet in very different circumstances.

At a new tournament played on the six courts of the Nice Country Club, situated a short distance from the Imperial Hotel, Suzanne won the handicap singles event. In 1922 this club became the main Nice venue, following the closure of the Place Mozart site. After entering doubles events only at the Metropole Hotel at Cannes, Suzanne finished her Riviera campaign on a high note by defeating Elizabeth Ryan in the final of the second Carlton Club meeting.

Playing with a knowledge of the game far beyond her years, Suzanne placed and drove beautifully and out-manoeuvred her opponent in the most wonderful fashion to win 6–3 3–6 6–2. The American did not play well and only in the second set did she show flashes of her true form. Suzanne, partnered by Alfred Dunlop, of New Zealand, lost a marathon mixed doubles final to Max Decugis and Elizabeth Ryan, 7–5 7–9 6–2.

Suzanne's growing stature in the game was recognised by the French Lawn Tennis Federation who added her name to the list of French premier players and invited her to compete in the French National Championships at the Racing Club de France in Paris, from 17th–23rd May. From the small entry of six, Suzanne won the All Comers' Singles after a bye and solid displays over Mme Germaine Golding, 6–2 7–5 and Mlle Marie Conquet, 6–4 6–2, but she could not sustain her effort and lost in the challenge round to Mlle Marguerite Broquedis, 5–7 6–4 6–3. Suzanne, with Germaine Golding, narrowly lost in the challenge round of the doubles to the twin sisters, Mlles Blanche and Suzanne Amblard, 6–4 8–6 but Suzanne, not to be denied a title, won the mixed event with Max Decugis.

Facing page: Suzanne and Elizabeth Ryan after their doubles victory at the World's Hard Court Championships at St Cloud, Paris, in 1914. The day before Suzanne had won the singles title at the age of 15.

Two weeks later Suzanne, just 15 years of age, reached new heights by majestically winning the World's Hard Court Championships at St. Cloud, near Paris. After accounting for Mrs Phyllis Satterthwaite, 6–3 8–6 and Mme Anne de Borman of Belgium, 6–2 6–3 she was given a hard fight by Suzanne Amblard in the semi-final but her superior steadiness and volleying ability tipped the balance, 6–2 4–6 6–3.

In the final, Suzanne enjoyed a comfortable 6–2 6–1 victory over Germaine Golding, who tried unsuccessfully to use her forehand drive attack but she usually faltered after three or four rallies. Also she seemed to lose heart after failing to bustle Suzanne out of her accuracy. Suzanne and Elizabeth Ryan beat the Amblard sisters in the doubles final, without losing a game, but in the mixed doubles, Suzanne, partnered by Austria's Count Ludwig Salm, had to be content with second prize.

Later in June, Suzanne added to her laurels by retaining her title at Lille, overwhelming Beatrice Butler in the final, 6–0 6–0, and winning the singles on her first visit to the Athletic Club in Amiens by defeating Mlle Vienne, at the last stage, 6–2 6–0.

In the weeks leading up to The Championships at Wimbledon there was the possibility that Suzanne would compete but after several communications her father decided that the venture was premature.

As the threat of the First World War loomed, towards the end of July, Suzanne competed at the Compiegne tournament where, to the great disappointment of the spectators, she defaulted in the final to Suzanne Amblard. Many wanted to interpret this withdrawal as a sign of defeat. Suzanne won the mixed doubles with Georges Gault. She intended to compete at the Etretat tournament, commencing 9th August, but five days before, German troops crossed the French border in Lorraine and for the next four years Europe was plunged into darkness. The Lenglen family left their home in the north to spend the duration of the war at Nice, where Charles Lenglen became Honorary Secretary of the Lawn Tennis Club.

During the long war years, Suzanne found no shortage of players with whom she could practise, as much of the Riviera became a haven for servicemen who were on leave or convalescing from the Western Front. Towards the end, a number of top-class players from the American forces also visited the area.

Suzanne gave tremendous support to the tournaments and exhibition matches arranged in aid of the French Red Cross and other relief organisations. These events, mainly held in Cannes during 1916 and 1917, quite often included singles matches against men, sometimes professional coaches. Suzanne, always the main attraction, seldom lost.

The signing of the Armistice on 11th November 1918 at last brought the war to an end. Her father had used the last four years to turn Suzanne into a completely equipped player, possessing correct stroke production and footwork, accurate in control and placing and without a weakness which any opponent could attack. As Suzanne's career unfolded she developed a few interesting idiosyncrasies. In doubles she usually turned around to watch the service of her partner. She also had a habit of gently blowing on her racket hand so as to cool or dry it, and occasionally she wiped the perspiration from her hand with the bottom of her skirt.

Suzanne with Count Salm, 1914

1919

Suzanne had to wait until the middle of February 1919 for lawn tennis to return to normal on the Cote d'Azur with the staging of the Carlton Club tournament. She was nearly 20 years old and eager to make up for lost time. Her game was not put to the test as she coasted through the singles to defeat Mme Doris Wolfson in the final, 6–1 6–1. The tournaments which followed at Monte Carlo, Menton, Nice and at the Beau Site Hotel, Cannes, offered no sterner opposition and, indeed, at Nice she won her first South of France Championship without losing a game. At the same meeting, Suzanne played in a handicap match for the last time, when she paired with Prince P. de Bourbon in the mixed doubles. During the season Suzanne won the five mixed doubles titles, four with Max Decugis and one with Pierre Albarran, who later became a noted international bridge player.

Apart from appearing in an exhibition match at Beau Site Hotel, Suzanne did not compete again until mid-May, when the first official tournament since the war was staged in the Paris region.

To some degree this meeting at the Racing Club de France was held to compensate for the loss that year of the French National Championships and the World's Hard Court Championships normally held around that time. The French Authorities had decided that contests of national importance would not be organised before the complete demobilisation of the army had taken place. Suzanne was in great form and captured all three events.

Facing page: Suzanne enjoying her first visit to The Championships at Wimbledon in 1919.

She stayed in Paris for the next week and as a spectator attended each day the Inter-Allied Army Individual Championships at the Racing Club. To the delight of the local enthusiasts Lt. Andre Gobert fought through a very high quality field from seven countries to win the singles title. On the last day Suzanne obliged by playing an exhibition doubles match and then announced she would be leaving soon to challenge for the title at Wimbledon.

Although Suzanne arrived in England early she chose not to compete in any of the preliminary meetings. However, she practised and visited the tournament at Queen's Club, West Kensington with her father and Max Decugis to view her possible opponents in action.

In those days The Championships at Wimbledon were staged at the old ground of the All England Lawn Tennis and Croquet Club, situated between Worple Road and the London and South Western Railway, approximately half a mile from Wimbledon Station. The ground capacity was approximately 10,000 and the Centre Court seating restricted to around 3,500.

Suzanne made her debut in the All Comers' Singles on Tuesday, 24th June versus Mrs Annis Cobb on No. 4 Court, where a stand had recently been erected. The match, which was delayed because Annis Cobb had arrived at the ground without her 'things', was watched by such a large gathering that the Centre Court seemed by comparison deserted. Although Annis Cobb could only win one game, in the second set, she played well enough to enable Suzanne to show her complete mastery of each stroke on the so unfamiliar grass surface.

A packed court at the Worple Road ground at Wimbledon in 1919 watches Suzanne easily defeat Ethel Larcombe, the 1912 Champion 6–2 6–1.

Her next opponent on Thursday was Mrs Ethel Larcombe, the 1912 Champion. Suzanne's first appearance on the Centre Court held no terrors for her as she proceeded to win with ease, 6–2 6–1. Many thought that Ethel Larcombe's drop shots and cut underhand service would worry Suzanne but this proved to be wrong as she hit the ball firmly with plenty of pace and immaculate length until an opening

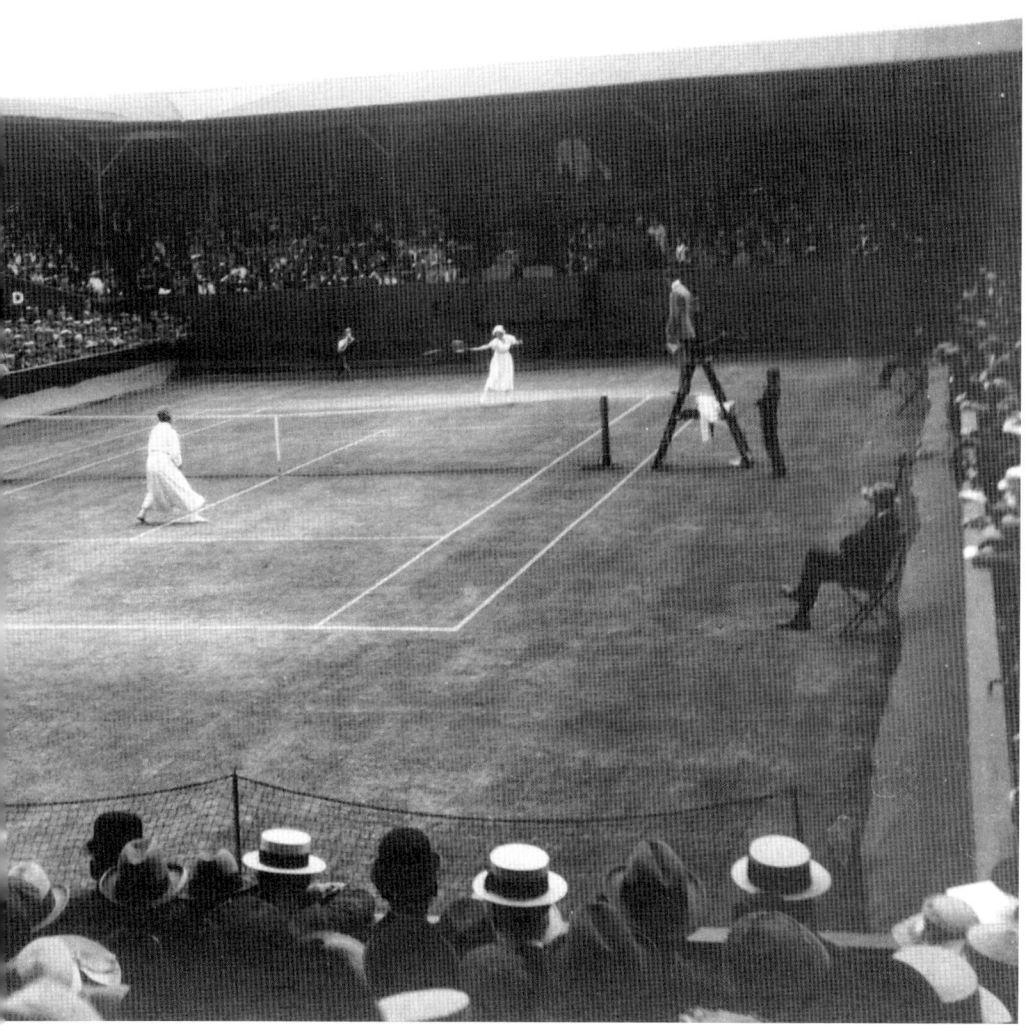

occurred for her to deliver the final shot. Only for the first three or four games was there any doubt as to the result of the match.

The following day Suzanne reached the last eight by completely overwhelming Mrs Doris Craddock, on No. 1 Court, 6–0 6–1. On the Monday of the second week, Suzanne continued in devastating style by defeating Britain's 'new hope', Miss Kathleen McKane, by dropping just one game in the second set. This match was contested before a packed house on No. 4 Court.

On the next day Suzanne was given much to think about against Elizabeth Ryan in the semi-final played on the Centre Court. Suzanne led 3–0 before Elizabeth Ryan settled down to capture four games in the first set. In the following set, Suzanne had two match points on her opponent's service at 5–2 40–15 but Elizabeth Ryan, with great courage, served her way out of this crisis and pulled up to 5–all. At 30–all in the next game rain stopped play for an hour. On resumption Suzanne won the next two points for 6–5. The next game was very long and at deuce Suzanne, with an air of determination, took off her cardigan. There followed some lively exchanges but eventually Elizabeth Ryan delivered a double fault on the fourth match point and a most exciting encounter closed at 6–4 7–5.

So to Wednesday and the final, which was too one-sided against Phyllis Satterthwaite to be of great interest. Suzanne, becoming acclimatised to the Centre Court, was able to remain comfortably in the middle of the court and dictate the play, forcing her opponent to run from side to side.

Phyllis Satterthwaite played with pluck and never gave up but she did not possess sufficient attacking strokes to be able to upset Suzanne, who triumphed 6–1 6–1.

Awaiting Suzanne in the challenge round was 40–year-old Dorothea Chambers, who had increased her tally of Wimbledon Singles titles to seven in 1914. For three weeks prior to the match certain sections of the press had been exclaiming that if Suzanne became the challenger, Dorothea Chambers would stand little chance of defending her crown against an opponent half her age. The critics were wrong and what took place was one of the most memorable matches in the history of the game.

Originally the match was scheduled for Friday, 4th July but rain which started at 2.30 pm never stopped all the afternoon and the match had to be postponed until the following day. Nearly 8,000 spectators, including King George V, Queen Mary and Princess Mary were present when the players came out on to the Centre Court around 3.30 pm Suzanne wore a flimsy, white, calf-length short-sleeved tennis frock with the skirt pleated, white stockings and a soft linen hat. Just below her waist was pinned a small monkey's paw mascot. Dorothea Chambers chose more traditional attire in the form of a white gored skirt, reaching to just below the calf, worn with a plain long-sleeved shirt, buttoned at the wrists.

Suzanne began badly by losing her service to love but hitting hard and confidently won the next four games. Fine service returns by Dorothea Chambers reduced the arrears to 4–3 but she could not deny Suzanne leading 5–3. Twice Suzanne was thwarted from winning the set when drop shots caught her out of position. Dorothea Chambers had two set points at 6–5 but Suzanne spectacularly saved both with attacking strokes. Eventually after leading 7–6 8–7 and 9–8, Suzanne broke through her opponent's service in the 20th game with a perfect volley, at 15–40.

In the second set, Suzanne made many unwise sorties to the net and failed to put away several of her volleys. Leading 4–1, Dorothea Chambers inexplicably abandoned her baseline game for the net and with Suzanne gaining more control, 4–all was called. Just in time the Englishwoman reverted to defensive play to edge out, amidst great cheering, at 6–4. Suzanne, a little distressed, called for brandy and rested a short while on a linesman's chair.

Somehow Suzanne found fresh vitality to lead 4–1 in the deciding set but this effort taxed her and Dorothea Chambers, hitting many great passing shots on the run, charged back to 4–all. Then two love games against service took the score to 5–all. At this stage the crowd was quite excited and noisy and the umpire repeatedly called for silence. After a long deuce game Suzanne eventually drove out to trail 5–6. When Dorothea Chambers had two match points at 40–15 in the next game the contest seemed virtually over. However, on the first point, Suzanne just managed to return a low lob over the net with the wood of her racket and on the second Dorothea Chambers, attempting a drop shot, netted the ball. From that point Suzanne moved steadily to victory. At 8–7 she captured her opponent's service to love and the tense duel, lasting just over two hours, was concluded at 10–8 4–6 9–7.

Suzanne hurried forward to shake hands with Dorothea Chambers before leaving the court, embraced by her excited parents. The King was keen to congratulate the contestants but both had returned to the dressing room quite exhausted and were not in a condition to reappear. Suzanne had won the match by 23 games to 21 and

THE 1919 CHALLENGE ROUND AT WIMBLEDON

Nearly 8,000 spectators including King George V and Queen Mary, were present on the Centre Court to witness Suzanne capture her first singles title at Wimbledon by defeating Dorothea Chambers, seven times champion, in a tense duel lasting over two hours.
Above: Suzanne serves from the east end. *Below:* Dorothea Chambers strides the baseline.
Facing page: Suzanne preparing for a forehand drive.

146 points to 134. She won four love games to Dorothea Chambers' six. There were six deuce games in the first set (five in succession), three in the second and four in the third, 13 in all, of which Suzanne won seven and her opponent six. Suzanne lost 12 of her service games and won 10. Her opponent won 9 and lost 13.

Three days later, Suzanne annexed a second title. Paired with Elizabeth Ryan she defeated Dorothea Chambers and Ethel Larcombe in the final of the doubles, 4–6 7–5 6–3, after being within two points of defeat. Earlier in the tournament Suzanne and William Laurentz were eliminated at the quarter-final stage of the mixed doubles. Despite losing an eye playing tennis in 1912, the Frenchman became his country's top ranked player for 1921. He died the following March, aged 26.

Back in France, Suzanne rested a while before competing at Cabourg, where a blistered hand forced her to retire at the semi-final stage. She then easily won the singles at Deauville and Le Touquet. At the former, Lord Wimborne presented Suzanne with the two gold medals she won at Wimbledon. In September, Suzanne wrote her first book, 'Lawn Tennis for Girls', published by George Newnes of London, (1s 6d) which contained stroke analysis and tactical advice for the beginner. She insisted that all the photographs illustrating the book were taken during match play and not posed.

During December, Suzanne was elected to the Committee of the Nice Lawn Tennis Club — a quite exceptional achievement for that era.

The year had been a tremendous success for 21 year-old Suzanne, who clearly established herself at a level of performance, not to be equalled in the next seven years. Her parents played a vital part in this achievement, being firmly behind her in all aspects of her career. They were particularly keen to have a presence at her matches and regularly sat at the courtside with Gyp, the family Belgian Griffon, nestling on the lap of Anaïse.

Facing page: Suzanne at Cabourg on the Normandy coast, 1919.

1920

On the French Riviera in 1920, Suzanne appeared at seven tournaments despite being unwell much of the time. She was always the centre of attraction. At the first meeting at the Beau Site Hotel, Suzanne beat Mrs Madeline O'Neill in the final of the singles, 6–1 6–0, but she had to work harder than the score suggests. In the final of the Carlton Club tournament, Suzanne found Elizabeth Ryan in very poor form and swept her off the court 6–0 6–1 in 20 minutes! At this meeting there was an unfortunate ending in the mixed doubles final, when Suzanne and Pierre Albarran were playing Major Ritchie and Elizabeth Ryan. A very stiff breeze which blew down the court distressed the French pair, who after making mistakes and having misunderstandings retired in the middle of the second set, much to the displeasure of the spectators.

In the title round at Beaulieu, Suzanne restricted Elizabeth Ryan to two games, both in the opening set. A week later at Monte Carlo, Suzanne defeated the American in the final, again by a wide margin, 6–1 6–2, but in the previous round she had an unusually severe match before overcoming Mrs Geraldine Beamish, 6–3 6–4. The Englishwoman pinned her to the back of the court for much of the time with her hard and good length drives.

Suzanne was due to meet Geraldine Beamish for the title at Nice but following a hard fought doubles final she was medically advised not to play, to the great disappointment of the crowd who had looked forward to the return contest. The

Facing page: Suzanne, with her father Charles, on the French Riviera in March, 1920.

13 Avenue Auber
.Nice

Dear Mrs Wightman -
I thank you very much for your nice letter....
I am not going over the States this year... perhaps some day I will have the opportunity.... but not soon I am afraid -
I think it would be a great fun to meet you and all your American players ...
You Know... my family does n't want to move so far... and I can't go alone !
I expect to play all the Riviera's tournaments this season...

In January 1920 Suzanne writes to Mrs Wightman, explaining why she cannot visit the USA.

Mrs Lambert Chambers is expected in February or March __ Miss Ryan is already here ...
I am very sorry you can't come in Europe ... perhaps will you be decided one day ...
Please forgive me for the very bad english I make ...
I am very glad my friend Mrs Ryan Kubb knows you .... So she will speak of you next April! ...
With thanks! yours sincerely!!!!

Suzanne Lenglen

25-1-20

following week Suzanne had not fully recovered so she confined her entry at the Cannes Club to doubles, an event easily won in partnership with Elizabeth Ryan.

During the last week of April, Suzanne returned to singles play at the last tournament of the season at the Beau Site Hotel. She had no opposition worthy of her skill and easily defeated Mrs Sigrid Fick, the Swedish champion, in the final, 6–1 6–1. During the week she partnered King Gustav V of Sweden to victory over Pierre Albarran and Sigrid Fick in an exhibition match, 6–4 6–2.

At the end of May, Suzanne entered the World's Hard Court Championships at St Cloud, Paris but was unable to defend the title she had won six years earlier owing to illness which forced her to withdraw at the last moment. She was sufficiently recovered a fortnight later to contest the French National Championships, which were decided at the Racing Club in Paris. Suzanne won the singles crown for the first time with three comfortable wins, over Mlle Elisabeth d'Ayen, 6–0 6–1, Germaine Golding, 6–2 6–3, Mme Jeanne Vaussard, 6–1 6–1, and a victory in the challenge round over Mme Billout, the former Marguerite Broquedis, who narrowly beat her for the title in 1914. Suzanne won the the first set 6–1 but was in danger of losing the second before edging out at 7–5. Suzanne won the doubles with Elisabeth d'Ayen, and retained the mixed doubles with Max Decugis. Elisabeth d'Ayen, a young Parisian, was the younger daughter of the 8th Duc de Noailles.

At Wimbledon, the public saw a smarter and more sophisticated Suzanne, dressed in clothes designed by Jean Patou, the Paris couturier, and sporting the new 'bobbed' hair style. On court she wore a loose, one-piece frock similar to the previous year and once again the monkey paw mascot was evident. Her dresses were always uncreased as she never sat, once dressed for tennis. The soft hat was replaced by what became known as the 'Lenglen bandeau', several yards of georgette, varying in colour from heliotrope to lemon, swathed around the hair. Later, Suzanne chose multi-coloured silk chiffon for the bandeau, which was usually held in place by a diamond arrow. With every match she changed the colour of the bandeau and matching cardigan. She scarcely ever wore jewellery.

Although Suzanne as defending champion had to stand out awaiting her challenger to emerge from the All Comers' Singles she kept match tight by competing in the two doubles events. Dorothea Chambers, determined to have another crack at Suzanne, played with great character and resolve to win through to the title round, culminating with crushing victories over four-times United States Singles

Champion, Norwegian born, Mrs Anna (Molla) Mallory, 6–0 6–2 and Elizabeth Ryan, 6–2 6–1, a truly magnificent performance from one approaching her 42nd birthday.

Because of this showing many observers anticipated a repetition of the mammoth struggle of a year earlier against Suzanne but the match played on Thursday, 1st July proved to be a great disappointment.

Only in the opening set was Dorothea Chambers able to contain, to a degree, the brilliant mastery of Suzanne, whose accuracy and anticipation had noticeably improved. Suzanne started the better of the two by out manoeuvring her opponent to lead 2–0 but then Dorothea Chambers hit some beautiful drives to even at 2–all. Suzanne, moving extremely well, won the next three games to love, mainly by keeping her opponent on the run until she was out of position and then delivering the decisive hard drive to the open court. Suzanne only ventured to the net when Dorothea Chambers hit a lofted return. Despite leading 30–love Suzanne made several bad errors to lose the next game but a couple of cross-court volleys and a service ace gave her the set 6–3. Suzanne scarcely made a mistake in the second set and hit winner after winner to capture six consecutive games, in 14 minutes, to retain her crown.

Two days later Suzanne became the first player to win three titles in one year. She retained the doubles with Elizabeth Ryan, defeating Dorothea Chambers and Ethel Larcombe in the final, 6–4 6–0, and captured the mixed doubles with Gerald Patterson of Australia, without losing a set in either event.

Suzanne stayed in England a further week. On the Sunday she played in an American-style invitation charity mixed doubles tournament, organised privately by Lady Sophie Wavertree at her home in Sussex Lodge in Regent's Park. The entry was unique and consisted of eight great pairs, Gerald Patterson and Suzanne, Bill Tilden and Molla Mallory, Randolph Lycett and Elizabeth Ryan, Stanley Doust and Dorothea Chambers, Charles Garland and Kathleen McKane, Brian Norton and Mrs Mabel Parton, Alfred and Geraldine Beamish and William Ingram and Mrs Aurea Edgington. Each match consisted of nine games and in a close contest the winners were Tilden and Mallory with 33 games followed by Patterson and Lenglen, 32 games and Lycett and Ryan, 31 games. A large and distinguished audience watched the proceedings. Although Suzanne had met Sophie Wavertree early in the year on the French Riviera, this occasion was really the start of a life-long personal friendship between the two. Suzanne always played in, or gave sup-

port to, the charity matches, which, for many years, became an annual feature at the conclusion of each Wimbledon.

Later in the week Suzanne visited the House of Commons with a group of leading players. At the weekend she watched the Davis Cup Tie between the United States and France at Devonshire Park, Eastbourne, during which she delighted the crowd by playing exhibition matches with Max Decugis and Gerald Patterson. At the dinner given for the teams by the British LTA at the Chatsworth Hotel, Suzanne was presented with the gold medals she had won at Wimbledon. She discovered to her delight that one of the items on the menu was 'Pêche Suzanne'.

In August, Suzanne visited Belgium for the first time to play at two tournaments in preparation for the Olympic Games. At Ostend Suzanne dropped just three games before beating Mrs Helen Leisk in the final, 6–0 6–0. The Knokke-Sur-Mer meeting was just another canter for Suzanne, who was far too strong for Anne de Borman, the Belgian Champion, at the last stage, 6–0 6–2.

The Olympic tournament held at Antwerp, 15th to 21st August, left much to be desired as the Beerchot Tennis Club courts were in close proximity to the Stadium and often the ecstatic applause intended for the athletes disturbed the progress of the matches. The courts and umpiring left much to be desired. Also, badly below standard was the dressing room accommodation which offered no hot water, soap or any drying facilities for clothes. However, little interrupted Suzanne's progress as she trounced Mme Marie Storms of Belgium, Mrs Winifred McNair and Sweden's Miss Lily Stromberg von Essen, each without losing a game. Then she beat Sigrid Fick, 6–0 6–1, and Miss Dorothy Holman 6–3 6–0 in the final, delayed for a day because of rain, to take the gold medal. Miss Holman's task was impossible once Suzanne had increased the depth and pace of her strokes. The King of the Belgians warmly congratulated Suzanne on her victory.

The best ladies match of the week was the doubles semi-final in which Suzanne and Elisabeth d'Ayen lost to Winifred McNair and Kathleen McKane in an exciting finish, 2–6 6–3 8–6. Suzanne and Elisabeth d'Ayen won the bronze medal when Marie Storms and Mlle Fernande Arendt of Belgium withdrew. Suzanne added another gold medal to her tally when she paired with Max Decugis to beat Maxwell Woosnam and Kathleen McKane in the mixed doubles final, 6–4 6–2.

On the way home, Suzanne captured the singles title at Boulogne, without losing a game, and won the singles cup outright at Le Touquet.

Facing page: Suzanne in action at Wimbledon in 1920.

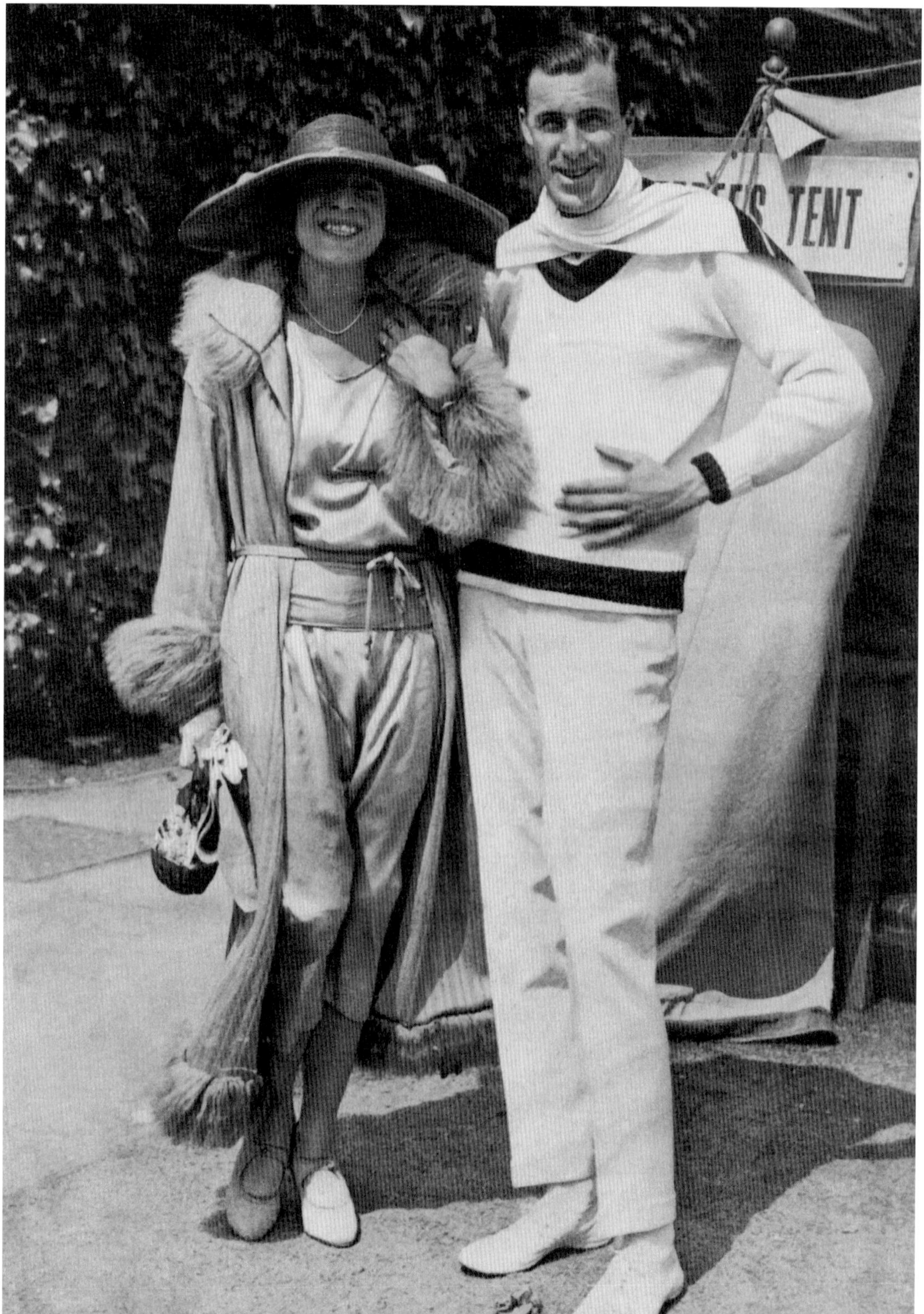
TENT

1921

The French Riviera circuit in 1921 was completely overshadowed by Suzanne who, in better health, appeared at 11 tournaments, played and won eight singles events and annexed a total of 13 doubles and mixed doubles titles. Her singles play was overwhelming to the point of embarrassment when she won half of her 34 matches without the loss of a solitary game and conceded just 29 games in all. The majority of these results were obtained against good class opposition, which included many leading players from England and national champions from the Continent.

At the opening gathering of the year at the Beau Site Hotel, Suzanne never lost a game in the singles. In the singles final of the next four tournaments at the Carlton Club, Nice, Carlton Club (second meeting) and on the new La Festa courts at Monte Carlo she defeated Elizabeth Ryan with ease, never allowing her more than two games per match. If there was any doubt remaining from the previous year of Suzanne's superiority over Geraldine Beamish it was soon dispelled when she beat her at the last two meetings, 6–1 6–0.

At the South of France Championships in Nice, Suzanne defeated Mlle M. Septier, 6–1 6–1 in the final of the singles and formed a notable partnership with the left-handed Russian Count Mikhail Soumarokoff to win the mixed doubles title. Suzanne ended the season with 6–1 6–0 victories over Phyllis Satterthwaite at the Carlton Club (third meeting) and Monte Carlo (second meeting). In Paris at

---

Facing page: The Wimbledon Singles Champions of 1921, Suzanne and the American, Bill Tilden.

the end of April, Suzanne was awarded the gold medal of the French Academie des Sports for her services to lawn tennis. Suzanne retained all three titles at the French National Championships, held at the Racing Club in Paris in the middle of May. In the singles she was not required to take the court as Germaine Golding withdrew after winning the All Comers' Singles. Suzanne had new doubles partners, Mme Germaine Pigueron and Jacques Brugnon.

After an absence of seven years, Suzanne returned to the World's Hard Court Championships at St. Cloud, where she first rose to fame. Great interest was created by the visit to Paris of Molla Mallory, the United States champion, and the prospect of her clashing with Suzanne in singles for the first time. Both reached the final which was staged before a packed and enthusiastic crowd of 4,000 on Sunday, 5th June. Suzanne won the encounter 6–2 6–3 but the American showed unexpected aggression and good mobility and might easily have captured more games. Suzanne was certainly not at her best and in the second set gave consideration to retiring due to blistered feet. She relied on solid defence and was content for Molla Mallory to make the errors. Both doubles titles fell to Suzanne, who paired with Germaine Golding and Max Decugis.

Leading up to this tournament there was much speculation by the press on the ability of Suzanne's play to be able to equal, or indeed overcome, Bill Tilden, undoubtedly by far the outstanding male player of his time. Clearly Suzanne was in a class of her own in women's tennis, but being pitched against the powerful and aggressive strokes of the American was another matter.

Somehow, a match between the two, consisting of a set, was arranged during one of the practice sessions and, with quite a number of spectators present, Tilden won, 6–0. Unfortunately, the tally of points in each game was not recorded for posterity but reports suggested that Tilden 'allowed' Suzanne two or three at the beginning of each game to present himself with more of a challenge. Apparently, several games went to deuce. A week or so later there was a photograph of the two in action shown in the London 'Field'.

Suzanne retained her crown at Wimbledon without being pressed. Her challenger, Elizabeth Ryan, had overcome an unkind draw by winning a series of difficult matches against Kathleen McKane, Geraldine Beamish, Molla Mallory and Mrs Irene Peacock and only in the final of the All Comers' Singles did she have matters her own way in beating Phyllis Satterthwaite. The challenge round played on Friday, 1st July, began unexpectedly with Elizabeth Ryan, using her cut and drop shots, leading 2–1 against a noticeably nervous opponent. Suzanne's response was to win the next 11 games with a beautiful display of accurate tennis whereby if Elizabeth Ryan came to the net she passed her and if she stayed back she out-manoeuvred her. There was little need for Suzanne to hit hard or to volley, so effective were her tactics.

With Gerald Patterson not competing, Suzanne partnered her fellow-countryman Andre Gobert in the mixed doubles but after they had narrowly won their opening match an injury to Gobert's ankle forced them to scratch. The doubles was dominated by Suzanne and Elizabeth Ryan, who never lost more than two games in any set and in the final beat Geraldine Beamish and Irene Peacock, 6–1 6–2. This was the last match ever played on the Centre Court at Worple Road, the last stroke being a smash by Suzanne. Prior to the First World War the facilities at the ground were expanded to meet the growing demand of the public and there was talk of moving to a larger ground. The arrival of Suzanne and the American star Bill Tilden emphasised this need and The All England Lawn Tennis Club took the decision to move to the present ground in Church Road, in readiness for the 1922 meeting.

Suzanne played at Sophie Wavertree's garden party and also took part in charity exhibitions at the Gipsy Club at Stamford Hill, before returning home.

Over the previous 18 months, Suzanne had received several invitations to visit the United States, including one from Mrs Hazel Wightman, four times United States champion, and an official proposal from the United States LTA, but she declined them all. However, during May, Miss Anne Morgan, Chairman of the 'American Committee for Devastated France', had visited Europe for several weeks, during which time she had convinced Suzanne that playing exhibition matches in the United States would be of great assistance in raising money for the relief work still being carried out in the war-torn regions of France.

Initially, Suzanne was reluctant to accept knowing that her father, a bad sailor, would not make the journey but a touch of patriotism and the knowledge that her mother and Albert de Joannis, Vice-President of the French Tennis Federation, and his wife would be by her side clinched the decision.

In June, Suzanne informed the French Tennis Federation that she had agreed to cross the Atlantic and would sail towards the end of July in the company of the French Davis Cup team.

Suzanne together with her mother Anaise (extreme right) and Mr and Mrs Albert de Joannis on board the 'Paris' just after arriving in New York in August 1921 to start her fund raising tour.

The tour was ill-fated from the start. Suzanne originally planned to leave Le Havre for New York on 23rd July, thereby allowing herself time to play some of the exhibition matches before competing in the United States Women's Championships at Forest Hills, New York, which opened on Monday, 15th August. However, plans for her to play at the Field Club of Greenwich, Connecticut on 3rd August,

Seabright L.T.C., N.J. on 6th August and at the Nassau Country Club, Glen Cove, L.I., on 7th August plus a short trip to the New England cities, were abandoned when she was forced to postpone her departure from France owing to an attack of bronchitis. A second departure, scheduled for 30th July, was also cancelled and eventually Suzanne embarked on the 'Paris' on 6th August and arrived in New York on Friday evening 12th August. She was sea sick for the first three days of the voyage but later managed to play some deck tennis on a court especially rigged for her. Her dancing was admired and it was said that she had eclipsed all the women aboard at the fancy dress ball. On the Saturday morning the 'Paris' docked at her pier at West Thirteenth Street and Suzanne dealt with a large gathering of the press and photographers. After being welcomed by officers of the United States LTA and a women's reception committee, Suzanne, wearing a large red hat, passed through the customs with her sixteen rackets and went directly to the Vanderbilt Hotel where she spent the remainder of the day resting.

The following morning the New York Times published a long article, written by Suzanne, in which she discussed the background to her visit, what she hoped to achieve and her health. This was the first of 13 articles, expounding on a whole range of tennis topics, which appeared carrying her signature. In the afternoon heavy rain prevented Suzanne practising so she requested that her opening match at Forest Hills, due to be played the next day, be postponed for 24 hours until the Tuesday. This was granted and she spent part of the Monday practising with Samuel Hardy, the U.S. Davis Cup captain.

The draw for the Women's Singles, which was unseeded in those days, found Suzanne and many of the leading Americans badly bunched in the third quarter. She was due to meet Miss Eleanor Goss in the first round and, if successful, the winner of the Molla Mallory – Mrs Marion Jessup match. On the Tuesday morning Eleanor Goss fell ill and defaulted to Suzanne. Molla Mallory, who had beaten Marian Jessop the previous day, and Suzanne then agreed to play their contest that afternoon, so as not to disappoint the large crowd which had arrived to see the Frenchwoman in action.

Just before five o'clock the two players, besieged by photographers, made their way from the club house to the centre court where a gallery of over 8,000 spectators awaited them. Before entering the enclosure Suzanne discarded her white fur coat and brilliant red cardigan to reveal an all white outfit apart from a broad, peacock-blue bandeau. Molla Mallory wore a dark brown cardigan over her white dress and she too had a hair band, light brown in colour.

During the knock-up both players appeared to be in good shape and full of confidence, with no indication of the drama that was to unfold. Suzanne soon realised that the quality of Molla Mallory's play was infinitely superior to their last meeting in early June. The American's determination was evident to all. She concentrated on each shot, moved freely and, above all, hit with tremendous power on each wing. In contrast, Suzanne controlled the ball well but her strokes were struck at a softer pace than normal.

Suzanne won the toss and elected to serve first. The first sign that she was in any difficulty occurred when she trailed 0–2 and love-40 and started coughing. This appeared to temporarily distract her opponent, who eventually lost the game after two deuces. However, the American soon regained her composure to lead 3–1. Although Suzanne's coughing, undoubtedly caused by her strenuous exertions, continued at intervals it did not affect her fighting qualities as she recovered to 2–3. The play that followed produced some magnificent tennis but gradually the continuous bombardment from Molla Mallory took its toll and Suzanne became discouraged. Three games in a row gave the American the set at 6–2.

In the second set, Suzanne lost the opening rally and then proceeded to serve a weak double fault. After hesitating for a moment she walked to the umpire's chair and announced, sobbingly, that she could not breathe and would be unable to continue. A slightly embarrassed Molla walked hastily towards the club house, while Suzanne, visibly trembling and in tears, left the court supported by Albert de Joannis and Joseph Jennings, the referee. Suzanne immediately left the ground and spent the remainder of the day in her room at the Forest Hills Inn. Feeling a little better on the next after-

Suzanne (left) and Molla Mallory in play during their second round match at the United States Championships, Forest Hills, New York on 16th August, 1921.

noon she returned to the tournament and chatted to Molla Mallory. Both expressed regret that they would be unable to play together in the doubles but hoped the opportunity would arise to allow them to meet again across the net before Suzanne returned to France.

A couple of days later, Suzanne was examined by a throat specialist who advised her to completely rest for a week to ten days. This necessitated her withdrawing from the United States Mixed Doubles Championship, which was due to commence the following Monday at the Longwood Cricket Club at Boston. On hearing the news her mother suggested they return home but Suzanne was determined to remain in the United States until she had fulfilled her commitment to the exhibition matches.

Before and after the historic match.
Left: Suzanne and Molla Mallory pose for the cameras.
Below: After defaulting, Suzanne in tears leaves the court supported by Albert de Joannis and Joseph Jennings, the referee.

Over the next week or so, Suzanne generally relaxed. She visited the West Point Military Academy and watched the baseball game between the New York Giants and the St. Louis Cardinals at the Polo Grounds in the Bronx.

Arrangements were made for her to play an exhibition match at the Newport Casino, Rhode Island against Molla Mallory or Eleanor Goss, on Wednesday, 31st August but this had to be cancelled. Eventually Suzanne made her first court appearance, since defaulting to Molla Mallory, on 30th August but this was strictly a practice session with Samuel Hardy at the Nassau Country Club at Long Island. The following day, after practising with Americans Dean Mathey and Leonard Beekman, Suzanne agreed to play an exhibition doubles with Vincent Richards against Willie Davis and Mrs May Bundy at Forest Hills following the United States v Japan Davis Cup tie. However, a few hours later this plan was cancelled when Suzanne's physician forbade her to play.

At last Suzanne's health improved and on Saturday, 10th September, in partnership with Mrs David Mills she defeated Miss Leslie Bancroft and Miss Martha Bayard, 7–5 9–7, at the South Orange Country Club, New Jersey. On the next day, Suzanne visited the Crescent Athletic Club at Bay Ridge for another exhibition but towards the end of the first set, in which she and Walter Merrill Hall were teamed against Harold Throckmorton and Leslie Bancroft, she became ill. Distressed, Suzanne managed to finish the set, which her opponents won 8–6, before collapsing and being assisted back to the club house. A meeting with Molla Mallory, scheduled for the following Friday at Philadelphia, was immediately cancelled.

Suzanne underwent a thorough examination by two physicians who agreed that she was unfit to play tennis for at least two or three months. Suzanne, quite upset, had no option but to make plans to return home. She had played just two exhibitions in aid of the 'American Committee for Devastated France' and these had raised only $1,600, which fell well short of the $3,600 used to bring Suzanne and her mother to the United States.

Suzanne departed from New York on board the 'La France' on Wednesday, 21st September without the same acclaim she received on arrival but nevertheless there was a considerable gathering to wish her goodbye. She said very little but expressed her thanks for the kindness shown during her stay.

Upon arriving in France, Suzanne proceeded to Pourville, where she rested for several weeks. She spent the winter at Nice during which time the Club at the Place Mozart moved premises to the Parc Imperial area, situated on the picturesque hillside overlooking the city and the Mediterranean, where new spacious accommodation provided 20 courts and good supporting services. The old site, which originated from 1890, was really too small. The ground, rented out from the local authorities, had a pavilion containing a restaurant, a reading room and changing facilities but there were only four courts, which were sometimes reduced to three to provide extra seating during tournaments. The Lenglen family moved from 13 Avenue Auber, facing Place Mozart, to Villa Ariem which overlooked the gates of the new Club.

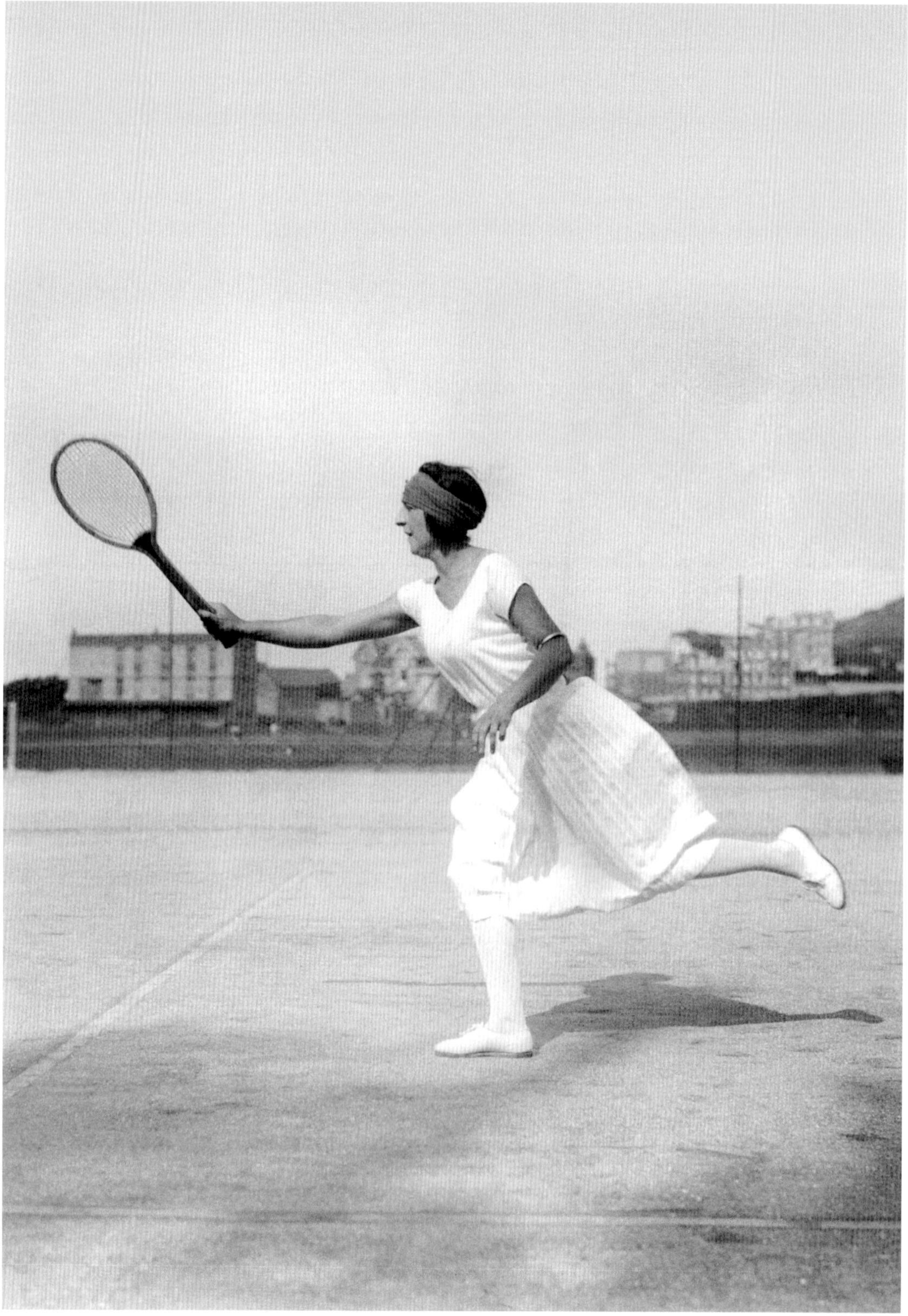

1922

Suzanne was expected to return to competitive play at the first Nice meeting in early February, but she contented herself with indulging in a few practice games. After an absence of nearly six months, Suzanne entered the South of France Championships held at the new Nice Club starting on the 13th March.

She did not contest the singles, but partnering Elizabeth Ryan and Count Soumarokoff sailed serenely through both doubles events. A fortnight later at the second meeting at the Beau Site Hotel, Suzanne entered the mixed doubles only and after reaching the final her partner Jean Borotra, making his debut on the Riviera, withdrew to fulfil an appointment in Paris to play in an Army Football match. However, he immediately returned to the Côte d'Azur and, despite an injured ankle, paired with Suzanne to win the mixed doubles at the Metropole Hotel tournament at Cannes.

The last tournament of the season at the Beau Soleil, Monte Carlo, the week of 17th April, was the scene of Suzanne's triumphant return to singles play. She won the event without dropping a game and in the final outclassed Eleanor Goss, who won just four points in the first set and eight points in the second. Suzanne also won the mixed doubles title with Alain Gerbault, who in 1923 was to cross the Atlantic single-handed in his 30–foot yacht 'Firecrest', taking 102 days.

Suzanne's participation in the closing weeks of the Riviera season had a remarkable influence on the 'gate'. Crowds at the new Nice venue were the largest on

---

Facing page: Suzanne playing at Pourville – one of her favourite clubs.

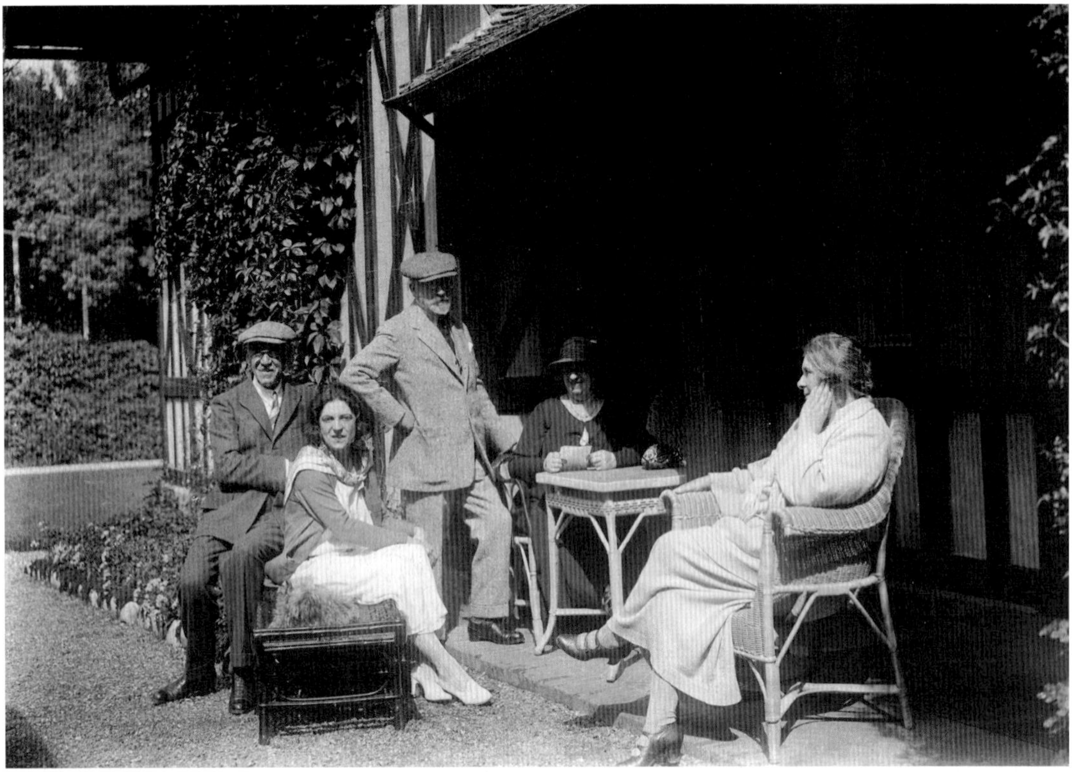

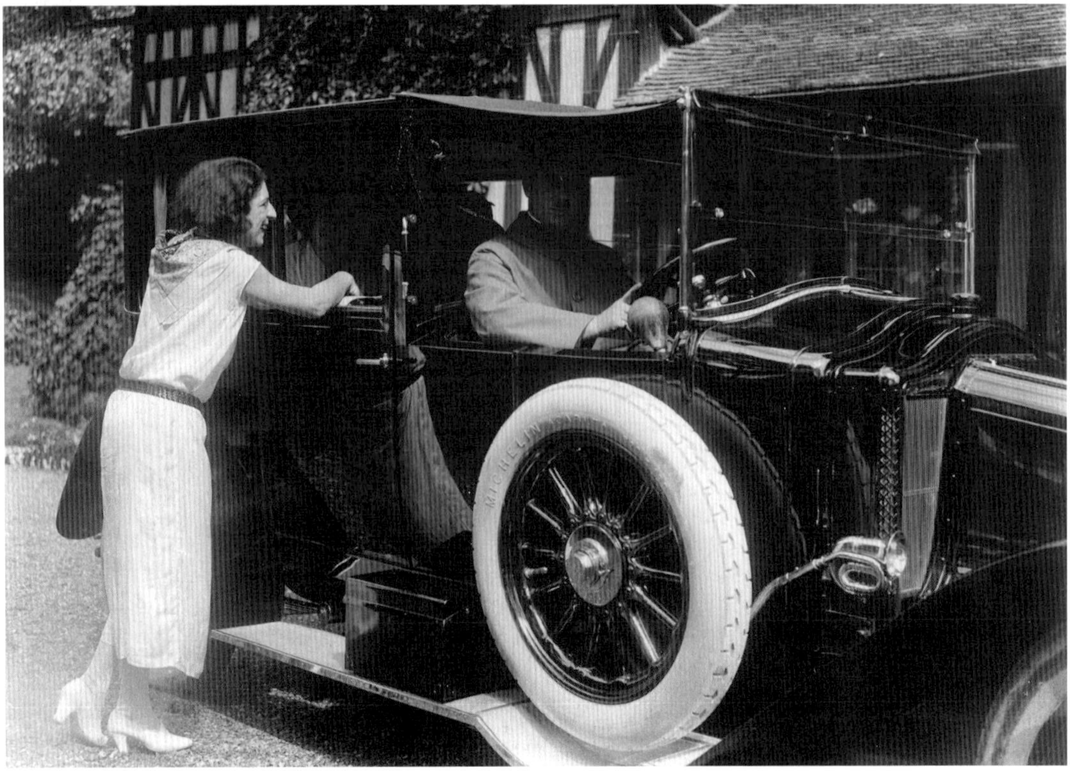
MICHELIN

Often when Suzanne required a holiday from tennis she would stay with her uncle and aunt, Alexandre and Eloide Hugot, at their beautiful residence, the Manoir de Mon Coin, near Pourville, on the north coast of France. This group of photographs was taken in April, 1922:
Left: A family gathering – left to right: Her father Charles, Suzanne, uncle Alexandre, mother Anaise and aunt Eloide.
Below left: Suzanne chats to the chauffeur of her uncle's car, a Renault 20.
Right: Reading a book by the fireside, Suzanne is seen wearing an engagement ring.
Below: Suzanne relaxing in the gardens with the dogs.

record, despite the grounds being situated well away from the town centre. Her one appearance at the Cannes Club, just to play an exhibition match, taxed the capacity of the ground, with every seat being taken up at 15 francs, while the tournaments at Beau Site Hotel, Metropole Hotel and Monte Carlo were also packed with sightseers.

By now Suzanne was becoming a well known public figure in Britain and as such was featured in a coloured cartoon published in the 1922 Punch Almanack. Entitled 'Popularity is to be achieved nowadays only through the Cinema', the print was divided into five, each showing a notable of the day such as Lloyd George, Lord Curzon etc. Suzanne is seen very athletically jumping over a range of mountains in 'A leap for life'.

Suzanne retained her singles title at the World's Hard Court Championships held at the Royal Leopold Club, Brussels in May but there was a brief period in her semi-final with Kathleen McKane when she seemed to falter and be likely to fail. However, she recovered herself in time to avert the crisis and having gained the ascendancy never let go. Watched by Queen Elizabeth of the Belgians, the drama occurred in the first set, when Kathleen McKane recovered from 0–3 to hold two set points on her service at 5–4, 40–15 but Suzanne with supreme steadiness saved the day. A great struggle ensued but after the Englishwoman led 8–7, Suzanne won the next three games fairly easily for 10–8. In the second set Kathleen McKane played into Suzanne's hands by going to the net too often and had to be content with two games. In the final, Suzanne had a routine win over Elizabeth Ryan, 6–3 6–2. She retained both her doubles crowns but with different partners from the previous year, Elizabeth Ryan and Henri Cochet.

From Brussels, Suzanne took the train to Bordeaux for a mixed doubles event, which she won with Jean Borotra, and then returned to Paris for the French National Championships, where she retained all three titles. Germaine Golding came through the singles to challenge Suzanne but after starting well, faded to 6–4 6–0. Her partners in the doubles events were Jacques Brugnon and Germaine Pigueron.

In early June, Suzanne visited Lille for the first time in eight years. She had a very conclusive 6–0 6–2 victory over Germaine Golding in the final but there was some cause for alarm in the round before when playing Doris Wolfson. Leading 30–love in the second game, Suzanne showed signs of physical distress and lost the next four points but unaccountably she recovered to win 11 successive games.

As a prelude to Wimbledon, Suzanne played an exhibition match on finals day at the Roehampton tournament, teaming with Jean Borotra to beat William Crawley and Kathleen McKane, 6–1 6–3.

Two days later on Monday, 26th June the new Wimbledon grounds were officially declared open by King George V, who at 3.30 pm stood in the Royal Box and gave three blows on a gong. Apart from the Centre Court, which had a seating capacity of 9,989 and standing room for approximately 3,600, there were only 12 other courts available that year as the No. 1 and No. 2 Courts had not been constructed. The meeting, one of the wettest on record and lasting to the third Wednesday, broke with tradition by abolishing the challenge round of the two singles and the men's doubles events. There had been much discussion over the years on this subject and in 1921 a poll of the players showed that a large majority was in favour of the holder playing through. Suzanne as champion was consulted and she agreed to the change.

Suzanne's first contest was not until the Wednesday when a brief appearance on No. 3 Court accounted for Mrs M.F. Ellis, 6–0 6–0. Two days later the match between Suzanne and Kathleen McKane drew the largest crowd ever seen at a tennis match in England up to that date. The capacity of the Centre Court was quite inadequate to the demands put upon it and hundreds were turned away. Suzanne controlled the ball well in the opening set, which she won without striking a volley, 6–1. In the second set, Kathleen McKane, keeping a much better length and volleying brilliantly, led 3–0. Suzanne's errors suddenly disappeared and playing superbly she won four games in a row. The Englishwoman squared the score and amidst tremendous excitement fought to within a point of breaking service for 5–4 but a perfect shot down the line from Suzanne saved the game. With the home crowd willing her on, Kathleen McKane tried desperately in the next few games but a relieved Suzanne edged through, 7–5.

On the Monday, Suzanne returned to No. 3 Court where, before a huge crowd, she overawed Miss Evelyn Colyer, a 19–year-old from London, 6–0 6–0. The following day Suzanne met Elizabeth Ryan on the Centre Court. After losing a tame opening set, 6–1, the American made a bold bid for the second. The intensity of her attack presented many problems to Suzanne who, visibly tiring towards the end, was a shade lucky to succeed, 8–6.

Irene Peacock produced some spirited play on the Friday against Suzanne in the first set of the semi-final, her driving on both wings being particularly effective.

Suzanne lost four games but was never really in danger. After dropping the opening game of the second set, Suzanne asserted herself and reeled off six games, although several of them were long and hard fought.

To the delight of most, Molla Mallory came through the bottom half of the draw, without losing a set, to contest the final against Suzanne on Saturday, 8th July. Spectators started queuing at dawn for a chance to witness what promised to be the match of the year in which the supremacy of one or the other would be established. The previous encounter on the Centre Court had been interrupted for two hours by rain and was not completed until just before 7 pm. Suzanne and Molla Mallory had no desire to postpone their match until the Monday, so at the unprecedented time for a Championship final of 7.01 pm they went on court. At 7.26 pm they came off with Suzanne triumphant, 6–2 6–0. From first to last her confidence and concentration never wavered. She volleyed only occasionally but the power and accuracy of her forehand and the invulnerability of her backhand gained her point after point. Molla Mallory played courageously throughout but she was never able to match the artistry of Suzanne who won the last nine games. Revenge for their previous encounter must have been very sweet.

Suzanne and Elizabeth Ryan had no difficulty in retaining their doubles crown, defeating Kathleen McKane and her elder sister Mrs Margaret Stocks in the final, 6–0 6–4. Suzanne also won the mixed doubles title with Australian, Pat O'Hara Wood.

After playing in Sophie Wavertree's annual garden party, Suzanne took part in a series of

The Ladies' final on the Centre Court at the 'new' Wimbledon in 1922. Suzanne (right) crushes Molla Mallory 6–2 6–0 in 25 minutes to gain revenge for her American defeat.

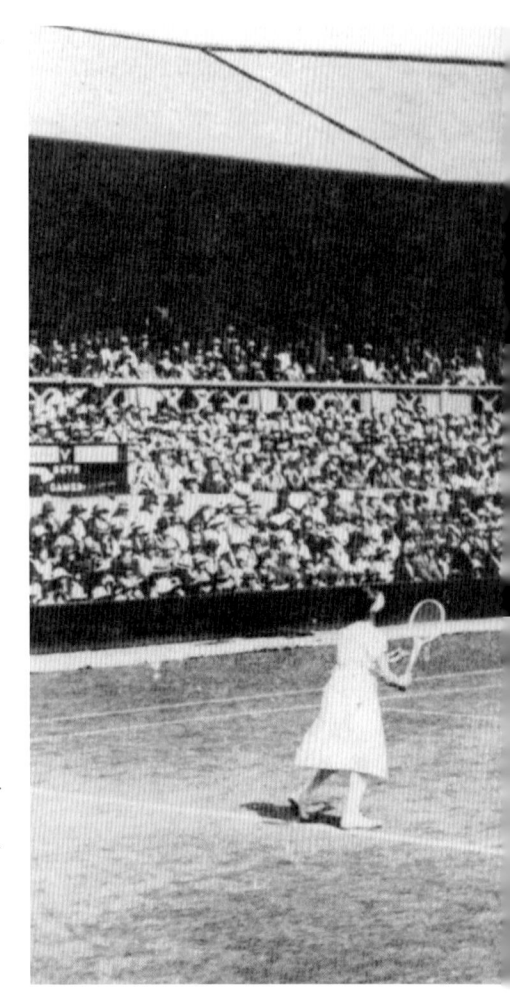

matches between the British Isles and France held on the Centre Court at Wimbledon on Friday, 14th July. The event, attended by the Princess Royal, was organised by the British League of Help in aid of rebuilding Verdun. Suzanne, partnered by Jean Borotra, defeated William Crawley and Kathleen McKane in an interesting match, 6–4 4–6 6–1 and later two of the rackets used by Suzanne were autographed and put up for auction, which realised 14 guineas.

Suzanne played continually for the next two months without being beaten in any event. A week in Central France at La Bourboule, where she routed Mlle Helene Contostavlos in the final 6–1 6–0, was followed by visits to six Channel resorts. A hollow win over Marguerite Billout in the title round at Deauville, 6–1 6–1, gave

Suzanne with a group of players on the seafront at Pourville, where they were competing in the local tournament. Next to her is Carlyle Blackwell, who before the First World War was an outstanding stage and screenstar in the United States.

Left: Carlyle Blackwell is seen explaining the intricacies of the camera to Suzanne.

Right: Suzanne arm in arm with Roger Danet, her regular partner in mixed doubles throughout the year. For a time they were engaged.

Below: Standing outside the American Bar, Suzanne points to her name on the poster for the follwing week's tournament at Le Havre. With her can be seen Jacques Brugnon, Marcel Dupont, Roger Danet, and Albert de Joannis and his wife.

Suzanne her only singles win on the coast, as rain prevented her playing Mme Marie Danet in the final at Pourville and at Le Touquet she was indisposed at the semi-final stage. Suzanne restricted her appearances to exhibitions at Boulogne and to doubles at Le Havre and Etretat. Her programme for the season concluded at Marseille with another simple win over Helene Contostavlos.

During the year Suzanne won 15 mixed doubles titles, seven of them pairing with Roger Danet, the 23–year-old son of Marie Danet. After victory at Lille during June, the couple played together week after week from mid-July to the end of September in the north of France, with a final flourish at Marseille. Their relationship blossomed and there were reports of an engagement with Suzanne wearing a ring in public, but by the end of the year the affair had faded.

In recognition of her continued success at Wimbledon, Suzanne was elected an Honorary member of the Nice Lawn Tennis Club.

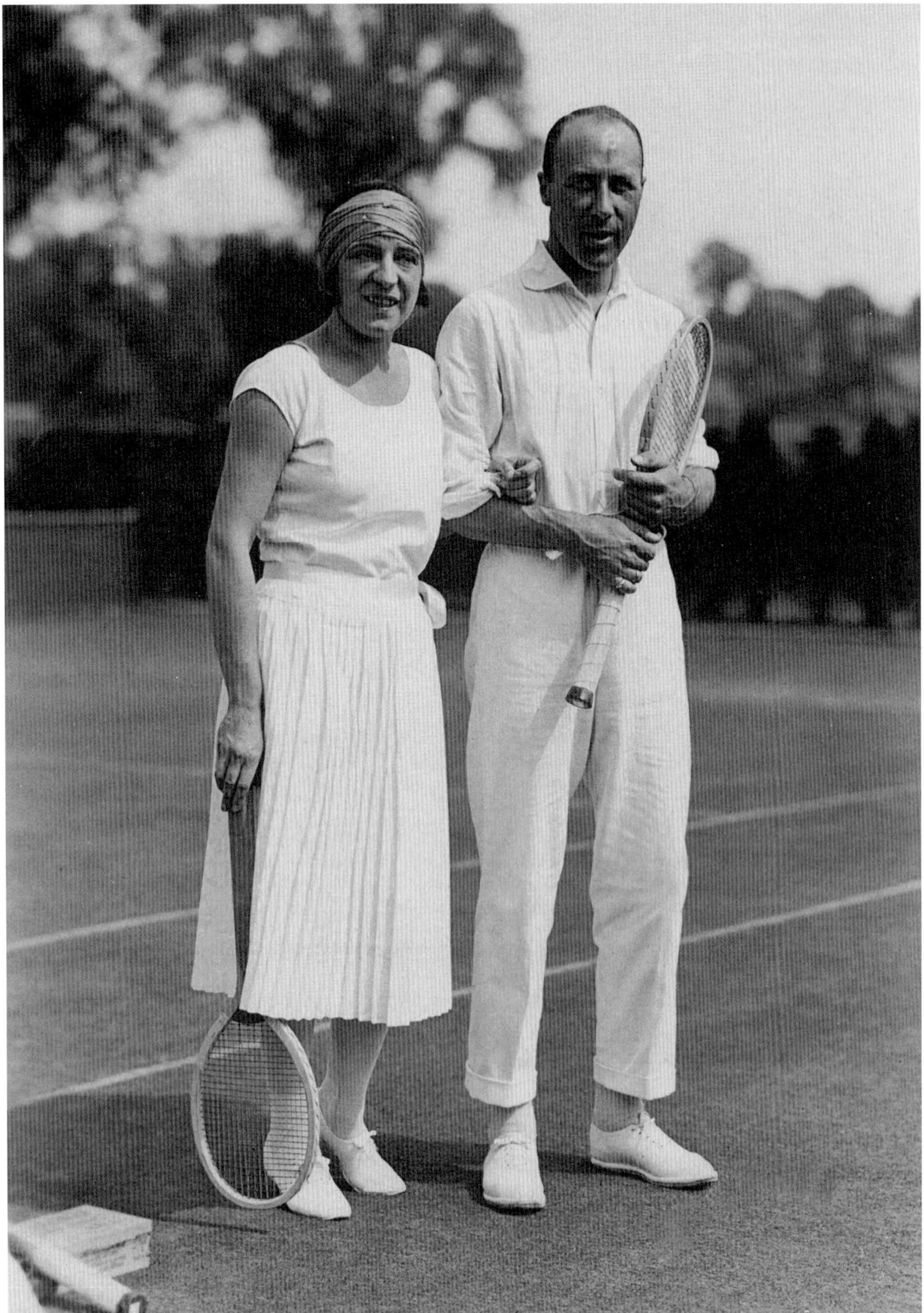

1923

Suzanne spent another enjoyable and rewarding season on the French Riviera in 1923, participating in ten tournaments but limiting herself to five singles events. At the Beau Site Hotel New Year meeting. Elizabeth Ryan's withdrawal from the singles, owing to a blistered hand, eased the way for Phyllis Satterthwaite to reach the final, where she put up a plucky fight against Suzanne before gradually fading, 6–4 6–2. At Nice in February, Suzanne was hardly bothered as she cruised through four rounds to find that Elizabeth Ryan had a severe cold and was unable to play in the final. A week later at the Carlton Club, the American, fully recovered, held Suzanne to 3–all but thereafter never seriously threatened again.

At Monte Carlo, Suzanne chose not to compete in the singles and Kathleen McKane, who made her Riviera debut two weeks earlier but had restricted her appearances to doubles, defeated Elizabeth Ryan in the final. Molla Mallory, playing for the first time in the South of France, never acclimatised to the conditions and lost easily to Phyllis Satter- thwaite at the quarter-final stage. The most thrilling match of the week was the final of the doubles, in which Suzanne and Elizabeth Ryan narrowly defeated Kathleen McKane and Dorothea Chambers, 6–1 3–6 6–4 after being led 4–3 in the final set. This was the only time the champion pair lost a set in open competition.

Facing page: Suzanne with Jean Washer, the Belgian Davis Cup player at Wimbledon in 1923. They contested the mixed doubles, but were eliminated in the semi-final by Randolph Lycett and Elizabeth Ryan, the eventual champions.

The singles entry at Menton for the Riviera Championships was quite superior to that of any tournament on the circuit and included Suzanne, Molla Mallory, Phyllis Satterthwaite, Geraldine Beamish, Elizabeth Ryan and Kathleen McKane. The possibility of Suzanne meeting Molla Mallory in the semi-final created much interest but the clash never materialised as the American was surprisingly well beaten in the second round by Miss Lesley Cadle, 6–0 7–5. Suzanne dismissed this relatively unknown Englishwoman from Durham, 6–0 6–1, before overwhelming Phyllis Satterthwaite, 6–0 6–0, to reach the final where Kathleen McKane awaited. Before a large crowd and on a very soft court Suzanne won this clash with some difficulty, 6–2 7–5, and was a little lucky in the second set when a net-cord tipped the balance at a crucial stage in the ninth game.

The much awaited match between Suzanne and Molla Mallory occurred the following week in the semi-final of the South of France Championships at Nice. Suzanne won without losing a game, almost entirely by deep drives of modest pace and heartbreaking precision to which the American had no answer. The encounter lasted 25 minutes with the winner scoring 50 points to 18. In the final Elizabeth Ryan made no headway facing Suzanne and had to be content with one game only. There was a major upset in the mixed doubles when Suzanne and Count Soumarokoff were beaten by Randolph Lycett and Elizabeth Ryan at the semi-final stage, 6–3 7–5, thereby failing to win the trophy for the third year in succession. This was Suzanne's first defeat in any match, that was fought to a finish, since the Olympic Games in 1920.

Suzanne closed her Riviera season by playing doubles at two tournaments in Cannes. Overall she had won eight doubles titles, all with Elizabeth Ryan, and six mixed doubles titles. A few days later Suzanne took part in an exhibition doubles at Toulon, prior to visiting Algiers, accompanied by Pierre Hirset, Maurice Germot, Marcel Dupont and Pierre du Pasquier, to play a series of matches against local players at the Municipal Stadium. Suzanne, who was given a marvellous reception wherever she went, easily beat Mlle S. Damin, the Algerian champion, and Mme Giroud, both without conceding a game.

The World's Hard Court Championships, which returned to St. Cloud in May, attracted an excellent attendance of around 6,000 each day in spite of the weather throughout being very unpleasant. For the third consecutive year, Suzanne won the singles title. She was not bothered until the semi-final when Geraldine Beamish maintained frequent baseline rallies, without securing more than one

At the South of France Championships at Nice in 1923, Suzanne and Count Mikhail Soumarokoff (left) were surprisingly beaten in the semi-final of the mixed doubles by Elizabeth Ryan and Randolph Lycett.

game in each set. Suzanne won the final from Kathleen McKane in two sets of nine games. At no time did play sparkle as both players made numerous unforced errors. Kathleen McKane's downfall was her lack of control on the backhand and her inability to seize volleying chances created by her own tactics. Suzanne retained the mixed doubles crown with Henri Cochet but with Germaine Golding offered weak resistance in the final of the doubles to Geraldine Beamish and Kathleen McKane and lost 6–2 6–3. Suzanne seemed reconciled to defeat from the start.

In June, Suzanne retained her three French National Championships at the Racing Club in Paris, where the organisers decided to follow the British lead and abolished the challenge rounds in all events. This made little difference to Suzanne who easily beat Helene Contostavlos, 6–2 6–0, and Jeanne Vaussard, 6–0 6–0, on the way to the final of the singles against Germaine Golding. Suzanne was led 4–0 in the second set of this match before she rallied in fine style to capture the next six games for victory at 6–1 6–4. Suzanne won the mixed doubles for the third time in a row with Jacques Brugnon and the doubles with a new partner from Marseille, 19–year-old Mlle Julie (Diddie) Vlasto, a cousin of Helene Contostavlos.

Following her normal practice, Suzanne stayed at Bailey's Hotel, South Kensington during the Wimbledon fortnight, which apart from the opening day was fine and sometimes hot. The attendance was greater than the year before and there was a record entry, including 70 in the Ladies' Singles. Suzanne won this event, for the fifth consecutive year, in such a convincing manner that she dropped only 11 games in six matches.

After a bye, Suzanne, on very top form, disposed of Miss Margaret (Peggy) Ingram who, despite not claiming a game, gave a plucky and spirited exhibition for one so young and unused to a packed Centre Court. In the next round, played on the newly opened No. 2 Court, Suzanne inflicted a 6–0 6–3 defeat on Mrs Phyllis Covell, who initially seemed nervous and out of touch. In the second set she was more in harmony when her driving and volleying were seen to good effect. Two days later on the Centre Court, Diddie Vlasto started strongly against Suzanne but after missing a few easy openings, succumbed, 6–1 6–0.

At the quarter-final stage, Mrs Marie Hazel contrived on No. 2 Court to get two games running from Suzanne before capitulating, 6–2 6–1. In the same round Geraldine Beamish played superbly to defeat Molla Mallory, in a very long match, but a couple of days later she could not reach the same heights against Suzanne who, giving no mercy, won twelve games without reply.

In the final, Kathleen McKane did her utmost to unsettle Suzanne by mounting a sustained attack but she was not sufficiently consistent to reap rich reward. Her smashing lacked its normal bite and often her backhand broke down but only because of the pressure it had to bear. Suzanne, playing within herself, hardly ever hit the ball hard and seemed content to wait for an opening to appear. The fact that the loser had captured 43 points out of a total of 106 was not reflected in the match score of 6–2 6–2.

Suzanne and Elizabeth Ryan strode majestically through the doubles event, defeating Evelyn Colyer and Miss Joan Austin, in the final, 6–3 6–1. This youthful British pair, who had thrilled the public during the week with a series of surprising victories over very useful couples, played with great zest and abandon, especially in the opening set when they reeled off three games in succession, amidst rapturous applause. Suzanne in tandem with Jean Washer of Belgium lost in the semi-final

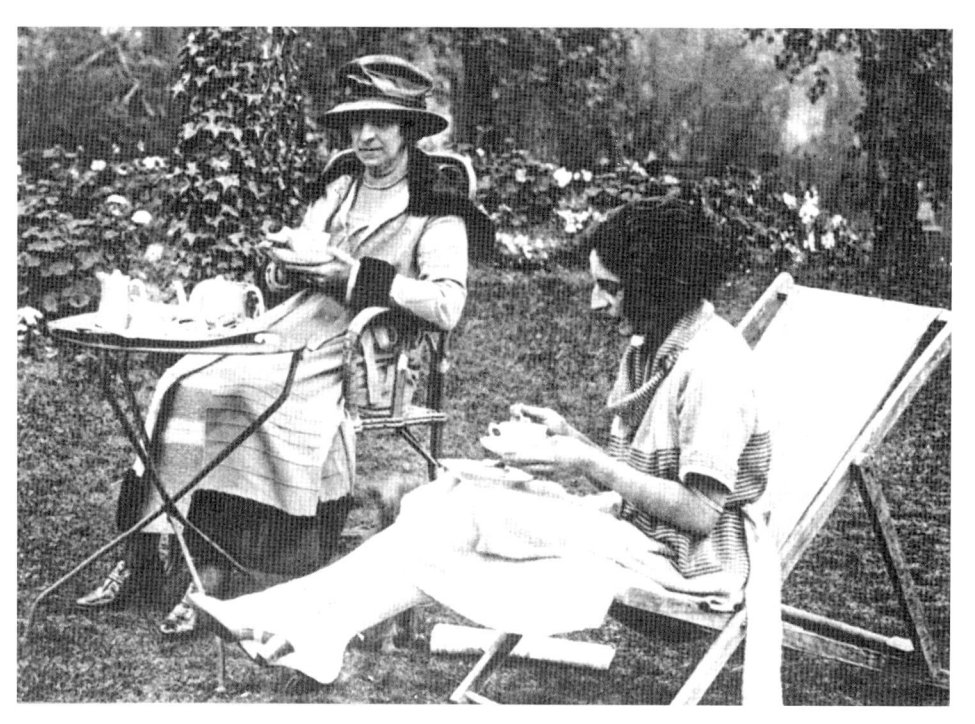

Suzanne at home: Tea in the garden with her mother Anaise.

of the mixed doubles to the eventual winners, Randolph Lycett and Elizabeth Ryan, 7–5 6–3.

This was the last year at Wimbledon when the 'World's Championships on Grass' was added to the traditional title of 'The Championships'. In 1913 the newly created International Lawn Tennis Federation had awarded this title to the British Isles in perpetuity for services rendered to the game over many years. The 'World Championships on Hard Courts and Covered Courts' were also started that year but they were allocated annually to different venues. All these titles were abolished as a condition of the United States joining the Federation.

On the Monday after Wimbledon, Suzanne played at Sophie Wavertree's garden party and the next day, partnered Eduardo Flaquer against Manuel, Count de Gomar and Christiaan van Lennep in an exhibition match during the Holland v Spain Davis Cup tie at Devonshire Park, Eastbourne, winning 6–2 7–5. During August, Suzanne appeared at four tournaments, Deauville, Pourville, Cabourg and in Belgium, at Chateau D'Ardennes and easily won the singles title at each,

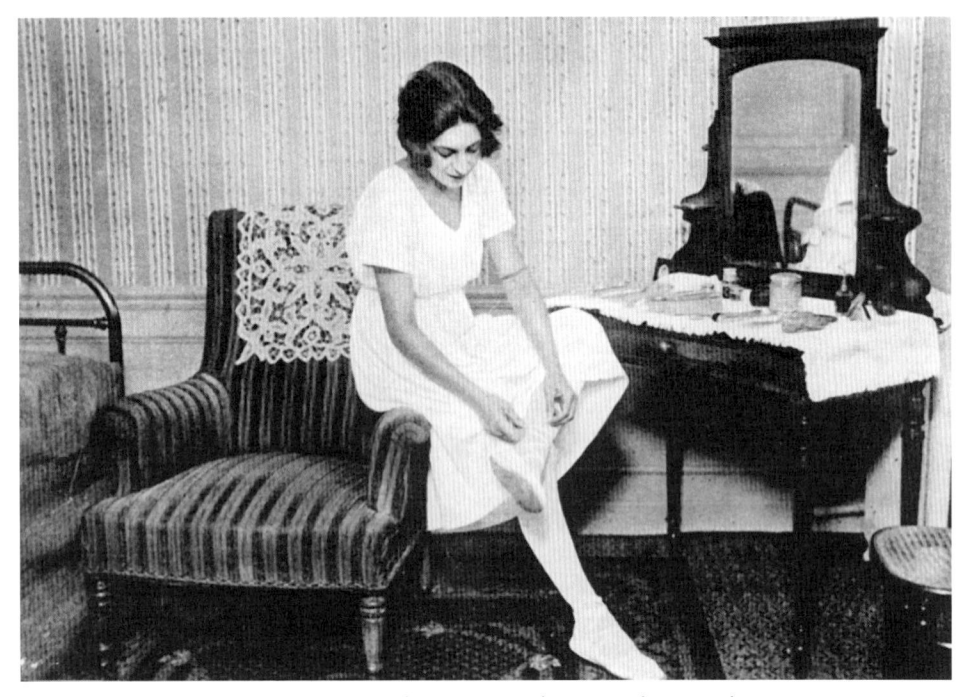

Suzanne at home – maybe preparing for a social game of tennis.

mainly against weak domestic opposition. At Pourville, Suzanne never lost a game in the singles event.

Early in September Suzanne began a very successful tour, mainly in Spain. Crowds flocked to see her play in the International Championships of Spain at San Sebastian where, before the King and Queen of Spain, she won the singles title by defeating Mme Nanette Le Besnerais in the final, 6–1 6–1 and Mme Germaine LeConte, in the challenge round, 6–1 6–0. Back in France at Biarritz, a week later, Suzanne beat the same two ladies in the singles and during the process of winning the event she did not drop a game. At both tournaments Suzanne won the mixed doubles title with Eduardo Flaquer.

Suzanne, accompanied by Eduardo Flaquer and Count de Gomar, then visited the Club Nautico de Las Arenas in Bilbao to play exhibition matches. A few days later Suzanne competed in the Portuguese International Championships at the Club de Cascais in Lisbon, where she won the singles title without losing a game, beating the local champion Sra Angelica Plantier on the way, and the mixed doubles with Eduardo Flaquer.

Suzanne then returned to Spain and on 2nd–4th October played exhibition matches at the Recreative Club in Huelva, where each day she partnered Eduardo Flaquer against two men, Count de Gomar and Raimundo Morales. Suzanne and Eduardo Flaquer lost the first match, 8–6 3–6 6–1 but won the other two, 2–6 6–2 6–1 and 7–5 6–3.

On 6th and 7th October, Suzanne watched the Men's International between France and Spain played in Barcelona, during which she and Maurice Cousin played an exhibition match against the brothers, George and Henri Gouttenoire. The following week Suzanne competed in the International Championships of Barcelona at the Tennis Club del Turo, and captured the singles title by defeating Srta Rosa Torras in the semi-final, 6–2 6–0, and Srta Maria Luisa Marnet in the final without the loss of a game. Suzanne also won the mixed doubles in partnership with Eduardo Flaquer. Her tour ended at Zaragoza on 17th and 18th October, when she played exhibition matches at the Sociedad Athletica Stadium. On both days she partnered Eduardo Flaquer to victory over Raimundo Morales and Jose Maria Tarruella, first 6–1 6–4 6–2 and then 6–4 6–2 6–3.

1923 was an outstanding year for Suzanne who won 45 titles, 16 in singles, 13 in doubles and 16 in mixed doubles.

An artist's impression of Suzanne – Almada of Portugal

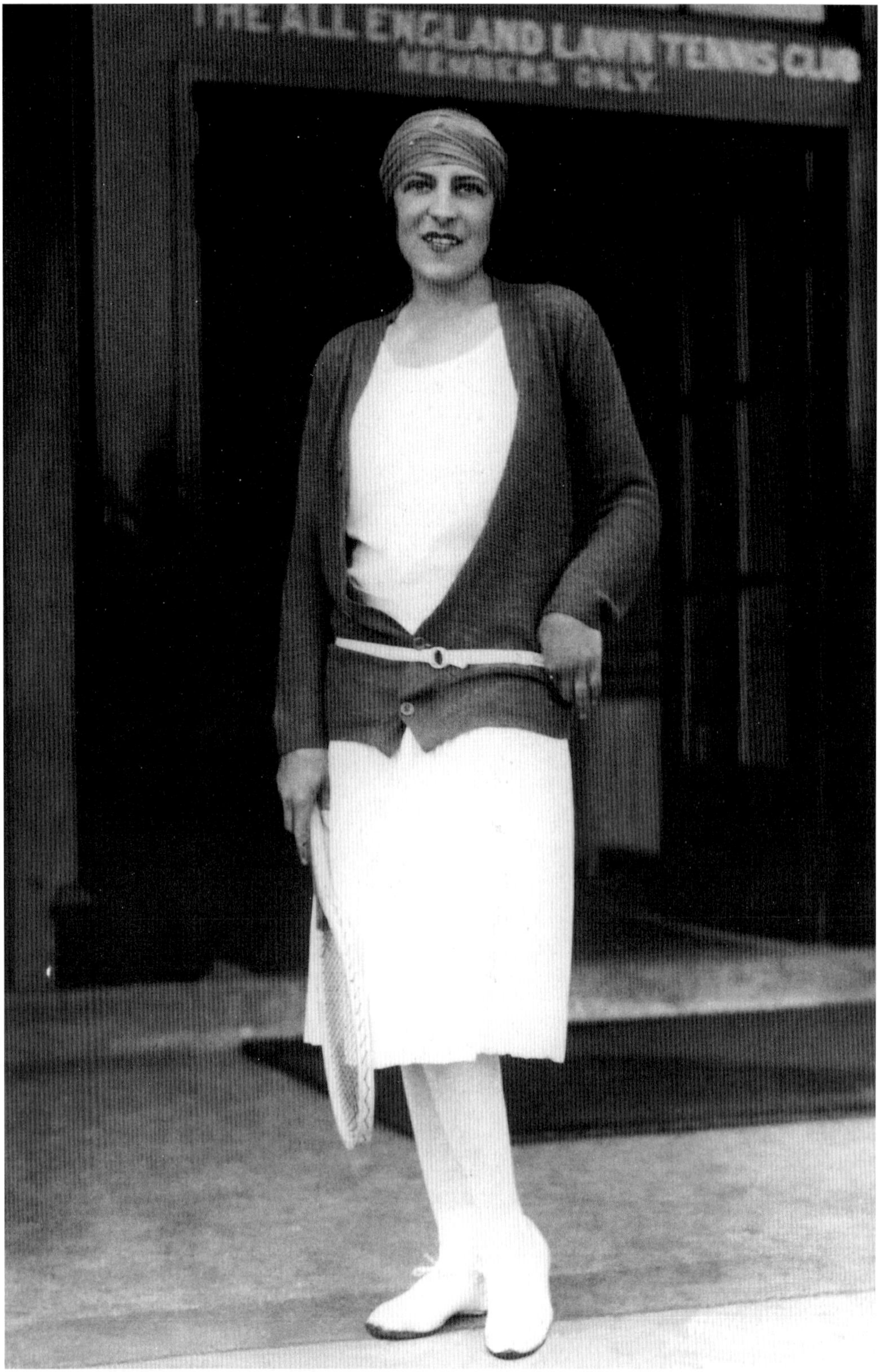
THE ALL ENGLAND LAWN TENNIS CLUB
MEMBERS ONLY.

1924

Suzanne did not enjoy the best of health during the 1924 French Riviera season and competed in only three singles events, although in all she participated in 10 tournaments. In January she confined her activities to doubles events and at the inaugural meeting of the Gallia Club in Cannes recorded the highest number of games she ever played in a set. This occurred in the mixed doubles final when in partnership with Col. Henry Mayes she beat Charles Aeschliman, the top Swiss player, and Elizabeth Ryan, 6–4 1–6 15–13. There was an incident during the doubles final, whereby, in the seventh game Suzanne was foot-faulted by a linesman and she declined to continue until the official had been changed. Apparently, the custom in France at that time was to give a warning to the player before calling a foot-fault. The linesman, an Englishman, was replaced and the match continued. The tournament was held on the five courts of the Club, adjacent to the Gallia Hotel, which was once the Casino of Cannes.

Suzanne won the singles final at the first Nice meeting, allowing England's Mrs Dorothy Barron one game in two sets. Much of the interest in the tournament was lost when a bad cold caused Elizabeth Ryan to retire early. The following week, Suzanne played doubles at the Carlton Club but was not sufficiently well to appear at Beaulieu and Monte Carlo. At Menton she won the singles title for the third time, dismissing Dorothy Barron, 6–4 6–0, Phyllis Covell, 6–2 6–1, and in the final, after a tense first set, Elizabeth Ryan, 7–5 6–1.

Facing page: Suzanne pictured in front of the Members' entrance at the AELTC.

When the circuit moved back to Nice for the South of France Championships, the competitors were able to take advantage of an extension to the pavilion, which included new luxurious dressing rooms, restaurant, dancing salon and roof accommodation for many spectators. Attached to each court was a nameplate. No. 1 Court was 'Suzanne Lenglen', No. 2, 'A.F. Wilding', No. 3 'Georges Gault', No. 4 'Lieut St. Cyr' and so on, all except the first paying a tribute to a hero of the war. In an entertaining match, Suzanne defeated Phyllis Covell in the final of the singles, 6–2 6–1.

At the Cannes Club, Suzanne partnered 46-year-old Australian, Norman Brookes, the 1907 and 1914 Wimbledon Singles Champion, who was making his first visit to Europe since 1919. Unfortunately he had an attack of influenza and withdrew after the second round. Two weeks later they joined forces again at the Metropole Hotel tournament for an invitation mixed doubles event, arranged on a 'round robin' basis. Six pairs, all of very high standard, played each other with Norman Brookes and Suzanne emerging on top without losing a set, let alone a match. Suzanne's season closed at Juan-les-Pins with an easy doubles win with Mrs Florence Gould. In all she had won eight doubles titles, seven teamed with Elizabeth Ryan, and eight mixed doubles titles.

In the middle of April Suzanne, in company with Alain Gerbault and Jean Borotra, returned to Barcelona to compete in the International Championships at the Tennis Club del Turo. She inflicted a crushing 6–0 6–0 defeat on Eleanor Goss in the semi-final of the singles and went on to retain her title by defeating Maria Luisa Marnet in the final, 6–1 6–1. Suzanne won the doubles with Eleanor Goss and the mixed with Eduardo Flaquer. Soon afterwards she suffered an attack of jaundice which left her unable to defend her French National title in early June and in her absence Diddie Vlasto became the new champion.

For a time there was doubt whether Suzanne would be fit to play at Wimbledon but ten days beforehand her entry was confirmed and the authorities gave a sigh of relief. She had become an idol. Whenever she played crowds packed the court and thronged the gangways in an attempt to get a glimpse of her in action. Whether she was engaged in a singles or a doubles match made no difference, the interest of the public was remarkable and because of this the Committee never dared to allocate any of her matches to a court other than the top two. Sometimes in mid-evening, Suzanne would take a box of balls and together with a colleague have a knock-up on an outside court. Within minutes the surround would be filled with hundreds of people hustling for a favourable position. Off court, she was constantly besieged by photographers and by admirers who, with their book or programme, jostled for her autograph.

The first week of The Championships must have seemed like a dream to Suzanne who, not having played competitive tennis for over two months, eased herself into the programme by winning three singles matches without losing a game. Her first two encounters took place on the new No. 1 Court, which had been constructed west of the Centre Court in readiness for the meeting, against Miss Sylvia Lumley-Ellis and

The No. 1 Court of the Nice Lawn Tennis Club at the Parc Imperial in 1924. Suzanne lived in the Villa Ariem at the entrance to the Club.

Miss Edith Clarke, who were quite outclassed. Her third victory was on the Centre Court versus Hazel Wightman. The American forced many games to deuce but lacked the confidence to apply the finishing touch.

On the second Monday, Suzanne met Elizabeth Ryan in the quarter-final on the Centre Court and few expected this match to unfold any differently from their many clashes in the past. Suzanne swept through the first set 6–2 when Elizabeth Ryan, striving for speed and placement, made frequent errors.

In the second set it soon became clear that the American had found her touch and, with Suzanne running more and more, she forged ahead to 4–1. However, at this stage the control of the play swung dramatically in Suzanne's favour as she hit harder and tightened up on her length to reach 5–4. Only one point had been conceded in the last three games. Elizabeth Ryan then countered by serving and smashing well and using the drop shot to good effect led 6–5. She was denied the set in the next game when a couple of line decisions went against her, but undaunted she kept her nerve to win the next two games and the set 8–6. The crowd erupted. This was the first set Suzanne had lost in Europe since the challenge round at Wimbledon in 1919

In the deciding set honours were evenly shared for four games, Suzanne being forced to hurry her strokes by the constant attack from Elizabeth Ryan. In the sixth game errors crept into the American's play and she fell behind but immediately retorted to 3–4. The critical game was the eighth, when Elizabeth Ryan brilliantly pulled up from 0–30 to 40–30 only to hit the next drive inches over the line. She tried to drop shot but Suzanne turned this into a winner. A double fault and her chance was gone. The excitement continued when Suzanne failed to clinch the match with her next service but hitting with great precision reached 40–15 in the tenth game. Elizabeth Ryan saved one match point but then a very relieved Suzanne hit another perfect drive to take the match. There was much cheering as they left the court together.

Suzanne perhaps unwisely played again that day when she partnered Jean Borotra in a mixed doubles match on No. 1 Court. The day's happenings had taken a great toll on Suzanne's physical and mental reserves and later in the evening she decided to withdraw from the mixed doubles in order to save herself for the other two events. This decision was officially announced on the following morning. Later in that day, Suzanne accepted her doctor's advice that she was unfit to continue and consequently withdrew from the tournament. When the sensational

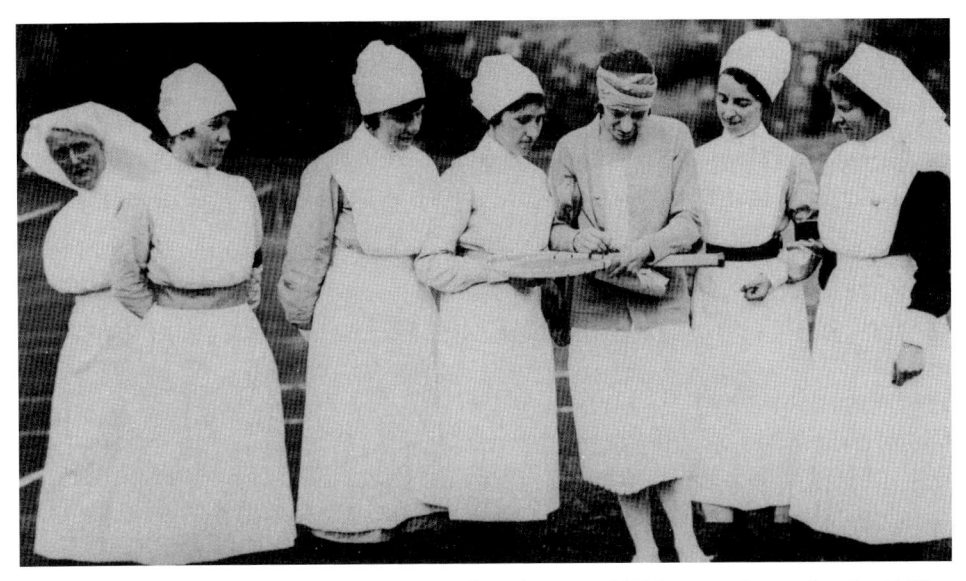

Suzanne often played for charity. In 1924, after playing exhibition matches at Stanford Hill, London, she autographed two rackets, which were raffled to raise money for the nearby Prince of Wales Hospital at Tottenham. She is assisted by nurse, Miss M. H. Billington.

news was made public on the Wednesday some of the press were critical but most accepted that her breakdown was the result of her exertions against Elizabeth Ryan coupled with the consequence of her recent illness.

Suzanne's retirement allowed Kathleen McKane a walkover into the final where, in a tremendous struggle, she recovered from a set and within a point of 5–1 down, to defeat the 18-year-old United States Champion, Miss Helen Wills, who was destined within a few years to take over Suzanne's mantle.

Although Suzanne's five year tenure of the title had come to an end, France remained to the fore. By winning the Gentlemen's Singles crown, Jean Borotra began his country's dominance of the event for the next six years, whereby he, Henri Cochet and Rene Lacoste each became champion twice.

Suzanne stayed until the end of Wimbledon and attended Sophie Wavertree's garden party as an onlooker. A week later, the Olympic Games was staged in Paris and Suzanne, disappointed at not being well enough to play, gave support as spectator. During the following weeks there were reports of Suzanne returning to play but as events proved she did not take to the court competitively until six months had expired. She spent much time at Nice with her father who was not well.

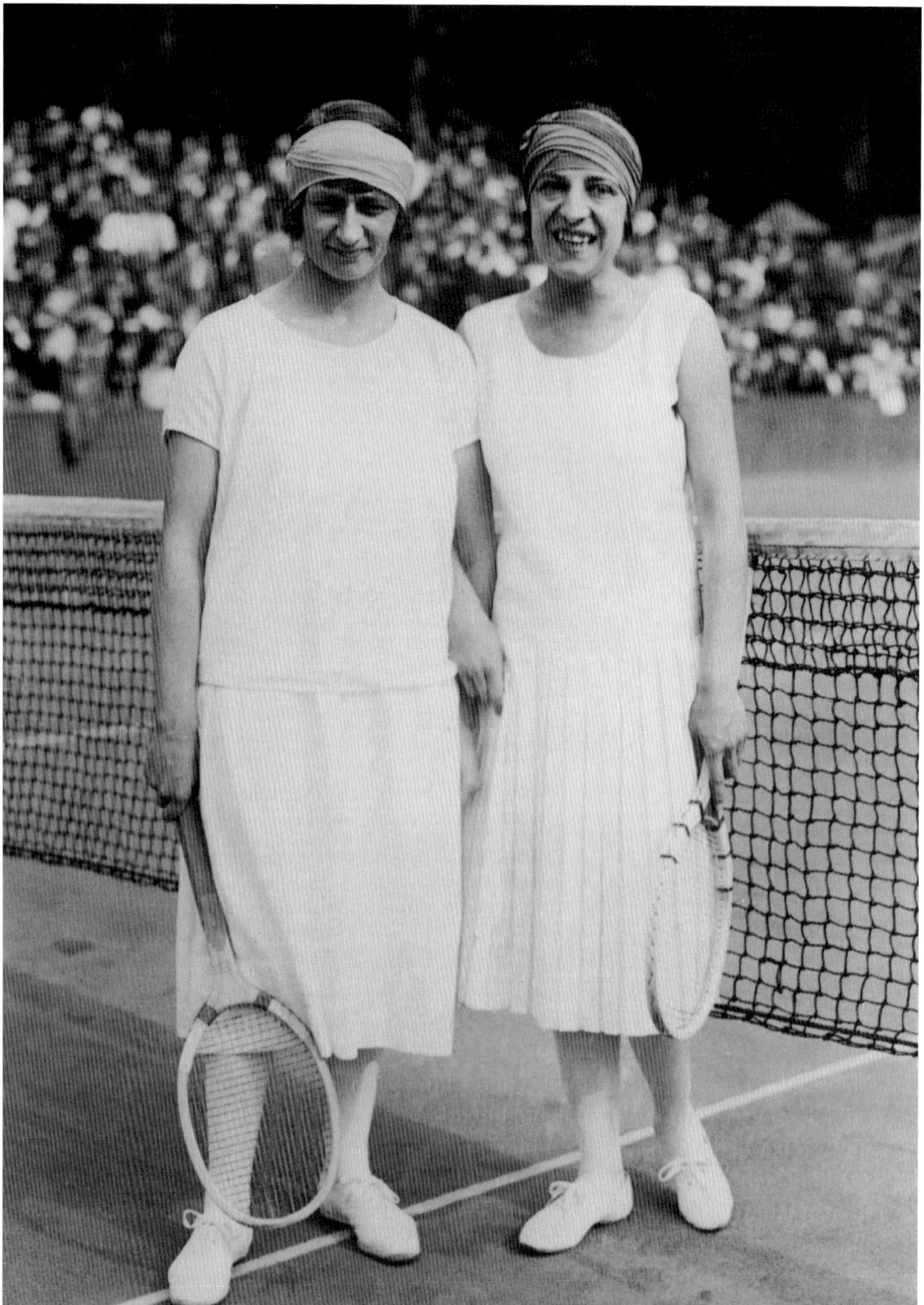

1925

Suzanne reappeared in public during the New Year meeting at the Beau Site Hotel, when she paired with Elizabeth Ryan to win the doubles. She was determined not to overtax herself during the Riviera season and therefore decided to severely curtail her singles appearances to the two Nice meetings.

At the February tournament, the entry for the singles did not contain anyone capable of causing Suzanne to display her real worth. In five rounds she dropped only two games, although her semi-final against Miss Eileen Bennett, one of England's promising players, was worth watching as she kept many rallies alive for a long period. In the final, Miss M. Tripp won one game. Suzanne comfortably won her fifth South of France crown in March. A series of easy victories over young English players took her to the semi-final against Diddie Vlasto, who promised much by winning the first two games but then faded. Suzanne won the title without taking the court as Miss Ermyntrude Harvey was taken ill beforehand with a 'temperature' and retired to her bed.

During the season two tournaments suffered severely due to bad weather. The second Monte Carlo meeting had three days in succession of thunder, lightning, hail, rain and snow, which forced play to be abandoned, the Men's Singles at the semi-final stage and the Ladies' Singles without playing the final. However, the inaugural Butler Cup, the Men's International Doubles, was decided but special arrangements had to be made to play the final a week later. During the week a

---

Facing page: Kathleen McKane and Suzanne – finalists in the French Singles Championship at St. Cloud, Paris in 1925. Suzanne won comfortably, 6–1 6–2.

presentation was made to George Simond on the occasion of his 21st year as referee and handicapper of the tournament. Well over a 100 names, royalty downwards, contributed to provide a pair of pearl studs and a portable dressing case. The presentation was made very privately by Suzanne and Wallis Myers and was followed by an informal dinner. George Simond, in his younger days a first class player, spent his life refereeing tournaments, all but one or two on the Riviera each year and throughout Europe in the summer. He continued until the mid-thirties. The Beau Site Hotel tournament, held in March, was throughout plagued by rain. Following a blank day, a start was made on the Tuesday morning, but after a dozen matches had been completed, the rain set in again and continued for three days, so that on the Friday evening the whole affair was shut down. Opinion was that never before had a Riviera tournament been abandoned, without hardly having started.

Over the season Suzanne competed at 11 tournaments and won nine doubles titles, seven with Elizabeth Ryan, and five mixed doubles. Her only reverse occurred in the mixed doubles final at the Cannes Club, where she and Charles Aeschliman lost to Baron Hubert de Morpurgo and Elizabeth Ryan, 6–3 6–3.

When the World's Hard Court Championships came to an end in 1923 there was a need for an open tournament in France which should have the same prestige. In 1924 the French were busy organising the Olympic Games but in 1925 they decided to enlarge the traditional French Championships, which hitherto had been confined to nationals, and allow foreign players to participate. This received the approval of the I.L.T.F. and the first meeting commenced at St. Cloud on 27th May.

Suzanne regained the three titles in grand style. In the singles she had whitewash victories over Mlle Simone des Landes de Danoet and Mrs Macready, the former Elisabeth d'Ayen, before eliminating Evelyn Colyer, 6–0 6–2, Helene Contostavlos, 6–2 6–0, and in the final Kathleen McKane, 6–1 6–2. This last match was played under a broiling sun with Suzanne using her accustomed skill to win the opening set. The Englishwoman speeded up in the second set in an attempt to drive her opponent from the net position but she was only partially successful as Suzanne won the last four games. Suzanne's partners in the doubles were Diddie Vlasto and Jacques Brugnon.

Immediately after the French Championships Suzanne crossed the Channel and travelled to Hayes, Middlesex where on 8th June she made a gramophone record,

Suzanne and Diddie Vlasto, who won the French Doubles Championships on three occasions 1923, 1925 and 1926. Diddie was French Singles Champion in 1924.

in Studio B of His Master's Voice Company, entitled 'Suzanne Lenglen on Lawn Tennis' (Cat No. B 2068). For just under six minutes, she gave instruction on the basic strokes of the game and a few tips on tactics. The record was issued in July.

Suzanne returned to Wimbledon in a blaze of glory, not just because she recaptured her singles crown but by the manner the achievement was attained. Her performance of losing a total of only five games is the most overwhelming victory ever recorded in the event, since the holder was required to play through. Nearly all the leading players were in Suzanne's half of the draw. She was not required to hit a ball in the first round as her opponent, Mrs Aurea Edgington, withdrew owing to a serious illness in her family. On the Thursday spectators filled the Centre Court to capacity to witness Suzanne play Elizabeth Ryan. When the American led 2–0 there seemed cause for thought that a repeat of the dramatic match of a year earlier might be at hand. However, any speculation in this direction was short lived because in the middle of the next game everything fell into place for Suzanne, who proceeded to reel off a succession of 12 games. She was supreme, especially in the second set when Elizabeth Ryan mustered just eight points. This was the 18th and last occasion that Suzanne and Elizabeth Ryan met in singles. Other than the first encounter at Monte Carlo in February, 1914, Suzanne had won every match.

The next day on No. 1 Court Suzanne demolished Miss Elsie Goldsack, 6–1 6–0, in 18 minutes. The loser was so nervous that she lost the first 15 points and in all claimed only 12. For the third day in a row Suzanne was in action and this time she overcame Geraldine Beamish, 6–0 6–0. The very experienced Englishwoman was quite outclassed and managed to win only 14 points, four of them in the second set.

In the semi-final on the second Wednesday, Suzanne defeated Kathleen McKane, the holder, 6–0 6–0, both sets lasting 15 minutes. Contrary to the score the match was closely fought at times and thoroughly interesting. From beginning to end the gallant Kathleen McKane adopted a policy of attack, endeavouring to break the fearsome strength of her opponent's all-round game. Many

Suzanne and Elizabeth Ryan winning their sixth doubles title at Wimbledon in 1925. This was the last tournament they played together.

observers reported that the Englishwoman had never played better which served to illustrate Suzanne's level of ability. Suzanne won 58 points to 27.

There was a great surprise when 19–year-old Miss Joan Fry from Staffordshire, making her debut at The Championships, emerged as a finalist. Suzanne won the title round on the Friday, 6–2 6–0, and basically all she had to do was to stay on the baseline and defend against a steady and persistent attack, unaccompanied by any volleying. Joan Fry moved exceptionally well and retrieved many shots that few other competitors would have saved. The sets lasted 15 minutes and 10 minutes, respectively, and in all Joan Fry notched 22 points.

Suzanne won her third 'triple' at Wimbledon. She took the doubles crown with Elizabeth Ryan, for the sixth time, beating surprise finalists, Mrs Kathleen Bridge and Mrs Mary McIlquham, 6–2 6–2, and annexed the mixed doubles title on the Monday with Jean Borotra.

During July, Suzanne brought out two books both published by George G Harrap & Co. of London. One, 'Lawn Tennis, The Game of Nations' (2s 6d) dealt in some depth with stroke production, footwork, tactics and handicapping, while the other 'The Love Game – Being the Life Story of Marcelle Penrose', (3s 6d) was a romantic novel about a professional tennis coach.

In the next couple of months, Suzanne limited her appearances to two tournaments. At Pourville in July she had an uninterrupted passage through the singles and beat Mlle Yvonne Bourgeois, sister of Germaine Pigueron, in the final, 6–0 6–0. During the last week of August, Suzanne visited Deauville, where a Ladies' International tie between France and Australia was staged in conjunction with the annual tournament. Suzanne played her part in ensuring that the home side won the fixture by seven matches to four. She defeated Mrs Sylvia Harper, 6–0 6–4, Miss Esna Boyd, 7–5 6–1, and paired with Diddie Vlasto to beat Esna Boyd and Miss Floris St. George, 6–3 3–6 6–3, despite suffering from a blistered hand. In the tournament, Suzanne won the singles title for the fourth occasion, when she outwitted Miss Daphne Akhurst, the Australian Champion, in the final, 6–2 6–2. Suzanne also won the doubles but withdrew from the mixed doubles in the semi-final, at one set all, when her partner Count Salm injured his wrist.

During the next two months, Suzanne travelled many miles visiting five countries. She was given a very warm reception on her return to the Chateau D'Ardennes tournament in Belgium during the first week of September. The weather throughout the week was appalling, but on the last afternoon there was a break in the rain and Suzanne consented to finish her programme by playing five matches. In the singles she beat Mme Marthe Dupont and Mme Simone Washer to capture the title.

In the middle of September, Suzanne competed at Biarritz and won the singles title with little exertion, defeating Marguerite Billout in the final, 6–0 6–0. Suzanne also won the mixed doubles event with Count Salm. From Biarritz, Suzanne journeyed through France across the Alps to the Villa d'Este Tennis Club on Lake Como and as an honoured guest watched the Men's International between France and Italy. A few days later, Suzanne played exhibition matches at the Tennis Club of Milan, at the special invitation of the Club president, Count Alberto Bonacossa.

Another train ride took Suzanne and her mother to Vienna, where a series of exhibition matches were held. The visit, organised by Count Salm was originally scheduled for 3rd and 4th October with Jean Borotra participating, but Suzanne eventually arrived on the 8th October and played the next three days.

Arrangements had been made for her to stay just south of the capital at Semmering, a health resort, or nearby Reichenau, the home of Count Salm, but an illness in his family prevented this and she stayed at the Hotel Bristol in Vienna.

The matches, played on the clay courts of the Vienna Athletic Club, were an outstanding success, with the 2,000 seats available each day being well over-subscribed. Diplomatic interest was shown by the presence of the French Ambassador. As usual, Suzanne wore a new outfit for each day and match.

On the Friday, Suzanne beat Frau Erna Redlich, the Austrian Champion, 6–0 6–0, and joined with Count Salm to lose to Karel Kozeluh and Frau Nelly Neppach, the German Champion, 6–3 6–4. Later in the day Suzanne paired with Karel Kozeluh to win a one-set match against Count Salm and Nelly Neppach, 6–0. On the following day, Suzanne beat Nelly Neppach, 6–1 6–1, but the match was tighter than the score indicates, with Suzanne winning 29 to 15 points in the first set and 25–11 in the second. Nelly Neppach was so keen to have the opportunity to play Suzanne that she had turned down an invitation to play in a good class tournament at Merano in Italy. Later Suzanne and Count Salm teamed to play two leading Austrian men, Paul Brick and Franz Glanz but Suzanne tired quickly and was forced to retire with the score in her opponents' favour, 7–5 3–1.

On the Sunday, Suzanne was in great form to defeat Erna's sister, Frau Maria Redlich, a former Austrian Champion, who was often known as Madi (little maid), 6–0 6–1. Suzanne then played two one-set mixed doubles matches, first with Count Salm against Paul Brick and Nelly Neppach, and then with Karel Kozeluh versus Count Salm and Nelly Neppach, and in both, won 6–3.

There was nearly an 'international incident' when Suzanne played Nelly Neppach. This was before the embargo was raised on allied nations playing with Germans after the First World War, although Austrians were already allowed to compete. The French Ambassador was on the point of intervening when it was suddenly remembered that Nelly Neppach was Austrian by marriage and the match was allowed to proceed. One newspaper named Suzanne, 'Angel of Peace'.

At the time there were rumours that Suzanne might get engaged to Karel Kozeluh, who was always a very close friend, or even marry Count Salm, but, as usual, both were just speculation.

Suzanne spent a couple of days sightseeing in Vienna before catching the train to Czechoslovakia to play further exhibition matches. The visit started on Thursday 15th October at Brno, where, on the Luzanky Park courts, she defeated Erna Redlich 6–2 (one set only) and joined with Count Salm to beat Friedrich and Gretel Rohrer, 6–1 7–5. As soon as play was over, Suzanne left for Prague where she was met in the evening at Wilson Station by a delegation from the Prague LTC.

The following day a near capacity crowd was present at the show court which was decorated in the colours of France and Czechoslovakia. Among the diplomatic presence was the French Ambassador. The conditions were not good as a fine rain persisted for some time, but players, eager to please, agreed to continue. Suzanne overwhelmed Mrs Maria Sindelarova 6–0 6–0 and with Count Salm defeated Jan Kozeluh and Miss Renata Zahnova, 6–2 6–2. The following afternoon, Suzanne beat Miss Anna Janotova, 6–1 6–1 and in partnership with Count Salm beat Jan Kozeluh and Anna Janotova, 6–4 6–3. Good crowds had attended both days. Unfortunately heavy rain prohibited play on the other two

Jacques Brugnon and Suzanne at the Covered Court meeting at Cromer in October, 1925. This is the only tournament Suzanne played in England, outside of Wimbledon. This team won the French Mixed Doubles Championship five times.

days when Suzanne was scheduled to play further singles and doubles matches and the money for the tickets had to be returned to the public. Suzanne's hosts were keen on her staying for a while to play further matches but she was concerned about her father's health and returned to Nice.

Being assured that her father was satisfactory and in the care of her mother, Suzanne decided to visit England, accompanied by Jacques Brugnon. On the evening of the 26th October, they were welcomed at London Victoria Station by their host, Commander Oliver Locker-Lampson MP who escorted them to Cromer to compete in the first tournament on the two covered courts he had recently erected in the grounds of the Newhaven Court Hotel.

The two En-tout-Cas courts were enclosed in one spacious building which gave ample surrounding room. All four walls had galleries and below, at the sides, were tiers of seats giving accommodation in all for 1,500 spectators. Artificial lighting was also provided.

Restricting their appearances to doubles events only, both visitors had a probable seven matches ahead of them if they were to successfully complete the tournament in two days on the Friday and Saturday. This they did without too much difficulty.

Suzanne and Jacques Brugnon won the mixed doubles final from Charles Kingsley and Eileen Bennett, 6–1 6–2, while Suzanne and Dorothea Chambers were given a walkover in the doubles final by Eileen Bennett and Ermyntrude Harvey, the latter exhausted by earlier play. Not to disappoint the spectators, Suzanne agreed to play an exhibition match with Jacques Brugnon against two men, Henry Mayes and Charles Kingsley, which was abandoned at one-set all. Apart from Wimbledon this was the only tournament Suzanne played in England. On the following Monday, Suzanne and Jacques Brugnon played an exhibition match against Henry Mayes and Nicholas Mishu on the hard courts at the Royal Botanic Society in London before returning to Paris in the afternoon.

On the 14th November, Suzanne was presented with the French Tennis Federation's Gold Medal for her services in the cause of lawn tennis. Max Decugis, Jean Borotra and Rene Lacoste were similarly honoured. Late in December, Suzanne's father underwent a serious operation in a Nice clinic. He stood up to this ordeal well and after a short period was allowed home to Villa Ariem. Earlier in the year the Lenglens had sold the house at Marest-sur-Matz.

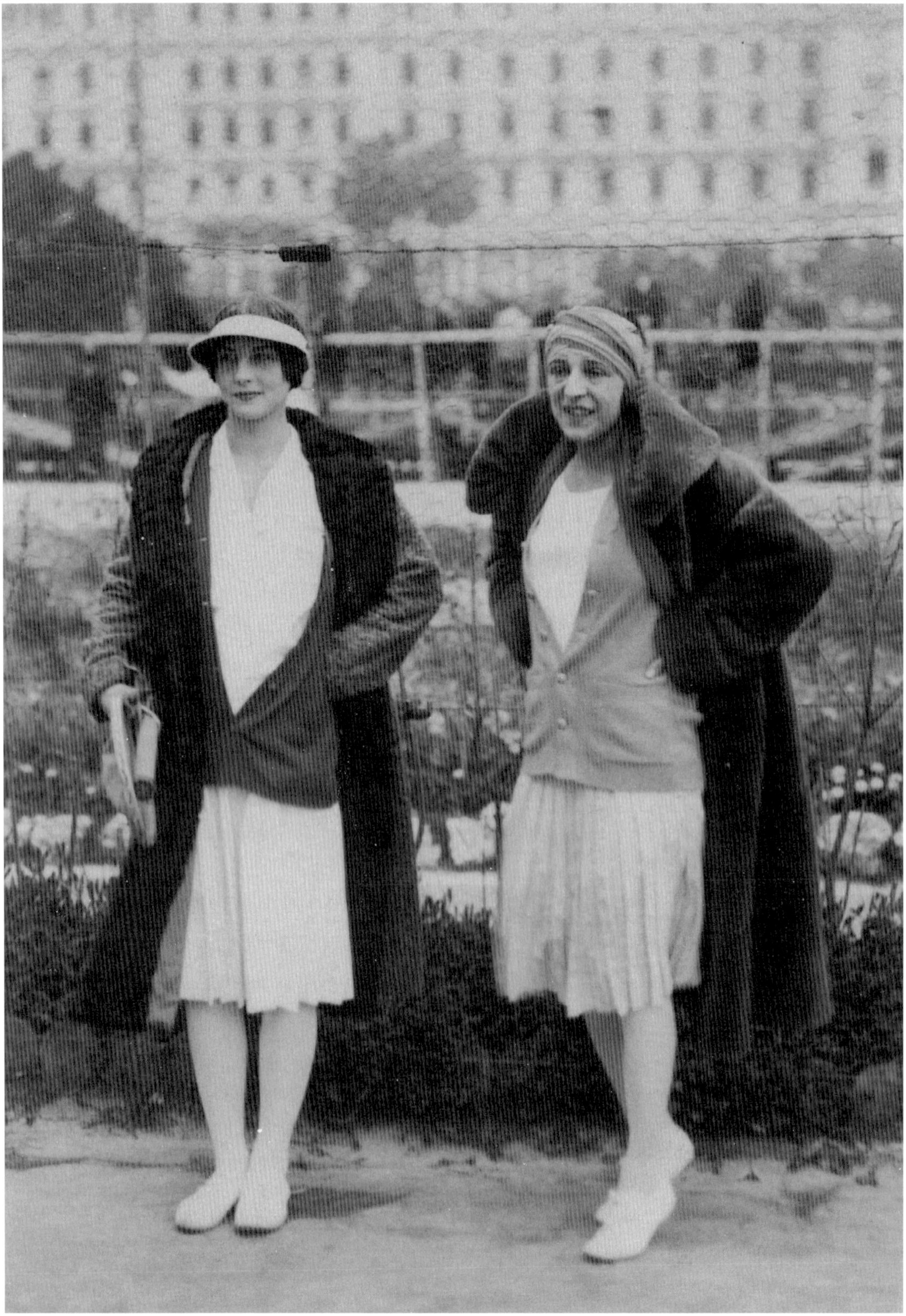

1926

There was a buzz of excitement on the French Riviera at the end of December when confirmation was received that Helen Wills would be competing there during the 1926 season. Ever since her successful visit to Europe in 1924, hopes had been high that a meeting with Suzanne would take place and speculation on the outcome of such a clash was a frequent topic of the press. In 1925 the American's stature had considerably grown when she led her country to victory in the Wightman Cup and a fortnight later captured the United States Singles crown for the third successive year. At the age of 20 she had more than proved herself at home and was keen to tackle Europe again and, in particular, pitch her skill against Suzanne.

From California to the South of France involved a journey of some 6,000 miles. Helen Wills, with her mother as chaperone, crossed the United States and left New York on 5th January on board the 'De Grasse' and arrived two days late at Le Havre on 15th January. The boat train was met in Paris by Jean Borotra and Pierre Gillou, the President of the French Tennis Federation, and later that day she caught the overnight Blue Train from Gare de Lyon to Nice in good time for a couple of days' practice before the commencement of the Metropole Hotel tournament in Cannes.

Suzanne had opened her season a little earlier than usual by competing at the La Festa Club in Monte Carlo, just prior to Christmas. She then played at the Beau

---

Facing page: Helen Wills and Suzanne pose for the cameras at the Nice Lawn Tennis Club in early February, 1926. They faced each other across the net for the first time in the final of the mixed doubles.

Site Hotel New Year meeting and at the inaugural tournament at the New Courts Club in Cannes. At all three venues Suzanne followed her normal practice early in the season of playing only in the doubles events. She teamed with Phyllis Satterthwaite as her regular partner, Elizabeth Ryan, was absent from the Riviera for the first time in many years, spending the winter playing in the United States. In between these tournaments Suzanne found time to compete in the Nice Club championships (members only) and captured the singles title for the seventh time.

At the Metropole Hotel Suzanne again confined her attention to doubles while Helen Wills opted for singles only, so their paths did not cross. The American, who came under close scrutiny by the Lenglen family several times during the week, won the final against Diddie Vlasto, 6–3 7–5. The next week, Suzanne did not play at the Gallia Club, as her father was unwell and in a not too strong field Helen Wills won again, beating Helene Contostavlos in the final, 6–3 6–2.

At Nice, Suzanne and Helen Wills faced each other across the net for the first time when they met in the final of the mixed doubles. This match was over very quickly with Suzanne and Hubert de Morpurgo defeating Helen Wills and Charles Aeschliman, 6–1 6–2. Helen Wills decided not to enter the singles, whereas Suzanne did and in a notable performance she went through five rounds without a game being taken from her. Suzanne's appearance in this event did much to quell the press who for weeks had suggested that she was trying to avoid the American. A clash with Helen Wills was avoided in the doubles when Suzanne's partner Phyllis Satterthwaite withdrew owing to an injury sustained when her car collided with a tram.

The announcement that Suzanne and Helen Wills would both be competing in the singles at the Carlton Club tournament, commencing on 8th February, began an upsurge of world-wide interest that had hitherto not been accorded to ladies' tennis. Scores of journalists gathered at Cannes during the week, all working overtime to obtain their exclusive stories of the daily happenings of the two players. The Club had a total of six courts situated in the grounds at the rear of the Carlton Hotel, with the entrance down a side road. The remote possibility that Suzanne and Helen Wills would not meet in the final was ignored by the authorities as they set about doubling the seating accommodation around the principal court to 3,000 by erecting a temporary stand on the adjacent second court.

Unfortunately, the weather had no regard for the programme. The rain came and for three days, Tuesday to Thursday, no play was possible and the proceedings

Diddie Vlasto and Helen Wills, just before their semi-final match at the Carlton Club, Cannes on 15th February, 1926.

were forced into a second week. There were no players really capable of testing the strength of Suzanne and Helen Wills until the semi-final. Suzanne then disposed of Helene Contostavlos 6–0 6–2, while Helen Wills, having taken the first set from

Diddie Vlasto 6–1, suffered a brief lapse in the second set to trail 1–4 but she quickly finished the match with a run of five games, much to the relief of all concerned.

The final was decided in perfect weather on Tuesday, 16th February. The interest in the match was tremendous. Every seat was sold in advance at 300 francs and the standing room at 100 francs was packed to the limit. Every possible view was taken up. Many spectators even risked injury by scaling the neighbouring roofs and eucalyptus trees. Distinguished guests assembled at the court side included ex-King Manuel of Portugal, Grand Duke Michael of Russia, Prince George of Greece, The Rajah of Pudakota, The Duke of Westminster, The Duke of Connaught, Baron de Graffenried and Count de Bourbel.

The Referee was George Simond. He carefully selected 'neutral' officials to take charge of the match. Commander George Hillyard, the former All England Lawn Tennis Club Secretary, was appointed umpire and among the linesmen chosen were Cyril Tolley, the amateur golf champion, Clement Cazalet, Roman Najuch, the professional at the Cannes Tennis Club, Sir Francis Towle, the hotel magnate, Lord Charles Hope and R. Dunkerley. There was no footfault judge. Seated together within the confines of the Court, a few feet along from the umpire, were Charles Aeschliman and Francis Fisher, the two main organisers of the event.

As the excitement and tension grew, Suzanne arrived in good time at the ground from Nice in a Voisin car. She was soon spotted by the crowd, who spontaneously cheered. When both players came on court soon after 11 am they were immediately besieged by photographers. Suzanne, relaxed and smiling, wore a

---

Suzanne playing Helen Wills in the final of the Carlton Club tournament on 16th February, 1926. The ground was packed and spectators risked injury by scaling the adjoining roofs.

salmon-pink bandeau with matching cardigan, while Helen Wills, quiet but confident, sported her usual white eyeshade. They shook hands, both left-handed.

Suzanne won the toss and started with a love game on her service but any prospect of an easy triumph soon disappeared when Helen Wills, getting the better of the exchanges from the back of the court, won the next two games. Suzanne captured the next ten points and eventually led 4–2, mainly by drawing errors from the American, who at this stage was intent on breaking down her solid defence. Helen Wills won the seventh game with her first volley of the match but she lost the next two games with only one point in each to her credit and the first set was Suzanne's, after 19 minutes, at 6–3. Suzanne, far from her best, had experienced more physical strain than anticipated as was shown by the need for the occasional sip of brandy.

The second set opened entirely in favour of Helen Wills, who took risks boldly on the drive and volley to go ahead 3–1. However, in the fifth game she moderated her pace and attempted to beat Suzanne by more purposeful placing. These tactics played into the hands of Suzanne, who recovered to 3–all. The seventh game was the longest of the match and required 14 points before the American won through.

Facing page: Suzanne at full stretch against Helen Wills in the final at the Carlton Club, 1926.

Before and after the match between Suzanne and Helen Wills at the Carlton Club. This was the only occasion when these players met in singles. Suzanne won 6–3 8–6.

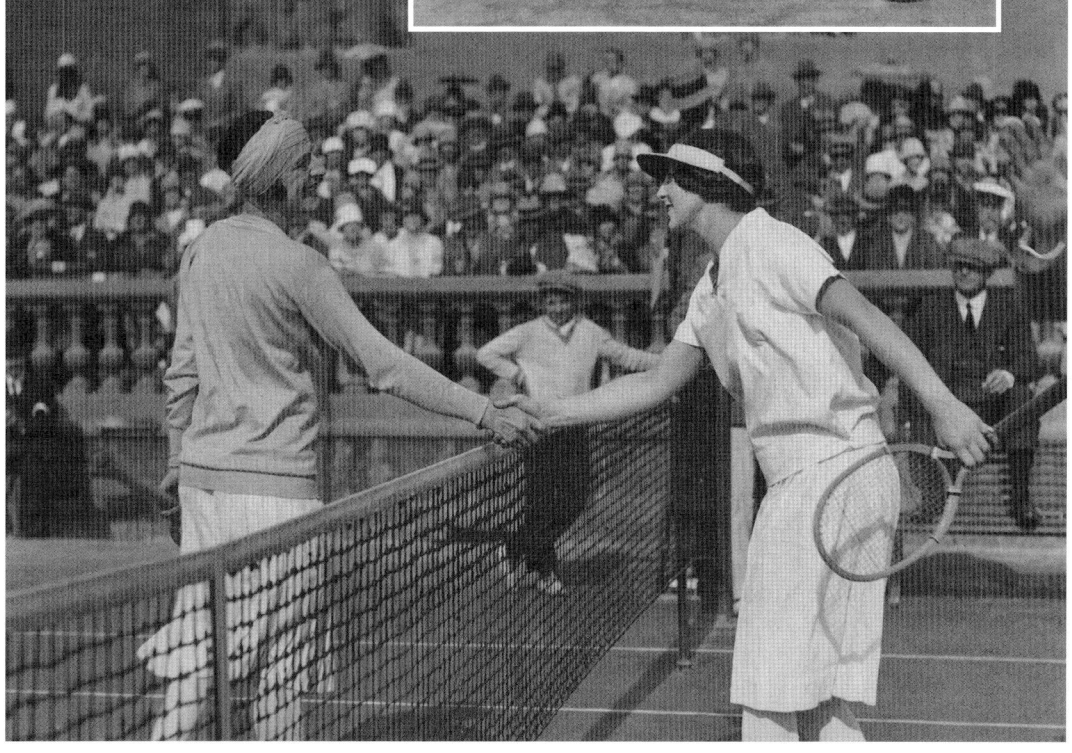

Suzanne wavered a little in the next game and at 30–all hit a forehand drive which Helen Wills thought was clearly out. However, the linesman, Cyril Tolley remained silent and the American's chance to lead 5–3 disappeared. She recovered to lead 5–4 but Suzanne won the next game to love by placing the ball very skilfully at half court, which brought the American forward to overdrive.

Suzanne advanced easily to 6–5 and appeared to have the match within her grasp in the 12th game when she reached 40–15 on her service. However, after a long rally Helen Wills hit a beautiful drive, which struck Suzanne's forehand line. The linesman, Lord Charles Hope, remained silent but from somewhere came a shout of 'out' and Suzanne, thinking that the match was over, advanced to the net and shook hands with Helen Wills.

Immediately the court was invaded by the many eager photographers and pressmen. Realising the situation, Charles Aeschliman rushed forward extending his arms to indicate to the surging mass that the match was not over. In the midst of the commotion, George Hillyard dismounted the umpire's chair, and, walking a few steps to the sideline, confirmed with Lord Charles Hope that the ball was good. He returned to the foot of the chair and, after informing the two players that the match must continue, ordered the court to be cleared.

The match resumed with the score at 40–30. Suzanne, nearly exhausted, still had a match point but she hit the ball over the baseline and soon the score was 6–all. There followed two tense games. Suzanne, after being a game point down, captured the American's service to lead 7–6. In the last game Suzanne double-faulted when within a point of winning but her coolness and experience triumphed in the end on her fourth match point, 8–6. The set had taken 41 minutes when the match ended at 12.25pm. The points tally in Suzanne's favour was 30 to 17 in the first set and 52 to 47 in the second set. Not once during the match did Suzanne remove her cardigan.

After a second handshake, Suzanne sat for a while by the side of the court surrounded by officials. Several huge baskets of flowers were brought on to court for presentation to the winner but a weeping Suzanne was too agitated to take much notice. Late in the afternoon, Suzanne returned to the court and in partnership with Diddie Vlasto defeated Helen Wills and Helene Contostavlos, in the final of the doubles, 6–4 8–6. Fortunately for her side Diddie Vlasto was in good form as Suzanne was too tired to do much more than play an occasional shot from the back of the court. She was helped off court in a half-fainting condition by two friends.

Carlton Club, Cannes, France
Ladies' Singles Final: 16th February, 1926
Suzanne Lenglen (FRA) v Helen Wills (USA)

FIRST SET

Game	Server		Points L	Points W	Games L	Games W
1	L	15–0, 30–0, 40–0, GL	4	0	1	0
2	W	15–0, 15–15, 15–30, 30–30, 40–30, GW	2	4	1	1
3	L	0–15, 15–15, 15–30, 15–40, 30–40, de, Adv W, GW	3	5	1	2
4	W	0–15, 0–30, 0–40, GL	4	0	2	2
5	L	15–0, 30–0, 40–0, GL	4	0	3	2
6	W	0–15, 0–30, 15–30, 30–30, 30–40, GL	4	2	4	2
7	L	15–0, 15–15, 15–30, 15–40, GW	1	4	4	3
8	W	0–15, 15–15, 15–30, 15–40, GL	4	1	5	3
9	L	15–0, 30–0, 30–15, 40–15, GL	4	1	6	3
			30	17	6	3

SECOND SET

Game	Server		Points L	Points W	Games L	Games W
1	W	15–0, 30–0, 40–0, GW	0	4	0	1
2	L	15–0, 30–0, 30–15, 40–15, 40–30, de, Adv L, GL	5	3	1	1
3	W	0–15, 15–15, 30–15, 40–15, 40–30, GW	2	4	1	2
4	L	0–15, 15–15, 15–30, 15–40, GW	1	4	1	3
5	W	0–15, 0–30, 15–30, 15–40, GL	4	1	2	3
6	L	15–0, 15–15, 30–15, 40–15, GL	4	1	3	3
7	W	0–15, 15–15, 15–30, 15–40, 30–40, de, Adv W, de, Adv L, de, Adv W, de, Adv W, G	6	8	3	4
8	L	15–0, 15–15, 15–30, 30–30, 40–30, GL	4	2	4	4
9	W	0–15, 15–15, 30–15, 40–15, 40–30, de, Adv W, GW	3	5	4	5
10	L	15–0, 30–0, 40–0, GL	4	0	5	5
11	W	15–0, 15–15, 30–15, 30–30, 30–40, GL	4	2	6	5
12	L	15–0, 30–0, 30–15, **40–15, 40–30**, de, Adv W, GW	3	5	6	6
13	W	0–15, 0–30, 0–40, 15–40, 30–40, de, Adv W, de, Adv L, GL	6	4	7	6
14	L	15–0, 15–15, 30–15, 30–30, 40–30, de, Adv W, de, **Adv L**, GL	6	4	8	6
			52	47	8	6

The match lasted 63 minutes (First set – 19 minutes, second set – 41 minutes)
LENGLEN WON 6–3 8–6

Later that week at the Beaulieu tournament, Suzanne played only in doubles and retired indisposed after winning one round with Phyllis Satterthwaite. The following week at Monte Carlo she was again far from fighting fit but nevertheless was able to win the newly instituted 'Beaumont Cup', for pairs of the same nationality, with Diddie Vlasto. There was a possibility that Suzanne would meet Helen Wills across the net in this event, but in the semi-final the American and her partner Leslie Aeschliman, formerly Bancroft, were well beaten by Eileen Bennett and Phyllis Satterthwaite. In the final they severely tested the French pair.

The stress of the past few weeks had taken its toll on Suzanne, who readily accepted an invitation from Count Alberto Bonacossa to relax for a few weeks in Italy, with Sophie Wavertree as companion. Originally Suzanne was to refrain from picking up a racket but soon a programme of exhibition matches was arranged to be played at Villa d'Este, Milan, Turin and Genoa during the whole of March. Many players contributed to the success of the tour, including leading Italian players, Placido Gaslini, Count Mimo Balbi di Robeco, Roberto Bocciardo, Sig.na Paola Bologna and Sig.na Rosetta Gagliardi. Phyllis Satterthwaite also joined the party for a short period.

Suzanne, restored to good health, returned to the French Riviera in time to play at the second tournament of the Carlton Club, which commenced on 29th March. She coasted to a doubles victory with Phyllis Satterthwaite, a formula repeated the next week at the Beau Soleil Championships at Monte Carlo.

A few days later, Suzanne returned to Italy and spent considerable time sightseeing in Rome. The last week in April she competed in the Rome Championships and, in a class far superior to the other players, won the singles title without losing a game. In the final she defeated Sig.na Maud Rosenbaum, who later emigrated to the United States and as Baroness Levi reached the semi-final at Forest Hills in 1930. Suzanne also won the doubles with Mlle Pat du Cros and the mixed doubles with Jacques Brugnon. While in Rome, Suzanne was granted an audience with the Pope.

After her defeat by Suzanne at the Carlton Club, Helen Wills stayed on the Riviera for another five weeks, during which time she annexed, in devastating style, the singles titles at Beaulieu, Monte Carlo, Menton, Nice and Cannes Club. For the next three weeks Helen Wills and her mother visited Italy and combined sightseeing with playing exhibition matches against Italian players. On the return journey from Rome they called at Florence and Milan before returning to Paris in the middle of April. A comparison of her timetable over this period of two months with that of Suzanne's showed that both players were in Italy at the same time for one week only, 22nd to 28th March. Many hoped that a return match might be arranged but this never materialised, mainly because both players were not really interested.

Around that time of the year, George G Harrap & Co intended publishing a book entitled 'The Secrets of Suzanne', with Henry Mayes and Suzanne being co-authors. However, the commission was cancelled and instead a book written by Henry Mayes called 'Keeping Fit' was issued, which contained a large wall chart showing Suzanne demonstrating the exercises. During May, the London 'Evening News' started a series of weekly articles by Suzanne, entitled 'How to Play Lawn Tennis and How Not to Play It'.

At the end of the month, two international ties were played at the Racing Club in Paris. Over three days, France met the United States, for the first time on a mixed team basis, and then, for two days, played Great Britain in a ladies only contest. On each occasion the home country was severely weakened by the absence of Suzanne who had decided two weeks earlier that she would not participate. Naturally, the American camp was extremely disappointed that a clash between Helen Wills and Suzanne would not take place. France lost both encounters, 8–3 to the United States and 9–3 to Great Britain.

The French Championships, which commenced on 2nd June at the Racing Club, were dogged throughout by bad weather. Suzanne asserted her supremacy once more by winning the singles crown for the sixth time, losing just four games in five matches. The outcome might have been different if Helen Wills had been able to contest the final instead of being forced to withdraw from the second round. Two days after defeating Germaine Golding, late on the opening afternoon 6–3 7–5, she became ill and acute appendicitis was diagnosed. A successful operation was carried out by a leading French surgeon at the American Hospital at Neuilly. Among the profusion of flowers sent by well-wishers was a large bunch of pink and yellow peonies from Suzanne. Although Helen Wills was up and about in a few days any chance of her playing in the Wightman Cup and Wimbledon later in the month soon vanished. There was universal regret at her misfortune, especially from the people of Paris who had looked forward to a possible return clash with Suzanne.

Suzanne began the defence of her singles title with 6–0 6–0 victories over Mrs Ilona Peteri, the champion of Hungary, Dorothy Barron and Mme Simone

Celebrities and fans gather in the Bois de Boulogne in Paris after Suzanne won the French Championships for the sixth time. Left to right: Mary Browne, Anaise Lenglen, movie stars Douglas Fairbanks and Mary Pickford, and Suzanne.

Mathieu. She had expected to meet Elizabeth Ryan in the semi-final; but the American was eliminated by Joan Fry in the previous round, after a marathon match of 41 games. Untroubled Suzanne beat Joan Fry, exclusively from the back of the court, 6–2 6–1. The final against Miss Mary Browne, of the United States, was played on a wet and slippery court. The American had not got the speed nor the length of drive to cause any real embarrassment to Suzanne stationed on the baseline. Despite reaching advantage in several games, Mary Browne won only the second game. Suzanne won the doubles easily with Diddie Vlasto and the mixed doubles with Jacques Brugnon, for the fifth time, after some splendid encounters.

The Jubilee Championship meeting at Wimbledon in 1926 opened on Monday 21st June with a most appropriate ceremony. At 3 o'clock King George V and Queen Mary, escorted by officials, walked on to the Centre Court amidst prolonged cheering and took up their stand at a table in the centre. On the east side of the court were lined up 34 surviving ex-champions, whilst at the ends of the court were grouped the competitors taking part in the tournament that year. After the National Anthem the ex-champions came forward, one by one, and were presented with a silver commemorative medal by the Queen, while the King, at her side, shook hands with each recipient. Suzanne, next to last in line, received one of the loudest cheers from the crowd as she made her curtsey. No one present on this memorable occasion could have possibly imagined the drama that was to unfold over the next week, when a chain of events culminated in Suzanne withdrawing from The Championships.

As soon as the ceremony was over, the net was put up for an exhibition set, in which Suzanne and Elizabeth Ryan were unexpectedly beaten 8–6 by Mrs Godfree, the former Kathleen McKane, and Miss Kornelia (Kea) Bouman of Holland. Under normal circumstances the loss of this exhibition set would not have bothered Suzanne but she knew that the match was her last in partnership with the American and a farewell win on the Centre Court would have been most satisfying. A few weeks earlier the French Tennis Federation had asked Suzanne to break her lifelong association with Elizabeth Ryan and instead play with a fellow countrywoman. The team of Suzanne and Elizabeth Ryan had never suffered defeat in open competition, and only once lost a set, since they joined forces for the World Hard Court Championships in May, 1914. They had won 40 titles including six at Wimbledon. Very reluctantly Suzanne agreed to the French request and Diddie Vlasto became her partner at Wimbledon. Unfortunately when the draw was made for the doubles event, Suzanne found she was due to meet Elizabeth Ryan in her

Suzanne receives her commemorative silver medal from Queen Mary on the occasion of the Jubilee Championships at Wimbledon in 1926. King George V looks on.

very first match. This considerably disturbed Suzanne, who openly expressed dissatisfaction at the situation.

When Suzanne played her opening singles match against Mary Browne before a packed Centre Court on the Tuesday, her display was far from impressive and at times she appeared listless. The American, always a courageous fighter, volleyed well but her ground strokes lacked the necessary control to put her opponent under pressure. Suzanne won by a fairly safe margin of 6–2 6–3 but in this one match she had conceded as many games as the year before in winning the title.

Suzanne did not visit the Referee's office at the close of play to enquire her programme for the following afternoon, as was her practice in previous years, when she would be escorted either by George Hillyard or a member of the French team.

What happened overnight is uncertain but one account is that before leaving the ground Suzanne was aware that her programme was a singles match against Mrs Evelyn Dewhurst on No. 1 Court at 2 pm and a doubles match with Diddie Vlasto versus Elizabeth Ryan and Mary Browne on the Centre Court at approximately 4.30 pm Suzanne, unhappy with this arrangement, stated she was not prepared to play the singles match before the doubles, which she felt had greater priority. Another version is that Suzanne was not aware of her programme until Diddie Vlasto read to her the order of play from a newspaper, late the following morning, by which time Suzanne had booked an appointment with her doctor. She asked Jacques Brugnon to telephone Wimbledon and inform the Referee's office that she would not be arriving in time to play the singles match. This he did but apparently the message never reached the Referee, Francis (Frank) Burrow. Whatever transpired, Suzanne clearly had no intention of playing the singles match as scheduled.

On Wednesday the No. 1 Court was crowded at 2 pm but Suzanne was not present. At 2.30 pm Suzanne was still absent and a public announcement was made that she was delayed and the second match would be put on court. At 3 pm Queen Mary arrived, a little later than usual as she had been lunching at Buckingham Palace with the King and the Prince of Wales, on the occasion of the Prince's 32nd birthday. The Queen always enjoyed watching Suzanne and undoubtedly was looking forward to seeing her perform on the Centre Court later.

When Suzanne arrived at 3.30 pm the majority of the Committee were waiting at the entrance to the Clubhouse. Immediately there was an exchange of words with the upshot that a sobbing Suzanne rushed hysterically to the dressing room. Jean

Borotra's assistance was enlisted but after being diplomatically guided into the ladies' dressing room he emerged minutes later to report that Suzanne was in no fit condition to play. By that time the Centre Court crowd, including the Queen, were patiently waiting for Suzanne to appear but when this seemed unlikely the next match on the programme was advanced.

The Committee was in an awkward position. To scratch the holder of three titles would have been a grave step to take and certainly very unpopular with the public. Also, Suzanne's opponents declined to accept a walkover. Rightly or wrongly, the decision was taken to postpone both her matches until the next day and the following statement was issued: "The Committee of Management regret that owing to the indisposition of Mlle S.Lenglen it was found impossible to carry out today's programme It is hoped that she will be well enough to play both matches tomorrow."

The Committee further bowed to Suzanne's wishes when they allowed her to play the doubles match before the singles on the Thursday. The Centre Court was filled to the brim with spectators eager to see this match which was second on court. At around 3.30 pm when Suzanne and Diddie Vlasto led Elizabeth Ryan and Mary Browne 3–2, a heavy storm deluged the ground and stopped play for an hour. On resumption the French pair soon took the opening set, 6–3, but the Americans fought back to win an exciting second set 9–7, after saving three match points in the 14th game. Suzanne and Diddie Vlasto were shaken by their failure to clinch victory and they offered comparatively little resistance in the deciding set, which the Americans won, 6–2. Suzanne was more or less her usual self and without doubt the best of the four players. Her partner, chained to the baseline, gave good support at times. Both Americans played well, especially Elizabeth Ryan in the third set.

Due to the delayed programme that afternoon there was insufficient time for Suzanne's contest against Evelyn Dewhurst to be put onto court and it was held over, once again, until the Friday. In this match, played on No. 1 Court, Evelyn Dewhurst produced some excellent shots and played with plenty of vigour but she was a little too erratic to make much headway against the accuracy of Suzanne, who won 6–2 6–2. Afterwards Suzanne complained of a pain in her arm.

On the Saturday, Suzanne's only commitment was a mixed doubles match with Jean Borotra versus Harold Aitken and Miss Beatrice Brown on the Centre Court. This resulted in an easy 6–3 6–0 victory for the French team but for the first time

Suzanne and Diddie Vlasto leave the Centre Court defeated by Mary Browne and Elizabeth Ryan.

in her career Suzanne was not received too well by a section of the crowd and it required the occasional clowning act from Jean Borotra to mask the situation.

Doubtless, the crowd were reacting to press reports which had exploited to the full the events of the week and suggested that Suzanne was discourteous in keeping the Queen waiting. This and the loss of her doubles match had a telling effect on Suzanne over the weekend and with the worsening of her arm injury doubt existed whether she would be fit to continue. Suzanne was due to meet Miss Claire Beckingham on the Monday and the unusual step was taken to add a precautionary note to her name in the programme stating "If well enough to play".

On the Monday morning, Suzanne decided she could not go on and it was left to the Secretary, Major Dudley Larcombe, to announce to the public:

"I have just spoken to Mlle Lenglen over the telephone and she tells me that, although she started to come to Wimbledon she was compelled to return to her hotel owing to severe pain she was suffering and that, therefore, she retires from the Singles Championship. She also asked me to inform the public how sorry she was not to be able to play and that she has done her best to carry on".

Suzanne's withdrawal opened the way for Kathleen Godfree to win her second singles title. In the final she beat Spain's Srta Elia (Lili) de Alvarez, 6–2 4–6 6–3.

Suzanne was left in the mixed doubles event but on the Tuesday it was announced that her arm was still causing her pain and she was therefore compelled to retire altogether from Wimbledon. Sadly, she was never to grace the courts again.

Usually after Wimbledon, Suzanne stayed in England for a few days, perhaps visiting friends or sometimes playing in an exhibition, but she had never competed in a tournament. However, this year she had entered, along with Jacques Brugnon, the Midland Counties Championship at Edgbaston followed by the Irish Championships in Dublin. Naturally there was great disappointment at both centres when she withdrew her entry, but she was in no frame of mind to oblige.

Upon returning to the Continent, Suzanne told friends of her intention to retire from the strain of championship play, which she felt had been very exhausting since the abolition of the challenge round a few years earlier. Despite medical advice that she would recover the full use of her injured arm, Suzanne was adamant she would not change her mind. Arrangements were made with the Palace Hotel, St. Moritz for Suzanne to stay awhile and recuperate. She agreed not to compete in any of the tournaments taking place there in August and eventually returned to Nice.

So Suzanne's amateur days ended. Over ten seasons, 1913, 1914 and 1919–1926, she had captured a total of 250 titles, 83 singles, 74 doubles and 93 mixed doubles. During her adult career from 1919 to 1926, she was beaten in singles once, by Molla Mallory in 1921, and conceded just three sets, to Dorothea Chambers in 1919, Molla Mallory in 1921 and Elizabeth Ryan in 1924. From the beginning of 1922 to her retirement she won 179 consecutive singles matches.

At Wimbledon, Suzanne played a total of 94 matches and lost only three, one in doubles and two in mixed doubles. She played 66 sets in singles, losing only two and winning 29 sets at 6–0. At the French Championships, Suzanne played a total of 55 matches and lost two, one in singles and one in doubles. She played 43 sets in singles, losing only two and winning 18 sets at 6–0.

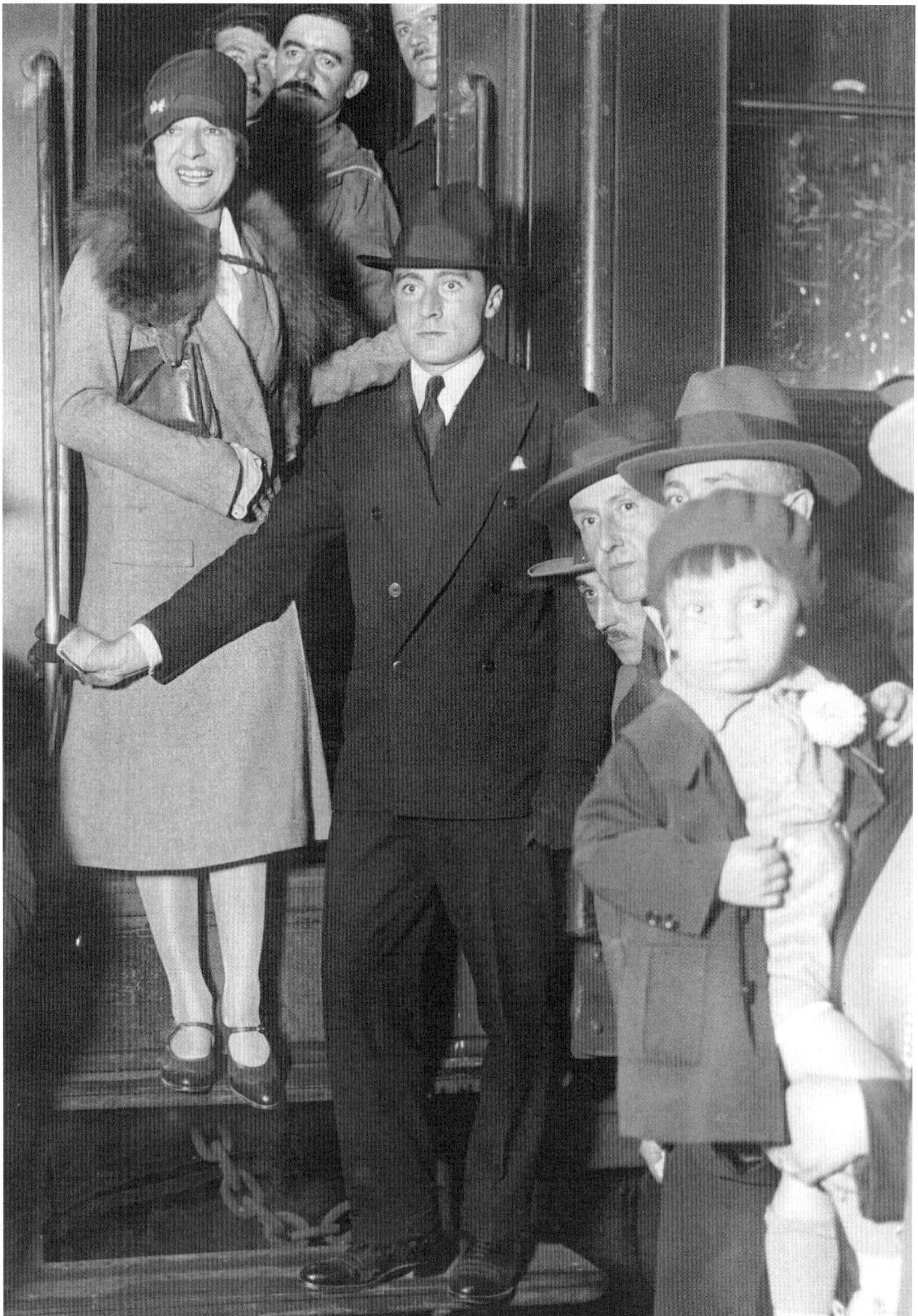

A Professional

For several weeks there had been rumours that Suzanne would turn professional, so there was little surprise when at a press conference, held in Paris on the 2nd August, the announcement was made that she had signed a contract. The chain of events which led up to this dramatic news had been started by the enormous upsurge of interest shown by the world of tennis in the match between Suzanne and Helen Wills, played early in February at Cannes.

Later that month at Los Angeles, Damon Runyon, a man of ideas, suggested to William Pickens, a promoter of bizarre sporting events and other profitable ventures, that as Suzanne attracted so much attention, why not arrange for her to tour the big cities of America under contract. William Pickens took the proposition to Charles (Cash and Carry) Pyle, a leading American sports and motion picture promoter, who agreed to back the plan.

Charles Pyle sent William Pickens to Nice in April to carry out preliminary negotiations with Suzanne and before long he was able to present a satisfactory report. Spurred on by the knowledge of Suzanne's recent emotional withdrawal from Wimbledon, Charles Pyle, accompanied by his attorney, William Hayward, travelled in July, first to Paris and then to Pourville, where Suzanne and her family were staying at her uncle's home.

From there the deal was struck. The contract called for Suzanne to tour the United States and Canada for four months commencing in October, for which she would

---

Facing page: Suzanne's professional career begins as she leaves Gare St. Lazare in Paris with Paul Feret to catch the boat to the United States.

At the beginning of August, Suzanne signs a professional contract with the American promoter, Charles Pyle, to tour North America for four months.

be paid $50,000 plus a share of the profits. William Pickens also was put under contract to be Tour Manager and he immediately set about making the complicated arrangements.

The tour was a history-making adventure. For many years there had been players who were professionals, making their living by coaching, either privately or attached to a Club or Association. The Tour was the first where a group of professional players were contracted to show their skills, 'night after night' at different venues, for a sustained period. Indeed, this tour set the pattern for the future. From then on, a continuous stream of the very top amateur players were persuaded over the years to relinquish their status until 1968, when the game became truly Open and all categories of players were allowed to compete together.

Having secured the services of the leading lady, Charles Pyle set about enrolling the supporting cast. He approached Helen Wills and Molla Mallory but neither was interested, so in the end he settled for the very experienced and instinctive fighter, Mary Browne, as the perfect foil for Suzanne, at a reported sum of $30,000.

35-year-old Mary Browne had a notable record, having won the United States singles, doubles and mixed doubles, three years in a row, 1912–1914, plus doubles in 1921 and 1925 and mixed in 1921. In 1926 she reached the singles final of the French Championships and captured the doubles crown at Wimbledon. She was also an outstanding golfer, reaching her peak in 1925, when she was runner-up at the United States Championship.

The signing of the men also caused Charles Pyle great difficulties. He was rebuffed by Bill Tilden and Bill Johnston, the two leading United States players, but was able to secure the No. 6 player, bespectacled Howard Kinsey, who earlier in the year had reached three finals at Wimbledon. He also obtained the services of Californian, Harvey Snodgrass, a former U.S. top ten ranked player, who had become a teaching professional and Paul Feret, the French Davis Cup International, who was still recovering from the death of his 19–year-old bride, Mlle Elena de Rivas, four months after his marriage. His signing as a professional was probably influenced by a desire to distance himself from the tragedy. Charles Pyle still had one more ace to play.

On the 23rd September Suzanne, together with her mother and Paul Feret, left on the boat train from Gare St. Lazare in Paris to Le Havre. There they embarked on the 'Paris' for the voyage to New York. She occupied one of the best cabins, where each day fresh flowers and champagne were placed on the instructions of Charles Pyle. Suzanne took aboard 25 dolls, representing herself, each wearing her famous bandeau, and these were auctioned during the voyage. The liner arrived in New York on the 29th and Suzanne was met at the pier by Charles Pyle, who presented her with a large bunch of red roses. Suzanne's luggage consisted of 10 trunks and 12 rackets. The following evening over 200 guests were assembled aboard the 'Paris' for a dinner given in Suzanne's honour by Charles Pyle. At the start of the proceedings the promoter took all present by surprise when he introduced his latest signing, Vincent Richards who, accompanied by his wife, Claremont, entered the gathering amidst hearty applause. At 23, Vincent Richards had established a fine reputation in the American game, having won the National Doubles five times, the Olympic singles and doubles and the Wimbledon doubles crown in 1924. The troupe was complete.

Suzanne stayed at the Vanderbilt Hotel and relaxed for a few days before starting to practise. She visited the Yankee Stadium to watch a World Series baseball game, had lunch with boxers Jack Dempsey and Georges Carpentier and attended several photographic appointments. On the 4th October, Suzanne and other members of the troupe practised for the first time on the private court of Dr. Horace Ayres at Richmond Hill. Sessions were also held during the following days on the Van Kilton public courts in Manhattan.

The setting for the inaugural evening was on Saturday 9th October at Madison Square Garden in New York, where about 13,000 people paid from $1.50 to $5.50 (total receipts – $34,000), for the privilege of watching four matches. The conditions were ideal with the lighting exceptionally good. The court was of dark green canvas tightly stretched over a matting of cork composition, which afforded an excellent playing surface. The court was portable and cost around $10,000.

A 16–page well-illustrated brochure, containing articles and biographies of the players, was on sale throughout the Tour, priced 25 cents. This allowed Charles Pyle and Suzanne a forum to express their view on professional tennis, with Suzanne being particularly forthright in condemning the amateur organizations for lining their pockets from the gate money at tournaments, while the players performed for virtually nothing. A single sheet giving the order of play was inserted in the brochure at each stop.

The State Governor and the Mayor of New York were in the audience to give support to the event. So was Bill Tilden, who was cheered loudly when announced. Play scheduled for 8.30 pm, started late with Vincent Richards holding control throughout to defeat Paul Feret, 6–3 6–4. Then followed the feature match of the evening when Suzanne, producing almost flawless tennis, proved too severe for Mary Browne, the sturdier, but noticeably shorter at 5 feet 2 inches, to the extent of 6–1 6–1 in 39 minutes. The men's doubles followed, in which Vincent Richards and Harvey Snodgrass beat Paul Feret and Howard Kinsey,

6–2, and the entertainment was brought to a conclusion when Suzanne partnered Vincent Richards to victory over Howard Kinsey and Mary Browne, 6–2. During the evening the programme was augmented by the appearance of the renowned baseball comedians, Nick Altcock and Al Schardt, who did their usual burlesque act, this time playing phantom tennis without a ball and mimicking the players.

The matches were repeated the following evening at the same venue, but before a rain-restricted crowd of 5,000. This time Suzanne defeated Mary Browne, 6–2 6–1. That weekend, 3,600 miles away in Paris, the French Tennis Federation expelled Suzanne and Paul Feret. Both were omitted from their national annual ranking lists for 1926. The United States acted similarly with the American players. Also, The All England Lawn Tennis Club withdrew Suzanne's membership.

About 13,000 people were present at the Madison Square Garden in New York on 9th October, 1926 to see Suzanne and Mary Browne make their debut as professionals

The pattern set in New York was repeated throughout the United States and four Canadian towns as the show moved from east to west, down the Pacific coast and back across the south, taking in Florida and Cuba, before returning to the New York area at the end of January, having visited some 39 towns. Attendances varied between 1,500 and 9,000. Normally four matches were played at each stop, always indoors and in the evenings, with Vincent Richards alternating against the other men, while Suzanne versus Mary Browne was a constant ingredient.

The players and entourage, about 14 in number, travelled from place to place almost entirely at night by train, which had a special carriage attached to transport the portable tennis court, which with accessories weighed nearly a ton. Two or three men went in advance of the train to arrange publicity. Suzanne accompanied by her mother, a maid and masseur, Bill O'Brien, enjoyed riding in the luxury Pullman coaches but found sleeping difficult. Everywhere her appearances created great interest by the press and there was no shortage of local people eager to entertain the visiting star.

So the show moved off to Toronto, Baltimore, Boston and Philadelphia at which juncture Charles Pyle reported that over $83,000 dollars had been taken in receipts from the 41,000 spectators who had given support.

A large appreciative crowd at Toronto, witnessed Suzanne sail past Mary Browne, 6–0 6–2. The American claimed just six points in the first set but fought courageously in the second to win 22 points. At Baltimore, Mary Browne ran herself into the ground while suffering a whitewash, 6–0 6–0. Afterwards, completely exhausted she withdrew from the mixed doubles and as a substitute match, Paul Feret and Howard Kinsey combined to quash Vincent Richards and Suzanne, 6–1. Two days later the troupe moved to Boston, where they were accommodated at the Lennox Hotel. Before 8,000 people, Mary Browne played her best so far on the Tour, but still could not do better than win three games. At Philadelphia, before a 3,000 crowd at the Sesqui Auditorium, Suzanne again won comfortably, 6–2 6–2 and Vincent Richards steamed on, but dropped his first set of the Tour to Paul Feret. The players were all based at the Ritz Carlton Hotel.

There were three further engagements during October, at Montreal, Buffalo and Cleveland. The pattern changed little as Suzanne continued to dominate Mary Browne and Vincent Richards confirmed his superiority. At Montreal, Suzanne was given tremendous support by the French speaking section of the large 8,500 crowd and at Buffalo a very appreciative audience included a personal appearance

Four of the professional troupe – Vincent Richards, Mary Browne, Suzanne and Paul Feret.

of Charles Pyle. There was another big attendance of over 10,000 at Cleveland to watch tennis played at the Public Auditorium for the first time.

Despite suffering from a bad cold for several days, Suzanne beat Mary Browne, 6–0 6–2. Nick Altcock and and Al Schardt were engaged and being very successful were signed to perform at the next six towns.

A few days later at Pittsburgh, Charles Pyle, anxious to create an atmosphere of greater competitiveness, introduced bonuses, whereby if Mary Browne took at least four games from Suzanne or any player won seven games from Vincent Richards they would receive $100. Also, a set taken from Vincent Richards, would be rewarded with $200. This may have inspired Howard Kinsey, as that evening, before 6,000 spectators, he was in sparkling form to inflict the first defeat on Vincent Richards, 7–5 6–4. Mary Browne had to wait a little longer for a bonus.

Suzanne took time off during the stay to visit the Carnenege Institute International exhibition of paintings.

More trains, more hotels as the troupe weaved west via Columbus, Detroit, Cincinnati, Minneapolis and Chicago. At Columbus, Suzanne stayed at the Neil House Hotel. She was delighted to be presented on court with a life-size portrait of herself, by local artist, Robert Vail. Just after Mary Browne pocketed her first bonus, by winning four games, two in each set. Before arriving at Detroit, Suzanne contracted a severe cold and there was doubt about her playing. However, the matter was settled when she declared she would play, regardless of her condition. The five games she conceded in singles gave Mary Browne another bonus, a feat repeated in Minneapolis. Over 7,000 were present in Chicago to see Mary Browne take Suzanne to an advantage set for the first time. She played superb tennis to reach 4–love, but doing so covered so much ground that the pace told on her and Suzanne was able to sweep through to lead 5–4 and eventually take the match, 7–5 6–1. That evening the American well earned her $100. Harvey Snodgrass came within a point of a bonus against Vincent Richards.

OFFICIAL PROGRAM

WORLD'S PREMIERE

International Professional Tennis Matches
Direction CHARLES C. PYLE

COLSIEUM, FAIR GROUNDS, Columbus, Ohio
Thursday, November 4th, 1926 at 8:30 P. M.

Local Officials will officiate
Program subject to change

First Match—Men's singles.
Vincent Richards of America vs. Paul Feret
Two out of three sets.
First set won by.........................
Second set won by.........................
Third set won by.........................

Second Match—Women's Singles.
Suzanne Lenglen of France vs. Mary K. Browne of America
Two out of three sets
First set won by.........................
Second set won by.........................
Third set won by.........................

Third Match—Men's Doubles.
Vincent Richards and Paul Feret
vs. Harvey Snodgrass and Howard Kinsey
Two out of three sets
First set won by.........................
Second set won by.........................
Third set won by.........................

Fourth Match—Mixed Doubles.
Suzanne Lenglen and Paul Feret
vs. Mary K. Browne and Howard Kinsey
Two out of three
First set won by.........................
Second set won by.........................
Third set won by.........................

At Kansas City the troupe were met at the station by local officials and taken by motor car to the Athletic Club, where Suzanne had been allocated a suite. She remarked that the land around was "so broad and beautiful and everyone so friendly". Suzanne was not extended in defeating Mary Browne, 6–1 6–3 but Vincent Richards was pushed hard to win a 22–game opening set against Paul Feret.

Despite a very tiresome journey to St. Louis, Suzanne soon settled into her suite at the Chase Hotel and, curled up on a divan, gave a sparkling performance to the reporters for over an hour. The next afternoon, prior to the matches,

Match programme for Columbus, Ohio on 4th November, 1926.

Suzanne was suddenly taken ill and confined to the hotel. At the commencement of her match against Mary Browne in the evening she noticeably lacked energy but after conceding the opening two games, threw off her outer cardigan and won 12 of the next 14 games. The crowd enjoyed the mixed doubles, as numerous times Suzanne leaped into the air in her characteristic style to make sensational shots. Leaving the town on the way to the west coast, the troupe stopped at Wichita as an extra engagement. The lighting at the Forum was bad but the meagre attendance of a few hundred was well rewarded as Mary Browne extended Suzanne to a 7–5 second set to win her fifth match bonus in a row.

Suzanne was tired from travel when the troupe reached Denver, the only stop in the Rocky Mountain region, and avoided the official reception at Union Station. Instead she went directly to bed at the Brown Palace Hotel, in the same suite that Queen Maria of Romania had occupied a week or so earlier. An enthusiastic crowd, numbering around 2,000 were at the Stockyards Stadium on the Saturday evening to see Suzanne retain her hold on Mary Browne, with the loss of three games, 6–2 6–1.

The Tour moved over the border to Victoria and the following evening to Vancouver. At the former, the matches were played at the Willows Arena, where there was much disappointment among the spectators when an announcement was made that Suzanne's match against Mary Browne would be confined to one set only, because of the cold weather. Some left their seats, but those who stayed saw Suzanne win 6–1 and later produce a stunning display in the mixed doubles. Earlier, Paul Feret, in great form brought about the downfall of a listless Vincent Richards to win a double bonus, 7–5 6–2. The troupe was accommodated at the Empress Hotel.

At Vancouver, Suzanne was hotly pursued by the press, particularly when they learnt she travelled with 11 trunks containing 55 costumes and accessories. The main conference at the Vancouver Hotel concentrated on her personality and fashionable clothes, not on tennis. Suzanne said she had received 32 proposals of marriage, including several from dukes and counts, and others from men of lesser rank but with possibly more money. Regarding clothes she made clear that "A woman's only sin was to be ill-dressed". In the evening Suzanne had Mary Browne on the run with her full repertoire of strokes to win, 6–2 6–2. Mary Browne, as usual, worked very hard throughout. Harvey Snodgrass fully tested Vincent Richards.

The following evening at Seattle, Suzanne was well in control, dictating play from start to finish, 6–2 6–0. As ever, her opponent fought tirelessly but still could only muster 10 points in the second set.

At Portland real drama unfolded as Mary Browne came within two points of taking a set from Suzanne. After dropping the opening game, Suzanne won the next five, only for Mary Browne to win the next four to put her on an equal footing. Suzanne then led 6–5 7–6 and 8–7 only for the advantage to be taken from her. In the 17th game the American battled to deuce and with two quick points broke through to lead 9–8. Serving for the set Mary Browne reached 30–love before Suzanne rallied to 9–all and with the loss of only two more points won the set, 11–9. With that Suzanne grabbed her coat, retired to the dressing room and collapsed. A little later a car was called and she was taken back to her hotel. Ben Crose, manager of the Tour, announced that the mixed doubles scheduled for later in the evening was cancelled as Suzanne was exhausted by playing four evenings in a row and had been suffering from a cold and lack of sleep for several days.

The troupe moved on to California and performed before excellent galleries at San Francisco and, on the other side of the bay, at Oakland, on the 7th and 9th December, respectively. Suzanne, clutching a huge bouquet of American Beauty roses, tied with a long streamer of French colours, arrived by train at the Golden Gate city and immediately attracted the attention of thronging reporters and photographers, before being whisked away by car to her suite at the Palace Hotel. She confirmed a complete recovery from the effects of her cold at Portland.

Mary Browne had noticeably improved, which resulted in her pushing Suzanne to an advantage set at both locations. Vincent Richards, playing below par, was taken to tight third sets by Howard Kinsey and Harvey Snodgrass. Helen Wills attended both evenings and also called on Suzanne at the Oakland Hotel.

The presence of Suzanne in the California area fuelled much speculation in the press on the possibility of another showdown with Helen Wills, but with such a complicated situation there was never a real chance of this occurring.

Although weary after playing at six cities over nine days, including travelling in between, the standard of play had been good, but the players were thankful for the scheduled rest following Oakland for a period of nearly two and a half weeks until after Christmas. For much of the time Suzanne and other members of the troupe, minus Harvey Snodgrass but plus Charles Pyle, settled in at the Hotel del

Coronado on Coronado Island, off the coast of San Diego. This luxury hotel, built in 1888, had tennis facilities but Suzanne chose to rest. With the other players she attended the Tijuana Race Track for the Ladies' Programme Day and in her honour the seventh race was named the Lenglen Claiming Handicap. When she entered the Judges' Stand La Marseillaise was played.

With Christmas approaching Suzanne practised a little, but the headlines she commanded in the local newspapers were replaced when some major baseball stars were accused in a scandal of throwing games for money. Then Suzanne learnt that Mary Browne was practising hard on her home court at Santa Monica, so she moved to Los Angeles to have workouts with Vincent Richards.

The Tour resumed on the 28th December at the Los Angeles Olympic Stadium. Over 9,000 spectators were quite shocked at the speed with which Suzanne dispatched Mary Browne, who won only the third game of the second set. Local teaching professional, Walter Wesbrook, was engaged for the evening to partner Harvey Snodgrass for the doubles. In their amateur days these two had been a notable team, winning the U.S. National Clay Court Championships in 1925. With great style they defeated Howard Kinsey and Vincent Richards in two ten-game sets.

While in California, Suzanne met Baldwin M. Baldwin, a rich, handsome American, grandson and heir to multi-millionaire, Elias Jackson (Lucky) Baldwin, who made his fortune from mining, large-scale racehorse breeding and many other enterprises. Suzanne was to happily spend the next five years with Baldwin Baldwin, but they never married as he already had a wife and two children. In the past Suzanne had enjoyed a close relationship with several men, mostly tennis players, including Roger Danet, Pierre Albarran, Placido Gaslini and Eduardo Flaquer, but these affairs never quite matured to the point of marriage. Baldwin Baldwin accompanied Suzanne and the troupe for the remainder of the Tour.

The troupe departed from the west coast by train for the very long journey to Texas, where three exhibitions were undertaken. On New Year's Eve Suzanne, together with Vincent and Claremont Richards, appeared in the ballroom of the St. Anthony Hotel at San Antonio, much to the delight of the merry-making guests. On the following morning Suzanne with her mother and Claremont Richards viewed the attractions around town in a Hudson, provided by the local motor company, while the rest of the party played golf. Suzanne told the press she would write a book about her memoirs during her American tour – but she never did. On the Sunday

Throughout the North American tour Mary Browne gained admiration for her courageous fighting spirit. Here she is seen signing her professional contract.

morning of the exhibition the whole party were taken six miles out of town to the Sunshine Ranch rodeo where Suzanne was delighted to see a 'real' cowboy. In the evening at the Municipal Auditorium the always popular Mary Browne played well to lead Suzanne 3–2 but from then she faded and won only a further game.

Next came Dallas, where despite being shown to the wrong suite at the Adolphus Hotel and still waiting the arrival of her trunks, Suzanne was in sparkling form to meet the press. She dealt with questions in her usual excellent English and captured those present with her warm personality and charming manner. Meanwhile the men were playing golf at the nearby Lakewood Country Club. The evening at Gardner Park did not attract a large crowd but those present well appreciated the competitiveness of the encounters. Suzanne coasted to a 6–2 6–1 win over Mary Browne.

At Houston, the press were again very eager to enquire into all facets of Suzanne's life. She stayed at the Rice Hotel and with her mother was shown the local sights and visited the Rice Institute. On court Mary Browne had a wonderful opportunity to win her first set from Suzanne. The American lost the opening set, 6–1 but increased the accuracy of her strokes to forge ahead 5–3. She then badly faltered by delivering two double faults and although she recovered to 30–all, Suzanne took the game. Mary Browne led again at 6–5 but Suzanne at her peak captured the next three games. It was apparent that a hand injured in the first set hampered Suzanne as she continued to rearrange the bandage, which had been hastily applied. The injury caused the cancellation of the mixed doubles thereby restricting the matches to three.

The southern States of Louisiana, Alabama and Georgia were next on the schedule. At New Orleans, the results of the matches played on the old Jai alai (pelota) Fronton court followed the usual pattern with Suzanne winning her singles, 6–2 6–2. Vincent Richards looked in good shape when he defeated Harvey Snodgrass and competed in the doubles, but later that evening he went down with a bout of influenza (and later jaundice) which forced him to stay in the town, while the remainder of the players moved on to Birmingham.

At this stop the weather was intensely cold, which affected the attendance. With Vincent Richards absent, Howard Kinsey beat Paul Feret, in the top spot, in a long tussle of 36 games, while Suzanne easily accounted for Mary Browne, 6–1 6–2. There was no doubles contest and the mixed doubles drew the proceedings to a close.

Suzanne Lenglen

NORTH-AMERICAN TOUR

Souvenir Program 25¢

Four days later at Atlanta, Vincent Richards was still absent and the programme was again restricted to three matches. Harvey Snodgrass, with his very powerful service, crushed Paul Feret, 6–2 6–0. Suzanne started badly against Mary Browne completely losing her direction to go 4–love down, but then changed to top gear to allow her opponent just two more games. At the morning press conference Suzanne was in a good mood and allowed an official to say that during her adult life she always endeavoured to keep in the best of condition and, if necessary, engaged in training to ensure that her weight was consistently around 125lb and never fluctuated outside the 125–130lb margin. Her waist was normally 25? inches and her chest 32 inches. She was a little above average height at 5 feet 7 inches.

Another long overnight train journey and another State brought the troupe to Tampa, Florida. The contest between Suzanne and Mary Browne was undoubtedly the spectacle of the Tour so far. There was no indication of this when Suzanne won the opening set, 6–0, but what followed was that the American, approaching perfection, caught Suzanne time and time again with her brilliant returns and accurate placements, which continually brought the crowd to their feet, to take the set, 6–2 – her first of the Tour. But from then on the dazzling attack from Suzanne was too deadly and her opponent fell victim to her cross volleys for victory at 6–0 2–6 6–1. Earlier Harvey Snodgrass outlasted Howard Kinsey and later Suzanne with the latter won the mixed doubles. Vince Richards was still absent and again the show consisted of three matches.

The next stop was Miami, where the troupe was based at the Nautilus Hotel. The matches were played on the Biscayne Jai alai Fronton court, before a sizeable crowd. Suzanne was on song, allowing Mary Browne just one game in each set, but nevertheless there were some good rallies that brought the crowd to their feet. At the conclusion of the match both were given a beautiful bunch of flowers. Vincent Richards, still missing, allowed Howard Kinsey to defeat Paul Feret, 6–3 6–2. Suzanne spent one evening as a guest of the Biscayne Kennel Club, during which she presented a trophy for a special race. By chance, Molla Mallory was at Miami at the same time as the troupe and she invited Suzanne to play a friendly mixed doubles practise match with her on the Flamingo courts. Suzanne declined but Mary Browne accepted.

To reach the next venue the troupe caught the boat across the Florida Sea to Havana in Cuba where they stayed four nights, giving them ample opportunity for

---

Facing page: Cover of the North American Tour programme.

sightseeing. The matches were played on the old Jai alai Fronton court at the Palace of the Shouts on the Wednesday evening. Harvey Snodgrass beat Paul Feret in an interesting three-set encounter, while Suzanne easily disposed of Mary Browne, 6–2 6–0. After a couple of games the American conceded the next ten to Suzanne's magnificent ground strokes and great service placements. To some degree the evening's play was overshadowed by the behaviour of some of the spectators who appeared to know little about the game and often applauded at the wrong time.

Suzanne found time during the visit to attend the races at the Havana Jockey Club in Oriental Park.

At the end of their stay the players returned to Miami and took the evening train for their long two night journey back to New York, where they arrived on Sunday morning, 30th January.

The Tour soon ran into difficulties when Suzanne was taken ill with tonsillitis and confined to bed at the Vanderbilt Hotel and Vincent Richards was still not well enough to play. The only option was to delay the remainder of the Tour programme. Consequently, the scheduled stop at Hartford for the 4th February was postponed until the 9th, likewise the other venues, Newark, New Haven, Brooklyn and Providence were put back. Fortunately ticket sales were not affected.

At Hartford the audience was informed that Suzanne was not fully recovered from tonsillitis, but not wishing to disappoint everyone, had agreed to play a one-set match against Mary Browne. For a while Suzanne managed to hold her own and reached 3–all but after resting for a while she started coughing. She recovered a little but resuming play soon lost control of the ball and victory went to the American, 6–3. Suzanne then retired to the Bond Hotel and the possibility of the mixed doubles being staged disappeared. A far from fit Vincent Richards reappeared but played doubles only and the singles tussle was given to Paul Feret and Howard Kinsey.

The last four meetings followed very quickly with each restricted to a three match programme. Suzanne, who looked ill most of the time, never played singles again and limited her appearances at each venue to mixed doubles. At Newark the players stayed at the Robert Treat Hotel. Paul Feret contested his last match at this fixture, because he had been recalled for service by the French military authorities and had arranged to leave for Paris on the following evening. His place for the final three exhibitions was taken by the youthful Charles Wood, who partnered Vincent Richards in the doubles.

One of the most fiercely contested matches of the Tour took place at New Haven, when Howard Kinsey eventually beat Harvey Snodgrass over 39 games, lasting two hours.

At Brooklyn, Vincent Richards played one more singles match but, noticeably far from his best, was beaten by Howard Kinsey, 8–6 6–4.

The final matches took place at the Rhode Island Auditorium at Providence on Monday 14th February. Advance publicity suggested that Suzanne would play Howard Kinsey in a best of three sets singles match, (Suzanne was to receive one point in each game), but when the evening came the idea was soon forgotten. Mary Browne was absent as her contract had run out, so Suzanne played a doubles match, partnered by Vincent Richards, against Howard Kinsey and Harvey Snodgrass. This gave the spectators a glimpse of Suzanne for just twenty minutes. In the very final match of the Tour, Howard Kinsey and Harvey Snodgrass defeated Vincent Richards and Charles Wood, 6–3 6–1. The players stayed overnight at the Biltmore Hotel before returning to New York. The great adventure was over, in many ways to the relief of the players, who had been put under considerable strain during the last few weeks, particularly as the two stars of the show, Suzanne and Vincent Richards, had been unwell.

Overall, Suzanne met Mary Browne 36 times in singles and conceded, towards the end, just two sets, one in Tampa and one in Hartford. She was never defeated in a three-set match played to a finish, but certainly lost once in the one-set contest at Hartford.

Mary Browne gained the admiration of all for her courageous fighting qualities and splendid spirit. She never flagged at any time. A short while after the Tour, Mary Browne wrote a long and very complimentary article on Suzanne in which she called her the "most marvellous player in the world" and also stated that in the months they had travelled together, chatting in hotel rooms and on trains, she had learned more about tennis than in the previous 20 years.

Although not fully capturing the imagination of the American public, the Tour was undoubtedly a success and not the least gave thousands the rare opportunity of watching Suzanne's uncanny racket wielding ability. Behind the scenes the organization required to give back-up to the troupe constantly on the move was outstanding.

Financially, all concerned appeared to be satisfied. William Pickens, on behalf of Charles Pyle, stated that Suzanne had been 'compensated' to the extent of $100,000, made up of a flat guarantee of $50,000 plus 50% of the net gate receipts. Richards had been guaranteed $35,000, Howard Kinsey, $20,000, Harvey Snodgrass, $12,000 and Paul Feret $10,000, while Mary Browne received $35,000 plus 5% of the receipts. The total takings from the Tour, including royalties from advertising, were stated to be $500,000, while Pyle's profit was estimated between $50,000 and $75,000.

There was talk of Charles Pyle placing fresh contracts with the same players for a world tour later in the year, but nothing materialised. He continued with his enterprises but never ventured into tennis again. He died in 1939, aged 56. Suzanne with her mother, accompanied by Howard Kinsey and Baldwin Baldwin left New York from the West Fourteenth Street Pier, aboard the 'France' at 11 am on Saturday, 19th February. Suzanne told reporters that her visit to America was most enjoyable and everywhere the Tour travelled the hospitality received was magnificent. She regretted being unable to attend the wedding of Diddie Vlasto to Jean (Johnny) Serpieri in Athens, two days earlier, but remarked "I bet she looked sweet". The party arrived at Le Havre a week later and after a few days in Paris, Suzanne and Baldwin Baldwin journeyed to Nice. Vincent Richards remained in New York for a week or so before travelling to Florida, while Harvey Snodgrass returned to his home in California. Mary Browne moved to Cleveland to manage a sports store and a few months later, the United States Golf Association barred her from competing in amateur tournaments on account of being a professional tennis player.

In the spring of 1927, Suzanne agreed to an approach by Charles (C.B.) Cochran, the London theatrical manager and producer and promoter of sporting events, to undertake a short exhibition tour of Great Britain, starting in late June. Cochran soon signed Howard Kinsey and Karel Kozeluh, a Czechoslovakian who was already a professional, but the problem was similar to the American tour to find a player who would be able to extend Suzanne in her matches, at least sufficiently to make the spectacle entertaining, if not exciting.

Very tempting offers were refused by Miss Betty Nuthall, a brilliant 16–year-old English girl, who in 1930 became the first foreigner to win the United States Women's Singles title, and Frl Cilly Aussem, the 18–year-old German, destined to become Wimbledon Singles Champion three years later. Both were at the outset

The British Professional tour of 1927. The line up of players, left to right, Karel Kozeluh, Evelyn Dewhurst, Suzanne, C.B. Cochran the promoter, Vivien Glasspool, Dora Koring and Howard Kinsey.

of their career and by abandoning their amateur status they would have lost much and, apart from the money, gained very little. Some reports suggested that Betty Nuthall was offered a contract of £20,000. Kathleen Godfree was approached to join the troupe but she also declined.

In the end Charles Cochran signed little-known 38–year-old Frl Dora Koring, the German champion in 1912 and 1913 and silver medallist in the singles at the 1912 Olympic Games, and Evelyn Dewhurst, who at the previous Wimbledon had played Suzanne in her last singles appearance as an amateur. She was reputed to have signed for £1,000 because she "desperately needed the money". Miss Vivien Glasspool was signed as a reserve. She was Irish and had played most of her tennis abroad.

Suzanne, with her mother and Baldwin Baldwin as her manager, arrived in London on the 26th June after a rough channel crossing from France. Suzanne said she had been "horribly sea-sick". The Tour was scheduled to make a total of eight appearances, spread over five towns, with each programme consisting of three matches. On each occasion, Karel Kozeluh met Howard Kinsey in the opening contest. Throughout they produced some exhilarating tennis and were always good value for money. Honours were evenly shared. Next on the bill came Suzanne playing a singles match, followed by a mixed doubles.

The show was to have opened at the Phyllis Court Club at Henley-on-Thames on the afternoon of Wednesday, 29th June but heavy rain caused the matches to be cancelled. However, on the following Saturday evening, a good crowd was present to witness the opening match, in which Karel Kozeluh outmanoeuvred Howard Kinsey, 6–1 6–2. The attraction of the evening followed when Suzanne showed flashes of her great skill by defeating Dora Koring, 6–1 6–2. At the end the German woman was gasping for breath while Suzanne was still perfectly cool and fresh. Suzanne then joined Howard Kinsey to win over Karel Kozeluh and Evelyn Dewhurst, 6–1 6–2.

The next three exhibitions took place on the evenings of Tuesday, Wednesday and Friday, 5th, 6th and 8th July in Kensington, London at the Holland Park Hall, which normally housed a roller skating rink. The lighting in the hall, using 50 artificial sunlight lamps, was so bright that all the players, except Suzanne, wore eye-shades. The price of the seats ranged from 2s 4d to 14s 6d and a programme was on sale at 1s 0d. On the first evening over 5,000 spectators were present when Karel Kozeluh edged out against Howard Kinsey, 7–5 7–5. Then after a cautious start, Suzanne ran away with the match, 6–3 6–0 against Dora Koring who frequently queried Suzanne's line shots, sometimes standing over the line, saying "Out, Out". Later, Suzanne and Karel Kozeluh fought a marathon duel before overcoming Howard Kinsey and Evelyn Dewhurst, 8–6 3–6 8–6.

Charles Cochran, disturbed by Dora Koring's behaviour and attitude on court decided to dispense with her services and replaced her by Evelyn Dewhurst in the singles match on the following evening. Under the circumstances Evelyn Dewhurst performed well and managed to extend the rallies on many occasions. The crowd aware of her uphill struggle, gave good support and enthusiastically clapped the capture of a game. Suzanne, never really in any danger, won comfortably, 6–2 6–2.

On the eve of Friday's matches there was conjecture that Suzanne would pair with Charles Read, the professional at the Queen's Club, to play against Howard Kinsey and Karel Kozeluh. When informed, Suzanne quickly refused to play the match and said "It is unorthodox for one woman and three men to play a doubles match and I think the idea stupid". That was the end of the matter and the usual programme proceeded. Suzanne displayed scintillating form and in quick time overwhelmed Evelyn Dewhurst, 6–0 6–1. The spectators then saw a lively match in which Suzanne and Howard Kinsey narrowly beat Karel Kozeluh and Evelyn Dewhurst, 9–7 6–4.

Dora Koring returned to Germany where she coached for many years. She was killed during the Second World War in the bombing of Dresden, her home town.

The last three engagements were staged on Association Football grounds where a purpose-built court was erected with a light green canvas laid over a board flooring, measuring 120×60 feet.

On Monday 11th July, Suzanne arrived by train at the Central Station in Glasgow, wearing a beige sports dress and dark blue sweater under a brown checked tweed coat. She was met by Charles Cochran, who presented her with a bouquet of red roses. She then settled in at the Central Hotel for her short visit to the city. On the Tuesday evening over 8,000 spectators were present at the Queen's Park Football Club at Hampden Park, where the court was positioned in front of the South Stand. Play commenced at 6.30pm in cool weather, with Howard Kinsey beating Karel Kozeluh, 4–6 7–5 6–2 in a match which received continuous applause. Suzanne followed and in dazzling form defeated Evelyn Dewhurst, 6–2 6–0 in 20 minutes. Suzanne with Karel Kozeluh then won the mixed doubles.

The following Friday the venue was the Blackpool Football Club at Bloomfield Road, where a crowd of 7,000 paid between 2s. and 10s. 6d. to watch the stars in action. As usual, Karel Kozeluh and Howard Kinsey began and the audience was treated to many long and exciting rallies before the Czech became a little lame towards the end and was defeated, 6–4 6–3. Suzanne, who did not arrive at the ground until 3.30pm, appeared on court wearing a squirrel fur coat over a white ivory accordion pleated jumper frock and two cardigans. Her bandeau was green. She easily won the opening set against Evelyn Dewhurst 6–1, but in the next her opponent put up a very spirited fight before losing, 6–4. As the last ball of the mixed doubles was struck there was a rush to the court to secure Suzanne's autograph but to everyone's disappointment she donned her coat and rushed to the dressing room.

The last stop was at the Manchester United Football Club ground at Old Trafford on the Saturday. Special trains were run to bring the spectators in from outlying districts. A chilly afternoon never deterred the excellent attendance of over 15,000, mostly young ladies, being present for the 2.00pm start. Parties of schoolchildren were encouraged to attend by offering a reduced rate of 1s. 6d per ticket. Suzanne arrived in town wearing a magnificent mink with a spray of orchids. She constantly complained of the cold and played solitaire with Baldwin Baldwin in the dressing room while Karel Kozeluh was beating Howard Kinsey, 7–5 4–6 6–2. However, Suzanne on top form, dealt severely with Evelyn Dewhurst, allowing her just two

A PROFESSIONAL

Cover of the British Professional Tour programme at Blackpool.

Left: The British Professional tour of 1927. Suzanne plays Evelyn Dewhurst before a crowd of over 8,000 at the Queen's Park Football Club at Hampden Park, Glasgow on 12th July.

games in the second set. She then paired with Howard Kinsey to take the mixed doubles. The Club received 10% of the gross takings but in return provided the stewards and gatemen.

Generally the short Tour had been very successful, despite the complete lack of interest shown by the national press. The attendances, particularly during the second week were amazing. The players' financial arrangements were never made public. At least the people living outside London had been given a rare opportunity to see Suzanne in action.

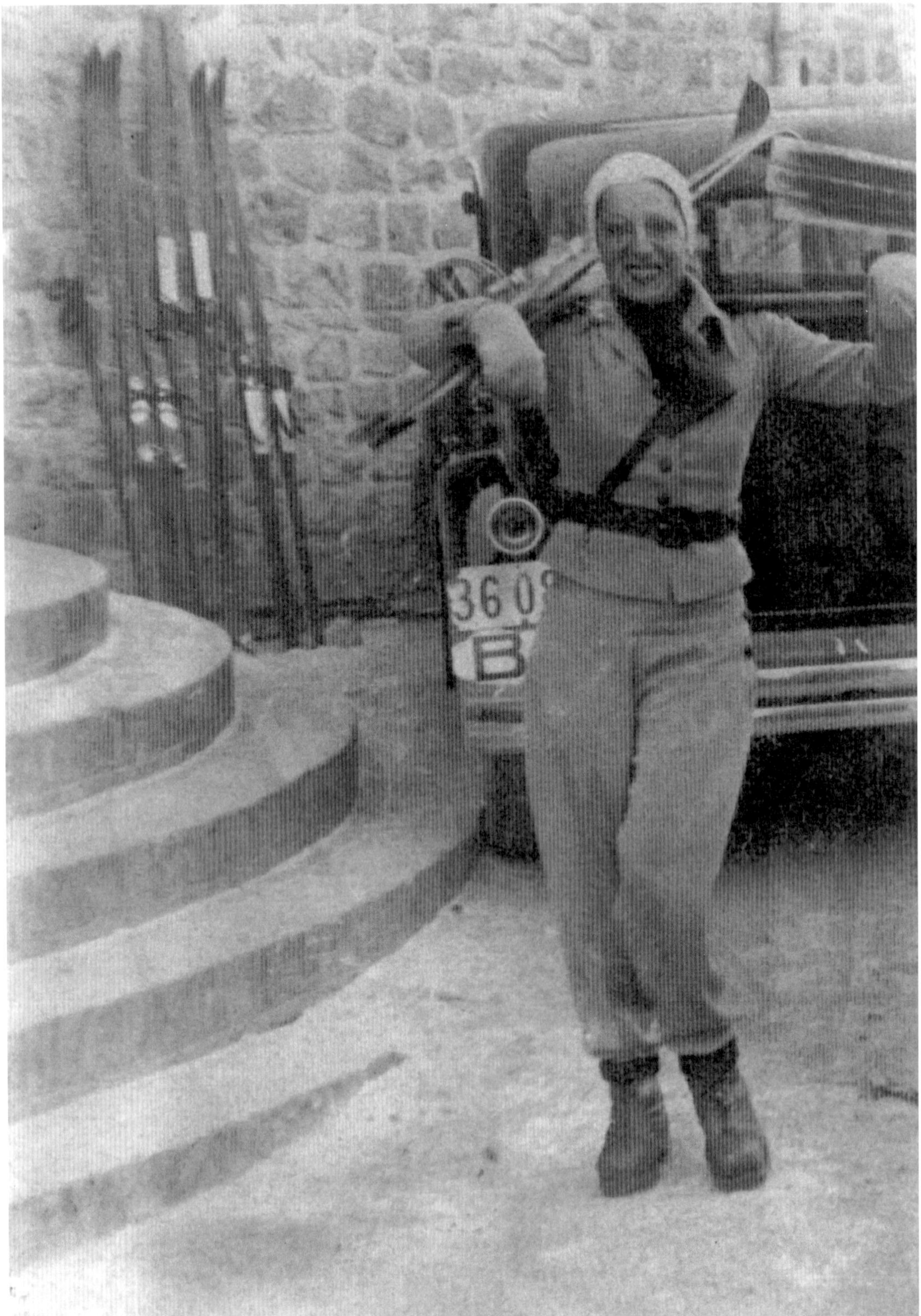
36 0
B

The Quiet Years

With the British tour over, Suzanne settled down with Baldwin Baldwin. She seemed happy to lead a life away from tennis, which gave her ample opportunity to pursue other interests such as driving, dancing and reading.

However, towards the end of 1928, Suzanne was in the headlines again when, accompanied by her mother and Baldwin Baldwin, she crossed the Atlantic aboard the Lloyd Sabaudo liner 'Conte Biancamano' and arrived in New York on 30th November. To avoid the French press they travelled from Nice to Gibraltar to pick up the Italian ship, instead of the usual journey to Paris for the boat train to Le Havre. During the voyage they travelled incognito with their names missing from the passenger list.

As soon as the ship docked, Suzanne disappeared leaving her mother and Baldwin Baldwin to arrange the taxis to convey the 20 pieces of luggage to the Savoy-Plaza Hotel.

A week later the party arrived by train at Trukee in California, where they stayed for three days at the Tahoe Lake Lodge as guest of Baldwin Baldwin's mother, Anita. Then they moved south to the Baldwin home in Arcadia, east of Glendale near Los Angeles. Mystery and rumour surrounded the visit with the speculation from the press that Suzanne and Baldwin Baldwin were engaged and about to be married. This was quickly denied by Anita Baldwin, who stated that her son was still married to his wife, the former Nell Maxime Wilson.

Facing page: Suzanne was a very enthusiastic skiier.

After about five weeks in Los Angeles, Suzanne and her fellow travellers returned to New York, where they boarded the 'Paris' on the evening of 25th January, 1929. Somehow several newspaper photographers had discovered the departure details and hustled Suzanne on her way up the gangway, which caused Baldwin Baldwin to have an altercation with two of the offending photographers, resulting in a broken camera.

The main reason for the visit to Los Angeles was undoubtedly for Baldwin Baldwin to negotiate with his wife for a divorce, but no agreement was forthcoming. The weekend that Suzanne departed from the United States, Nell Baldwin confirmed she would not aid her husband to obtain a divorce which he might seek in Paris but which, without her co-operation, he would be unable to secure.

When Suzanne returned home to Nice on 7th February, she found her father unwell. Three weeks later on 1st March, Charles Lenglen died, with his wife and Suzanne at his bedside.

Although there were times when Suzanne's relationship with her father was tempestuous, she realised that her achievement at tennis was entirely due to his drive, ambition and foresight in the early days. Suzanne and her mother were forced to relinquish the Villa Ariem and moved to 17 rue des Perchamps in Paris. They also purchased a house in the country at Septeuil.

In July, 1930 there were rumours that Suzanne would apply to the French Tennis Federation for reinstatement as an amateur but this she emphatically denied. Later in the year plans were being made for Suzanne to play in Berlin during November but this did not materialise because of the financial demands she made. There was a suggestion that she would have played singles matches against Karel Kozeluh and Roman Najuch.

During the early part of 1932, Suzanne and Baldwin Baldwin parted. He returned to the United States while she set up home at 4, Square Jean Paul Laurens in Paris. Suzanne began to take an interest in lawn tennis again and on the morning of 1st July, Suzanne, with little notice, flew from Paris to Croydon where Sophie Wavertree was waiting to escort her to Wimbledon. This was her first visit to the tournament since retiring in 1926 and she was soon the centre of an admiring throng. That afternoon she saw her successor as 'Queen of Wimbledon', Mrs Moody, the former Helen Wills, win her fifth singles title by defeating the American, Miss Helen Jacobs.

The following afternoon, Suzanne was again on the Centre Court to witness Ellsworth Vines of the United States overwhelm England's Henry (Bunny) Austin in the final. Over the weekend, Suzanne played in private at Sophie Wavertree's home and also suggested she take part in the annual charity matches but a British Lawn Tennis Association rule prohibited amateurs playing with professionals where gate money was charged. Suzanne, not wishing to cause any embarrassment, withdrew her offer and instead umpired a mixed doubles match.

Back home, Suzanne was obviously searching for some means to get involved in lawn tennis again. She raised the question of reinstatement as an amateur with the French Tennis Federation but was told to reapply in three years. This particularly upset Suzanne as Paul Feret had been reinstated and, indeed, had competed at the Wimbledon she had just visited. In the meantime she practised frequently and played a few exhibition matches at tournaments with Martin Plaa, the French professional.

In May, 1933, Suzanne was appointed director of a coaching school at the Roland Garros Stadium in Paris. During the French Championships, Suzanne coached Helen Jacobs on an outside court for an hour and a half, much to the delight of many people who eagerly assembled to watch. Early in July Suzanne, back in London, watched the concluding rounds at Wimbledon. She described Jack Crawford's win over Ellsworth Vines in the Gentlemen's Singles final as the most marvellous and perfect tennis she had ever seen.

While in London, Suzanne negotiated the final details of her year's contract with Selfridges, the giant department store in Oxford Street. She was to make 120 appearances to give demonstration lessons and advice on the selection of rackets and dresses.

On the opening day, Monday, 18th September, Suzanne, dressed in a unique linen combination outfit of coatee-skirt-shorts and wearing a bright orange bandeau, gave a demonstration on how to drive, serve and volley on a specially built half-court and canvas surface, laid out on the fourth floor of the store. Afterwards she gave lessons and answered queries.

Suzanne let it be known that she was never able to play on wood. She had tried twice, once when a girl and again when grown up, but each time she quit. It was not the light nor the pace but she felt there was something about a wooden floor that beat her. She had never entered a tournament played on wood. Suzanne also stated that she approved of the wearing of shorts in private but not in public. She spoke English quickly and fairly fluently with a surprisingly low voice.

During the first week, Suzanne gave a demonstration twice a day, at 11.30 am and 3 pm but afterwards her appearances usually consisted of one hour on the court, followed by an hour each in the sports and dress departments. Normally she was available for a week or ten-day period. Occasionally, Suzanne gave lectures in the Palm Court.

On the evening of Saturday, 21st April, 1934 accommodation was made on the roof of the building for 500 spectators to watch, for two hours, rising junior players entertain with skilful tennis on a purpose-built court. These exhibitions, on which Suzanne gave a running commentary through a microphone, were held as part of Selfridges 25th Anniversary celebrations. The area was floodlit, which was an innovation for those days. The court was used for demonstrations throughout the following summer.

While in London, Suzanne played a small part in the British comedy film entitled 'Things are looking up', starring Cicely Courtneidge. The production company was Gaumont, who began filming in July at the Islington Studio. In the film a tennis match takes place between Martha Bombarde, played by Suzanne and Bertha Fytte, acted by Cicely Courtneidge, on the Centre Court at Wimbledon but in fact the contest was filmed on the recreation courts of Gainsborough Studios. Bertha Fytte defeats Martha Bombarde who, in a fit of temper, throws her racket to the ground and storms off court without shaking her opponent's hand. The film, which lasted 78 minutes, was released in 1935.

For some years Suzanne had the idea of setting up a school of lawn tennis. She had motored throughout France visiting many tennis clubs, mainly away from the recognised centres with which she was familiar, making a detailed study of coaching methods. The conclusion she reached was that those who really needed lessons were not the gifted few who could hope to become really proficient at the

---

Facing page: In 1935 Suzanne appeared in the British film 'Things are looking up', playing in a tennis match against the star, Cicely Courtneidge. Supposedly, the contest was staged on the Centre Court at Wimbledon but in fact the film was shot at Gainsborough Studios.

Stills from the film show:
Above: Suzanne and Cicely Courtneidge posing for the cameras.
Below: the players in action during the opening game.

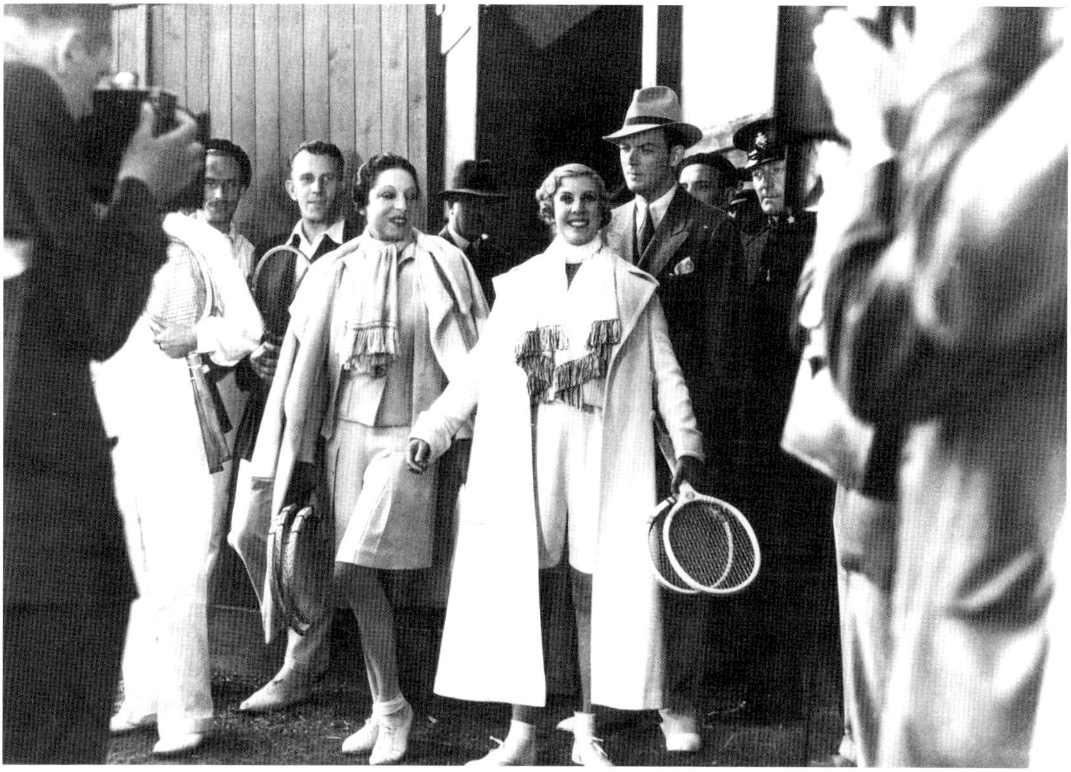

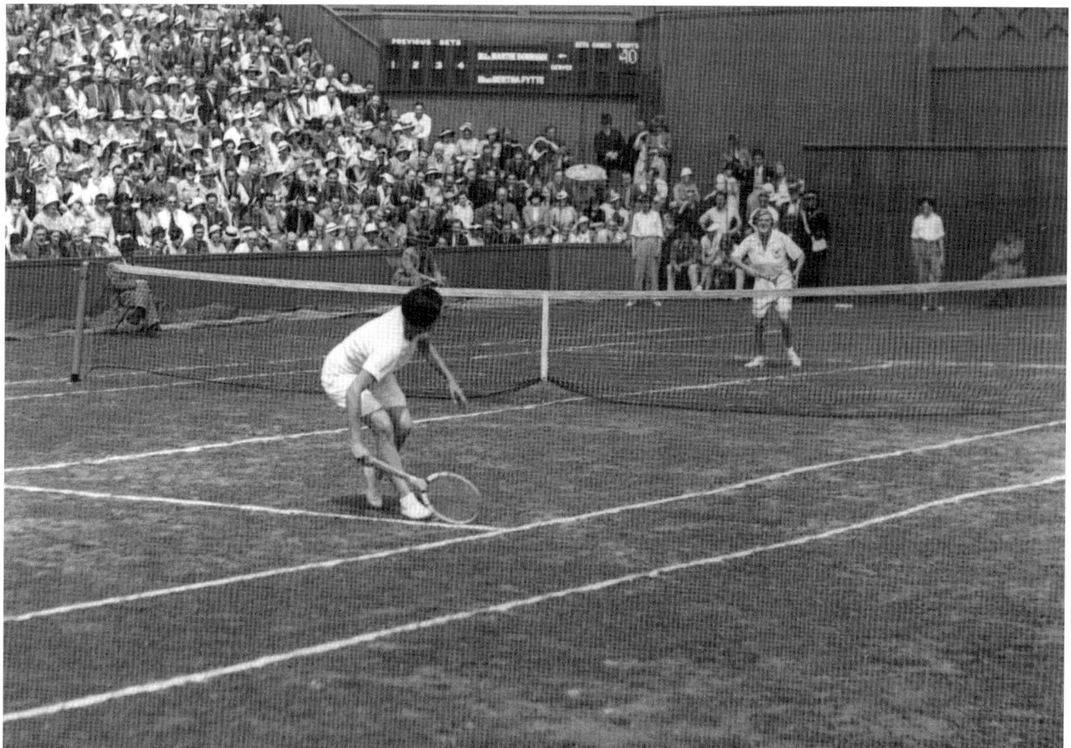
PREVIOUS SETS
1 2 3 4
40

game but those vastly more numerous who without lessons would never succeed in playing properly. She found there was a lack of understanding of the very principles involved in the execution of the strokes.

Eventually Suzanne, with the full backing of the French Tennis Federation, opened her coaching school at the Tennis Mirabeau, Auteuil, Paris during March, 1936. The venture was inaugurated by an outstanding exhibition doubles match with Suzanne and Jean Borotra playing Albert Burke and Raymond Rodel, both noted professionals.

In July, Suzanne visited Wimbledon again and was one of the first to congratulate the new champion, Helen Jacobs, in her dressing room.

In 1937 Suzanne expanded her tennis school and for the first time she provided classes for adults. The same year Suzanne collaborated with Margaret Morris, who had spent a lifetime studying the techniques of movement, in producing their book 'Tennis by Simple Exercises', published by William Heinemann of London. The first part of the book, contributed by Suzanne, outlined the essential requirements of lawn tennis to enable a player to lay a sound foundation for a good all-round game. The second part, written by Margaret Morris, listed a multitude of exercises which she had specifically designed for the lawn tennis player.

That year, far away in Phoenix, Arizona, Baldwin Baldwin married Mrs Rowena Schneider Wilson on 21st October, the day his divorce decree from Nell Baldwin became final in Los Angeles. This marriage was actually his third, as his second wife, Margaret Wilson of Indianapolis, had obtained an annulment of her marriage when a court ruled that a former divorce from the first Mrs Baldwin in Riga, Latvia was invalid. Baldwin Baldwin died in Orange, California on 21st September, 1970, aged 66.

On the 14th May, 1938 the French National Tennis School was opened at the Stade de Coubertin in Paris, with Suzanne as director. The school had been set up by the Ministry of Education to train games teachers at secondary schools.

Suzanne had hardly taken up the reins of this new challenge when she became ill at her home in Paris on 15th June, complaining of undue fatigue. She rapidly grew weaker and blood tests revealed she was suffering from pernicious anaemia.

Ten days later she was reported to be much improved after receiving a blood transfusion but after a couple of days her health deteriorated and she died at her home at 6.30 am on Monday, 4th July at the age of 39 years. She had last played tennis at the beginning of June.

Suzanne at the Roland Garros Stadium in Paris demonstrates the backhand stroke to a squad of juniors.

The following day the Cross of the Legion of Honour was awarded posthumously to Suzanne for her services to French Sport. This was presented to her mother by M. Zay, the Minister of Education. Many prominent French players and officials called at her home to pay their last respects and telegrams of condolence were received from all parts of the world.

The funeral service was held at the Church of Notre Dame de l'Assumption at Auteuil on Wednesday, 6th July, followed by the burial in the family grave at the Cemetery of Saint Ouen. Jean Borotra spoke on behalf of the French Tennis Federation, Pierre Gillou on behalf of the International Lawn Tennis Federation and Humbert Sabelli, on behalf of the Lawn Tennis Association. Also present were representatives of French government departments and the French Olympic Committee. Many tennis players, including Jacques Brugnon, Christian Boussus and Bernard Destremau, and other sports celebrities attended. Among the hundreds of floral tributes and wreaths received were those from the British and United States Lawn Tennis Associations, the All England Lawn Tennis Club and the King of Sweden.

In July 1939 the French Tennis Federation announced that a statue to commemorate Suzanne's prowess would be erected at the Roland Garros Stadium, home to the French Championships since 1928, but a few weeks later the outbreak of the Second World War caused the plan to be abandoned.

However, visitors to the ground today have a constant reminder of Suzanne, as one of the main entrances is 'Porte Suzanne Lenglen'. This leads into 'Allee Suzanne Lenglen' which, prior to the enlargement of the site in 1984, was a public road named 'Rue Suzanne Lenglen'.

In 1994 a bronze relief statue of the champion in action was erected on the avenue leading to a new stadium court, named in 1997 as 'Court Suzanne Lenglen'. The trophy presented annually since 1987 to the winner of the Ladies' Championship at the French Open is designated 'Coupe Suzanne Lenglen'.

Suzanne is also held in high regard by her home town of Nice where 'Avenue Suzanne Lenglen' may be found adjacent to the Nice Lawn Tennis Club in the Parc Imperial area.

Facing page: The tomb of the Lenglen family at the Cemetary of Saint Ouen in Paris. Suzanne's very distinctive signature features prominently.

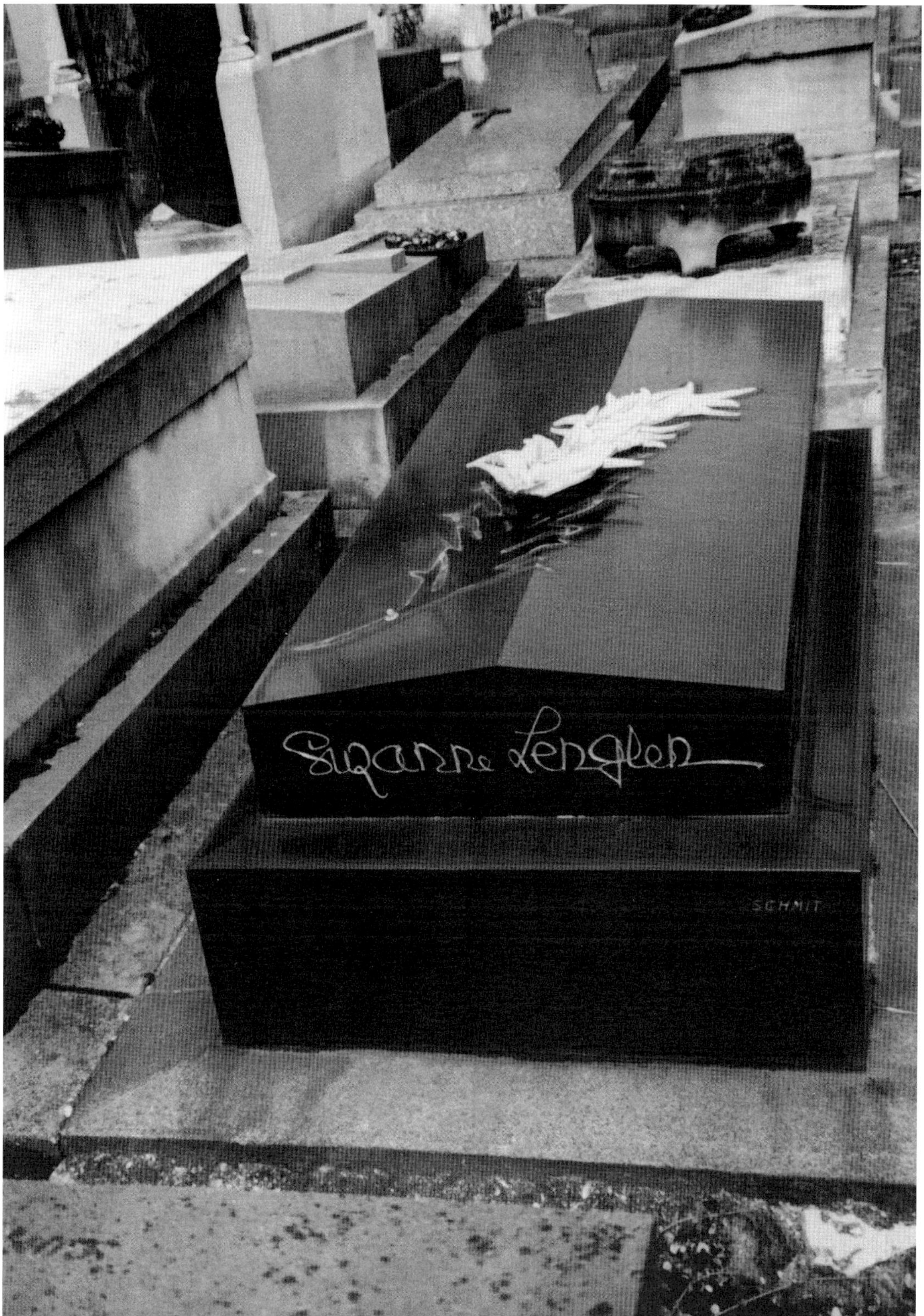
Suzanne Lenglen
SCHMIT

With the passage of time it is difficult to judge Suzanne's true overall position in the annals of the game. Undoubtedly, she was one of the greatest players, universally recognized as an icon, along with Helen Wills, Maureen Connolly, Margaret Court, Billie Jean King, Martina Navratilova and Steffi Graf.

Suzanne's meteoric rise to fame coincided with the end of the First World War. People wanted something different, particularly the ladies, who sought liberation. Suzanne helped to lead the way with her outstanding athleticism, daring dresses and sparkling charisma.

The lifestyle of the twenties will never return, nor will the like of Suzanne.

Suzanne – a study by Helen Wills

The Principal Characters

Mlle Suzanne Rachel Flore Lenglen
born Paris, France, 24th May, 1899
died Paris, France, 4th July, 1938

Charles Lenglen
born Paris, France, 19th April, 1858
died Nice, France, 1st March, 1929

Mme Anaise Lenglen (née d'Hainault)
born Paris, France, 1871
died Paris, France, 8th October, 1957

Miss Mary Kendall Browne (Mrs Kenneth Smith)
born Santa Monica, California, USA, 3rd June, 1891
died Laguna Hills, California, USA, 19th August, 1971

Mrs Dorothea Katherine Chambers (née Douglass)
born Ealing, Middlesex, England, 3rd September, 1878
died Kensington, London, England, 7th January, 1960

Mrs Maud Evelyn Ray Dewhurst (née Marshall)
born Ruislip, Middlesex, England, 12th January, 1902
died Chelsea, London, England, 17th April, 1988

Frl Dorothea (Dora) Koring
born Chemnitz (Dresden), Germany, 11th July, 1888
died Dresden, Germany, 13th February, 1945

Miss Kathleen McKane/Mrs Godfree
born Bayswater, London, England, 7th May, 1896
died Barnes, London, England, 19th June, 1992

Mrs Anna Margrethe (Molla) Mallory (née Bjurstedt)
born Oslo, Norway, 6th March, 1884
died Stockholm, Sweden, 22nd November, 1959

Miss Elizabeth Montague Ryan
born Anaheim, California, USA, 5th February, 1892
died Wimbledon, London, England, 6th July, 1979

Mrs Phyllis Helen Satterthwaite (née Carr)
born Kensington, Middlesex, England, 26th January, 1886
died Kensington, London, England, 20th January, 1962

Mlle Julie Penelope (Diddie) Vlasto (Mme Serpieri)
born Marseille, France, 9th August, 1903
died Lausanne, Switzerland, 2nd February, 1985

Miss Helen Newington Wills/Mrs Moody (Mrs Roark)
born Berkeley, California, USA, 6th October, 1905
died Carmel, California, USA, 1st January, 1998

Pierre Henry Maurice Albarran
born West Indies, 1893
died Paris, France, 24th February, 1960

Baldwin M. Baldwin
born Los Angeles, California, USA, 21st March, 1904
died Orange, California, USA, 21st September, 1970

Jean Robert Borotra
born Arbonne, Basses-Pyrenees, France, 13th August, 1898
died Arbonne, Basses-Pyrenees, France, 17th July, 1994

Jacques Brugnon
born Paris, France, 11th May, 1895
died Paris, France, 20th March, 1978

Roger Marie Robert Danet
born Paris, France, 22nd February, 1899
died Paris, France, 8th May, 1974

Max Omer Decugis
born Paris, France, 24th September, 1882
died Biot, France, 6th September, 1978

Paul Feret
born Paris, France, 27th February, 1901
died Paris, France, 3rd February, 1984

Eduardo Flaquer
born Barcelona, Spain, 4th September, 1894
died San Sebastian, Spain, 18th August, 1951

Alain Jacques Georges Marie Gerbault
born Paris, France, 17th November, 1893
died Dili, Timor, 16th December, 1941

Howard Oreon Kinsey
born St. Louis, Missouri, USA, 3rd December, 1899
died San Francisco, California, USA, 26th July, 1966

Karel Kozeluh
born Prague, Czechoslovakia, 7th March, 1896
died Prague, Czechoslovakia, 27th April, 1950

Vincent Richards
born New York, New York, USA, 20th March, 1903
died New York, New York, USA, 29th September, 1959

Harvey Burton Snodgrass
born La Crosse, Wisconsin, USA, 29th April, 1896
died Sun City, Arizona, USA, April 1983

Records

Complete list of Open titles won by Suzanne Lenglen 1912–1926

The Championships, Wimbledon

Singles 1919, 1920, 1921, 1922, 1923, 1925
Doubles 1919, 1920, 1921, 1922, 1923, 1925
Mixed   1920, 1922, 1925

World's Hard Court Championships

Singles 1914, 1921, 1922, 1923
Doubles 1914, 1921, 1922
Mixed   1921, 1922, 1923

French Championships, Paris

Singles 1920, 1921, 1922, 1923, 1925, 1926
Doubles 1920, 1921, 1922, 1923, 1925, 1926
Mixed   1914, 1920, 1921, 1922, 1923, 1925, 1926

South of France Championships, Nice

Singles 1919*, 1921, 1923, 1924, 1925
Doubles 1921, 1922, 1923, 1924, 1925
Mixed   1919, 1920, 1921, 1922, 1924, 1925

Cannes Championships, Cannes (Beau Site Hotel)

Singles 1919
Doubles 1924
Mixed   1919, 1923, 1924

Cote d'Azur Championships, Cannes (Cannes Club)

Doubles 1920, 1921, 1923, 1924, 1925
Mixed   1923

Riviera Championships, Menton

Singles 1919, 1923, 1924
Doubles 1921, 1923, 1924, 1925
Mixed   1919, 1924 (Int), 1925 (Int)

Picardie Championships, Pourville

Singles 1913
Mixed   1913

Amiens

Singles 1914
Mixed 1914 (div)

Beaulieu

Singles 1920
Doubles 1921, 1923, 1925
Mixed 1920, 1921

Biarritz

Singles 1923*, 1925
Mixed 1923, 1925

Bordeaux

Mixed 1922

Boulogne

Singles 1920*
Doubles 1920

Cabourg

Singles 1923
Doubles 1923
Mixed 1923

Cannes (Beau Site Hotel) New Year Meeting

Singles 1914, 1920, 1921*, 1923
Doubles 1925
Mixed 1920, 1921, 1923, 1924

Cannes (Beau Site Hotel) April Meeting

Singles 1920
Mixed 1916 (War), 1920

Cannes (Carlton Club) New Year Meeting

Singles 1914, 1920, 1921
Doubles 1923, 1925
Mixed 1914, 1921, 1923, 1925

Cannes (Carlton Club) February Meeting

Singles 1919, 1921, 1923, 1926
Doubles 1921, 1923, 1924, 1925, 1926
Mixed 1919, 1921, 1923, 1924

Cannes (Carlton Club) April Meeting

Singles 1914, 1921
Doubles 1926

Cannes (Gallia Club)

Doubles 1924
Mixed 1924

Cannes (Metropole Hotel)

Doubles 1924 (Int), 1926
Mixed 1922, 1924, 1926

Cannes (New Courts Club)

Doubles 1926
Mixed 1926

Compiegne

Mixed 1913, 1914

Deauville

Singles 1919, 1922, 1923, 1925
Doubles 1919, 1922, 1925
Mixed 1919, 1922, 1923

Etretat

Doubles 1922
Mixed 1922

Juan-les-Pins

Doubles 1924

La Bourboule

Singles   1922
Mixed   1922

Le Havre

Doubles 1922
Mixed   1922

Le Touquet

Singles   1913, 1919, 1920
Doubles 1920, 1922
Mixed   1919, 1920, 1922

Lille

Singles   1913, 1914, 1922
Mixed   1914, 1922

Marseille

Singles   1922
Doubles 1922
Mixed   1922

Nice, February Meeting

Singles   1921, 1923, 1924, 1925, 1926*
Doubles 1923, 1925
Mixed   1921, 1923, 1924, 1925, 1926

Paris (Racing Club de France)

Singles   1919
Doubles 1919
Mixed   1919

Pourville

Singles   1922 (div), 1923*, 1925
Mixed   1922 (div), 1923, 1925

Wimereux

Singles   1913

Beausoleil Championships, Monte Carlo

Singles   1921, 1922*
Doubles 1925, 1926
Mixed   1922, 1925

Monaco Championships, Monte Carlo

Doubles 1926
Mixed   1926

Monte Carlo, February/March Meeting

Singles   1919, 1920, 1921
Doubles 1919, 1920, 1921, 1923, 1926 (Int)
Mixed   1919, 1920, 1921

Chateau d'Ardennes

Singles   1923, 1925
Doubles 1923
Mixed   1923, 1925

Knokke-sur-Mer

Singles   1920
Doubles 1920
Mixed   1920

Ostend

Singles   1920
Mixed   1920

Barcelona Championships, Barcelona

Singles   1923, 1924
Doubles 1924
Mixed   1923, 1924

San Sebastian

Singles   1923
Doubles 1923
Mixed   1923

Portuguese Championships, Lisbon

Singles 1923*
Mixed   1923

Rome Championships, Rome

Singles 1926*
Doubles 1926
Mixed   1926

Cromer (CC)

Doubles 1925
Mixed   1925

Olympic Games (Antwerp)

Singles 1920 (Gold)
Mixed   1920 (Gold)

* Singles event won without the loss of a game.
Int – International event
div – title divided

Summary of titles won

Year	Singles	Doubles	Mixed	Total
1913	4	0	2	6
1914	6	1	5*	12
1916†	0	0	1	1
1919	9	4	8	20
1920	12	7	11	30
1921	11	9	9	29
1922	9*	9	15*	33
1923	16	13	16	45
1924	4	9	9	22
1925	8	13	11	32
1926	4	9	6	19
Total	83	74	93	250

* includes title divided
† wartime

The following record lists every open tournament at which Suzanne competed from 1912 to 1926 and, with few exceptions, the detailed scores of every match she played, including singles, doubles and mixed events. In the early years Suzanne entered handicap events and details of these supplement the other results.

Nearly all the married ladies' initials relate to their own forenames and not those of their husbands.

1912

South of France Championships, Nice (Place Mozart), March 4–10

Singles Handicap (30.3)

1   a bye
2   bt. Mrs F.B. Lacey w.o.
3   bt. Mrs E.M.F. Nutcombe Quicke w.o.
4   lost to Mrs M. Barger-Wallach 1–6 3–6

Compiegne, July 21–27

Singles

1   bt. Mme F. Zambaux w.o.
2   bt. Cesse d'Esclaibes 7–5 6–2
S   lost to Mlle J. Matthey 3–6 1–6

Mixed (Butin)

1   a bye
2   lost to R. Wallet and Mme K. Fenwick 6–8 1–6

Singles Handicap (5.6)

1   a bye
2   bt. Cesse d'Esclaibes 6–3 6–4
3   bt. Mlle Bruyere 6–2 6–1
S   bt. Mme Gautier 6–2 6–3
F   bt. Mme S.A. Puget 6–1 6–3

Mixed Handicap (Jourdan) (3.6)

1   a bye
2   bt. F. Zambaux and Mme F. Zambaux 3–6 6–3 6–2
3   bt. Butin and Mlle M. Nativelle 6–2 6–1
S   bt. M. de Seroux and Mme S.A. Puget 6–0 6–4
F   bt. Marechal and Mme de Valroger w.o.

Le Touquet, September 9–15

Doubles Handicap (Mme S.A. Puget (3.6))

    S   bt. Miss B. Collis and Mrs Meade 6–4 4–6 6–3
    F   lost to Miss M.M. King and Miss E. Lane 6–2 1–6 1–6

1913

Nice, New Year Meeting, January 6–12

Singles Handicap

    1   bt. Miss D. Liversidge 6–3 6–2
    2   bt. Mlle V. de Contes de Bucamps 6–2 6–4
    S   bt. Mrs Rowedder 6–4 6–2
    F   bt. Miss A. Hulbert 6–5 6–4

Mixed Handicap (P. Duchartre)

    1   bt. X. de Poligny and Mrs V. Cornwall 6–4 6–5
    2   lost to S. Glen Walker and Mlle V. de Contes de Bucamps 6–4 3–6 2–6

Monte Carlo, (Condamine), February 24 – March 1

Doubles Handicap (Miss E.M. Ryan) (Scr)

    S   bt. Miss Black and Miss E. White 6–2 6–2
    F   lost to Miss O. Ranson and Miss M.E. Stuart 3–6 6–2 5–7

South of France Championships, Nice (Place Mozart), March 10–16

Singles

    1   bt. Miss D.G. Beckett 6–1 6–1
    2   lost to Frl D. von Krohn 1–6 3–6

Mixed (B. Marco)

    1   a bye
    2   lost to F.W. Rahe and Countess C von der Schulenburg 1–6 1–6

Mixed Handicap (G. Gault) (3/6)

    1   bt. Mr and Mrs Harding 6–1 6–4
    2   lost to H. Williams and Mrs Hall Walker w.o.

RECORDS – 1913   137

Picardy Championships, Compiegne, May

   Singles

      F bt. Mlle L. Marcot

   Mixed (P. Prisse)

      F bt. A. Bacquard and Mme Vanni 6–4 7–5

Lille, June 18–22

   Singles

      1 bt. Mme A. Fockedey 6–0 6–0
      2 bt. Mlle E. Le Blan 6–1 6–4
      3 bt. Mlle D. Camsuset 6–1 6–1
      S bt. Mlle S. Descamps 6–2 6–2
      F bt. Mlle B. Butler 6–1 6–1

   Mixed (P. Fontaine)

      1 a bye
      2 lost to W.H. du Vivier and Mlle E. Le Blan 4–6 3–6

   Singles Handicap

      F bt. Mme L. Wilbaux 6–1 6–2

   Mixed Handicap (P. Fontaine)

      1 bt. G. Preaux and Miss N. Butler 6–5 6–3
      S bt. E. Dixon and Miss Dixon 2–6 6–3 6–1
      F bt. R. Motte and Mlle C. Lescornez 6–4 6–3

Chantilly, July 6–12

   Singles

      1 bt. Mlle Pluche 6–1 6–3
      2 bt. Mlle M. Lucas-Championniere 6–0 6–1
      F lost to Mlle J. Matthey 5–7 1–6

   Singles Handicap (owe 1.6)

      1 a bye
      2 bt. Mlle S. Arangi w.o.
      S bt. Mlle Solascroup 6–2 6–3
      F bt. Mlle D. Kulp 6–3 6–1

Mixed Handicap (E de Koning) (30.1)

    1   lost to E. Blanc and Mme K. Fenwick 5–6 4–6

Compiegne, July 20–26

Singles

    S   bt. Mme M. Decugis 6–3 2–0 retd.
    F   lost to Mlle J. Matthey w.o. [1]

Mixed (G. Gault)

    1   bt. de Sibert and Mlle Sequin 6–0 6–3
    S   bt. A. Canet and Mlle Acoulon 6–0 6–2
    F   bt. M.O. Decugis and Mme M. Decugis 6–3 3–6 6–4

Singles Handicap

    1   bt. Mlle P. Nativelle 6–2 6–2
    2   bt. Mlle de Failly 6–0 6–1
    S   bt. Mlle G. Nativelle 6–1 6–2
    F   bt. Mlle L. Marcot 6–1 4–6 6–3

Mixed Handicap (Duchartre)

    1   a bye
    2   lost to de Lestrange and Mlle L. Marcot 6–2 4–6 3–6

Wimeraux, August 24–29

Singles

    1   bt. Mlle A. Screpel w.o.
    2   bt. Mrs G.W. Picton 6–0 6–0
    3   bt. Miss E. Tighe 6–2 6–0
    S   bt. Mrs M.R. Galloway 6–1 6–1
    F   bt. Mrs B.G. Colston 4–6 9–7 3–2 retd.

Mixed (H. Diffre)

    1   a bye
    2   bt. A. Oswald and Mme Leblane 6–0 6–1
    3   bt. F. Lumiere and Mme Lechot 6–1 6–3
    S   bt. E.A. Miller and Mrs M.R. Galloway 6–4 6–0
    F   lost to G. Manset and Mrs B.G. Colston 1–6 6–1 10–12

Note: [1] Suzanne withdrew – exhausted after playing final of mixed doubles.

Le Touquet, September 7–13

Singles

    1   a bye
    2   bt. Miss M.A. Wright 6–4 6–3
    S   bt. Mrs Holloway 6–0 6–4
    F   bt. Mrs B.G. Colston 6–0 2–6 6–1

Mixed (E.R. Allen)

    S   bt. E.W. Hicks and Mrs Holloway 6–3 6–1
    F   lost to A.F. Wilding and Mrs B.G. Colston 3–6 6–3 2–6

Doubles Handicap (Mme S.A. Puget)

    S   bt. Mrs F.A. Jackson and Miss M.A. Wright 3–6 6–3 6–3
    F   bt. Miss Savill and Miss O. Saville 6–3 6–3

Mixed Handicap (P. Le Blan) (5.6)

    S   bt. C.H. Glendinning and Miss Stubbs 6–5 6–3
    F   bt. W.P. Wright and Miss M.A. Wright 6–2 6–1

Nice (Place Mozart), December [2]

Singles Handicap (owe 50)

    F   bt. Miss Street 6–2 6–1

1914

Cannes (Beau Site Hotel), New Year Meeting, December 29–January 4

Singles

    1   a bye
    S   bt. Miss A.N. Topham 6–0 6–1
    F   bt. Miss M. Ward 6–0 6–0

Mixed Handicap (N. Pearson) (2.6)

    S   lost to F.E. Cox and Miss A.N. Topham 6–3 3–6 5–7

Note: [2] Tournament was held as a prelude to 1914 season. No other details available.

Cannes, Carlton Club, New Year Meeting, January 5–11

Singles

    1 bt. Miss 'other' w.o.
    F bt. Miss R. Winch 7–5 3–6 6–1

Mixed (A.F. Wilding)

    1 bt. A. Tachihatchef and Mlle G. Nativelle 6–0 6–0
    F bt. A.W. Myers and Mrs R. Winch 6–3 6–4

Beaulieu (Hotel Bristol), February 9–15

Mixed (A.W. Myers)

    1 bt. S. Glen Walker and Mrs A.A. Hall 6–1 4–6 6–2
    2 bt. C.E.L. Lyle and Mrs Lyle 6–2 6–0
    S bt. H. Kleinschroth and Miss E.M. Ryan w.o.
    F lost to F.G. Lowe and Miss J. Tripp 1–6 5–7

Mixed Handicap (W. Caudrey)

    1 a bye
    2 lost to Ionides and Mrs Ionides 1–6 4–6

Monte Carlo (Condamine), February 23–March 3 [3]

Singles

    1 bt. Mrs A.A. Hall 6–2 6–3
    2 bt. Miss E. Hardcastle 6–0 6–0
    3 lost to Miss E.M. Ryan 3–6 4–6

Doubles (Miss M. Tripp)

    1 a bye
    2 lost to Miss E.M. Ryan and Miss J. Tripp 6–8 2–6

Mixed (A.F. Paulin)

    1 bt. Baron Haillard and Miss B. Collis 6–4 6–0
    2 lost to Count L. Salm and Mlle L. Isnard 4–6 4–6

Note: [3] Meeting extended from February 29 to March 3 due to bad weather.

RECORDS – 1914   141

South of France Championships, Nice (Place Mozart), March 9–15

Singles

    1 bt. Miss M. Tripp 6–1 6–3
    2 bt. Miss Street 6–1 6–1
    3 bt. Miss M. Towler 6–1 6–3
    S lost to Mrs D.K. Chambers 3–6 3–6

Mixed (C. Biddle)

    1 bt C.H. Hote and Miss L. Cadle 6–3 6–0
    2 bt. Comte Almasy and Miss Street 6–0 6–1
    3 bt. A.C. Hunter and Mrs D. Crossfield 6–2 9–7
    S lost to M.O. Decugis and Miss E.M. Ryan 7–9 2–6

Mixed Handicap (W. Caudrey) (owe 3/6)

    1 bt. S. Glen Walker and Mlle L. Isuard 4–6 6–2 8–6
    2 bt. G.A. Grieg and Miss M. Towler 6–2 5–6 6–4
    3 bt. J. Thomas and Miss O. Ranson 6–3 6–4
    4 bt. A.C. Hunter and Miss M.A. Wright w.o.
    S lost to M.D. Hick and Miss E. Kelsey 4–6 5–6

Nice (Country Club), March 16–23 [4]

Singles

    1 lost to Mrs Perrett w.o.

Doubles (Mme M. Gondoin)

    1 bt. Mrs D. Crosfield and Mrs S.Hall Walker 6–1 6–0
    2 bt. Mrs F.A. Jackson and Miss M.A. Wright 6–1 6–0
    S lost to Mrs A.A. Hall and Miss M. Towler 4–6 2–6

Mixed (G. Gault)

    1 a bye
    2 lost to M.O. Decugis and Miss E.M. Ryan w.o.

Singles Handicap (owe 15.3)

    S bt. Miss E. Kelsey 5–6 6–2 6–4
    F bt. Miss E.M. White 6–1 6–2

Note: [4] Meeting extended from March 22 to 26, due to bad weather.

Cannes (Metropole Hotel), March 31–April 5

Mixed (A.W. Dunlop)

- 1 bt. G.A. Greig and Miss H. Greig 6–1 6–1
- 2 bt. A.C. Hunter and Miss M.A. Wright 6–0 5–7 6–2
- S lost to M.O. Decugis and Miss E.M. Ryan 5–7 4–6

Mixed Handicap (Count L. Salm) (owe 15.3)

- F bt. F.J. Ganzoni and Miss H. Greig w.o.

Cannes (Carlton Club), April 6–12

Singles

- 1 bt. Mrs A.A. Hall 6–2 6–3
- 2 bt. Miss E.M. White 6–0 6–0
- S bt. Miss M. Tripp 7–5 6–1
- F bt. Miss E.M. Ryan 6–3 3–6 6–2

Mixed (A.W. Dunlop)

- 1 a bye
- 2 bt. A.F. Wilding and Mrs D. Crosfield w.o.
- S bt. A.L. Resuge and Miss M. Ward 6–3 7–5
- F lost to M.O. Decugis and Miss E.M. Ryan 5–7 9–7 2–6

Mixed Handicap (A.L. Resuge)

- F bt.

French National Championships, Paris (Racing Club de France), May 17–23

Singles

- 1 a bye
- S bt. Mme G. Golding 6–2 7–5
- F bt. Mlle M. Conquet 6–4 6–2
- CR lost to Mlle M. Broquedis 7–5 4–6 3–6

Doubles (Mme G. Golding)

- 1 bt. Mme K. Fenwick and Mme M. Conquet w.o.
- CR lost to Mlle B. Amblard and Mlle S. Amblard 4–6 6–8

Mixed (M.O. Decugis)

    1 bt. A.F. Poulin and Mme G. Golding 7–5 6–3
    S bt. G. Gault and Mlle D. Oustaniol 6–0 6–2
    F bt. M. Germot and Mlle S. Amblard 6–4 6–1

World's Hard Court Championships, Paris (St. Cloud), May 29–June 8

Singles

    1 a bye
    2 bt. Mrs P.H. Satterthwaite 6–3 8–6
    3 bt. Mme A. de Borman 6–2 6–3
    S bt. Mlle S. Amblard 6–2 4–6 6–3
    F bt. Mme G. Golding 6–2 6–1

Doubles (Miss E.M. Ryan)

    1 bt. Mme A. de Borman and Miss M. Fergus 6–3 6–3
    S bt. Mme S. Fick and Mrs P.H. Satterthwaite 6–1 6–3
    F bt. Mlle B. Amblard and Mlle S. Amblard 6–0 6–0

Mixed (Count L. Salm)

    1 a bye
    2 bt. A.C. Simon and Mme Dahl 6–2 8–6
    3 bt. M. Germot and Mlle S. Amblard 6–4 6–1
    S bt. A.W. Myers and Mrs P.H. Satterthwaite 6–1 6–4
    F lost to M.O. Decugis and Miss E.M. Ryan 3–6 1–6

Lille (New LTC), June 11–15

Singles

    1 a bye
    2 bt. Mlle A. Poissonier 6–0 6–0
    3 bt. Mme F. Gamuset 6–0 6–0
    S bt. Mme L. Wibaux 6–1 6–0
    F bt. Miss B. Butler 6–0 6–0

Mixed (A.G. Watson)

    1 bt. R. Landry and Mlle A. Datom 6–0 6–0
    2 bt. J. Descamp and Mlle Guilon 6–0 6–2
    3 bt. R. Motte and Mlle C. Lescorez w.o.
    S bt. J. Sabes and Mlle J. Cuvelier 6–2 6–0
    F bt. M. Fremaux and Mme Gallay 6–1 6–1

Amiens (Athletic Club), June 16–21

Singles

- 1 a bye
- S bt. Mlle T. Requier 6–0 6–0
- F bt. Mlle Vienne 6–2 6–0

Mixed (G. Manset)

- 1 a bye
- S bt. Thivel and Mlle Burel 6–0 6–1
- F v Leroy and Mlle Vienne – divided [5]

Compiegne, July 18–25

Singles

- 1 a bye
- 2 bt. Mlle P. Nativelle 6–0 6–0
- S bt. Mlle de Montozon 6–1 6–0
- F lost to Mlle S. Amblard w.o. [6]

Mixed (G. Gault)

- 1 a bye
- 2 bt. P. Lefebvre and Mme Requillard 6–0 6–4
- S bt. Thivel and Mlle L. Marcot 6–0 6–4
- F bt. Lamy and Mlle S. Amblard 6–1 8–10 6–0

Notes:

[5] Final not played due to rain (4 pm).
[6] Suzanne withdrew.

1915

Cannes (Cannes Club), April 22–24 [7]

    Singles Handicap (owe 50)

        1 a bye
        2 bt. Miss Jones w.o.
        3 bt. Mlle Hirsch w.o.
        S bt. Mrs V. Cornwall 6–3 3–6 6–0
        F bt. Mrs MacLean 6–2 6–0

    Mixed Handicap (I. Relecom) (owe 30)

        1 bt. C.P. Hatch and Mlle M. Nativelle 6–4 4–6 6–4
        2 bt. J. Van Praag and Mlle Hirsch 6–4 6–2
        S bt. G. Gougoltz and Mlle P. Nativelle 6–3 6–2
        F bt. J.E. Hoy and Mrs V. Cornwell 6–2 6–4

Cannes (Beau Site Hotel), April 27–29 [8]

    Singles Handicap (owe 50)

        1 bt. Mme Joseph w.o.
        2 bt. Miss D.M. Topham 6–2 6–2
        S bt. Mlle du Veyrier 6–5 6–1
        F bt. Mlle M. Nativelle 6–4 6–4

    Mixed Handicap (R. Dunkerley) (owe 30)

        1 a bye
        2 bt. I. Relecom and Mlle M. Nativelle 6–1 2–6 6–3
        S bt. Prince Ph de Bourbon and Miss D.M. Topham 6–5 6–4
        F bt. Prince G. de Bourbon and Miss A.N. Topham 0–6 6–2 6–2

Notes:
    [7] War charity tournament in aid of the Continental and Saint Charles hospitals in Cannes.
    [8] War charity in aid of the South Africa Ambulance Hospital in Cannes.

1916

Cannes (Beau Site Hotel), April 26–30 [9]

Mixed (B. Marion Crawford)

    F bt. G.M. Simond and Mme S.A. Puget 1–1 retd. [10]

Doubles Handicap (Mlle M. Nativelle) (owe 40)

    F bt. Mlle E d'Ayen and Mme S.A. Puget 6–4 6–5

1919

Cannes (Carlton Club), February 24–March 2

Singles

    S bt. Mlle G. Nativelle 6–1 6–1
    F bt. Mme D. Wolfson 6–1 6–1

Mixed (M.O. Decugis)

    S bt. M. Fremaux and Mlle A. Visart de Bocarme 6–1 6–0
    F bt. N. Mishu and Mme D. Wolfson 6–2 6–3

Monte Carlo (La Festa), March 3–9

Singles

    1 a bye.
    2 bt. Mlle A. Doublet 6–0 6–0
    S bt. Mme Vassal 6–0 6–1
    F bt. Mme D. Wolfson 6–0 6–0

Doubles (Mlle G. Nativelle)

    1 bt. Mrs Gallene and Miss Jones 6–0 6–1
    F bt. Mme D. Wolfson and Mme Vassal 6–1 6–1

Notes:
    [9] War charity tournament in aid of the South African Ambulance Hospital in Cannes.
    [10] Simond retired – ankle injury.

Mixed (M.O. Decugis)

    1 a bye
    2 bt. Major Hugessen and Mrs Hugessen
    S bt. J.C. Devereau and Mme Vassal
    F bt. P.H.M. Albarran and Mlle G. Nativelle 6–4 6–2

Riviera Championships, Menton, March 10–16

Singles

    F bt. Mlle A. Doublet 6–0 6–1 (one match only)

Mixed (M.O. Decugis)

    1 bt. F.R. Devereax and Mrs Dollfuss 6–0 6–0
    S bt. Capt. B. Bradford and Miss D. Wilson 6–0 6–1
    F bt. M. Fremaux and Mme Vassel 6–2 6–1

South of France Championships, Nice (Place Mozart), March 17–25

Singles

    1 bt. Miss D. Wilson 6–0 6–0
    2 bt. Mme Gerbault 6–0 6–0
    3 bt. Mrs F.A. Jackson w.o.
    S bt. Mme Vassal 6–0 6–0
    F bt. Mme D. Wolfson 6–0 6–0

Mixed (M.O. Decugis)

    1 bt. Dechartre and Miss Street 6–0 6–0
    2 bt. G. Deshayes and Mme G. Deshayes 6–1 6–0
    S bt. J.C. Deveraux and Mlle S. Voet 6–0 6–1
    F bt. N. Mishu and Mme D. Wolfson 6–2 6–2

Mixed Handicap (Prince P. de Bourbon) (owe 15)

    1 bt. Laporte and Mlle Neveu 4–6 6–2 6–2
    2 bt. Hoppeindur and Castelli 5–6 6–2 6–1
    S bt. Ruemont and Mlle Bedel 6–3 6–3
    F bt. Lieut. G. de Chazal and Miss Street 6–2 6–1

Cannes Championships, Cannes (Beau Site Hotel), March 25–30

Singles

    1 a bye.
    2 bt. Mrs Philbrick 6–0 6–0
    S bt. Mlle Lecaron 6–0 6–1
    F bt. Mlle E. d'Ayen 6–0 6–0

Mixed (P.H.M. Albarran)

    1 a bye
    2 bt. Capt. Barton and Miss Edwards 6–0 6–0
    S bt. M.O. Decugis and Mlle G. Nativelle 6–0 6–4
    F bt. A.H. Gobert and Mlle E. d'Ayen 6–2 8–6

Paris, (Racing Club de France), May 18–25

Singles

    1 bt. Mlle S. Deve 6–1 6–2
    S bt. Mlle M. Carbonnal 6–0 6–0
    F bt. Mme J. Vaussard 6–0 6–1

Doubles (Mme J. Vaussard)

    F bt. Mlle M. Conquet and Mme M. Danet 6–0 6–2

Mixed (M.O. Decugis)

    1 a bye
    2 bt. Bonnal and partner w.o.
    S bt. F. Restrepo and Mme G. Pigueron 6–0 6–2
    F bt. P. Guillemaut and Mme J. Vaussard 6–1 6–1

The Championships, Wimbledon, (Worple Road), June 23–July 5

Singles

    1 bt. Mrs A. W. Cobb 6–0 6–1 (Tue 24/6 No. 4)
    2 bt. Mrs E.W. Larcombe 6–2 6–1 (Thu 26/6 CC)
    3 bt. Mrs D. K. Craddock 6–0 6–1 (Fri 27/6 No. 1)
    4 bt. Miss K. McKane 6–0 6–1 (Mon 30/6 No. 4)
    5 bt. Miss E.M. Ryan 6–4 7–5 (Tue 1/7 CC)
    F bt. Mrs P.H. Satterthwaite 6–1 6–1 (Wed 2/7 CC)
  CR bt. Mrs D.K. Chambers 10–8 4–6 9–7 (Sat 5/7 CC)

Doubles (Miss E.M. Ryan)

- 1 a bye
- 2 bt. Mrs F.H. Leisk and Mrs A.R.K. Tuckey w.o.
- 3 bt. Mrs A. Cobb and Miss K. McKane 6–2 6–1
- S bt. Mrs W.A. McNair and Mrs M.B. Parton 6–2 6–1
- F bt. Mrs D.K. Chambers and Mrs E.W. Larcombe 4–6 7–5 6–3

Mixed (W.H. Laurentz)

- 1 a bye
- 2 bt. C.A. McConchie and Miss Bristowe 6–0 6–1
- 3 bt. O.G.N. Turnbull and Mrs A.R.K. Tuckey 7–5 4–6 6–1
- 4 lost to R. Lycett and Miss E.M. Ryan 6–2 4–6 2–6

Cabourg, (Garden Tennis Club), August 11–17

Singles

- 1 a bye
- 2 bt. Mme Donnaud w.o.
- 3 bt. Mlle Breton 6–0 6–0
- S lost to Mlle B. Amblard w.o. [11]

Mixed (M.O. Decugis)

Deauville, (Sporting Club), August 25–30

Singles

- F bt. Mme M. Billout 6–1 6–3

Doubles (Mme D. Wolfson)

- F bt. Mlle D. Speranza and Mlle M. Sichel 6–0 6–1

Mixed (M.O. Decugis)

- F bt. P.H.M. Albarran and Mlle M. Sichel 6–1 6–3

Note: [11] Suzanne withdrew from tournament owing to a blistered hand.

Le Touquet, September 8–13

Singles

1 bt. Mme Mallet Stevens 6–0 6–0
2 bt. Miss Burke 6–0 6–0
S bt. Mlle J. Marion 6–0 6–0
F bt. Mrs M.A. O'Neill 6–0 6–1

Mixed (C.E.L. Lyle)

S bt. Capt. L.F. Davin and Mrs Seacombe w.o.
F bt. A.E. Beamish and Mrs M.A. O'Neill 6–1 6–0

1920

Cannes (Beau Site Hotel), New Year Meeting, January 5–11

Singles

1 bt. Lady D. Crosfield 6–0 6–0
S bt. Mme M. Storms 6–1 6–0
F bt. Mrs M.A. O'Neill 6–1 6–0

Mixed (P.H.M. Albarran)

1 bt. A.J. Gerbault and Miss J. Sanders 6–1 6–1
2 bt. A.C. Hunter and Lady D'Abernon w.o.
S bt. M.J.G. Ritchie and Miss E.M. Ryan 7–5 6–1
F bt. A.W. Myers and Mrs M.A. O'Neill 6–3 6–2

Cannes (Carlton Club), New Year Meeting, January 12–18

Singles

1 a bye.
2 bt. Lady D. Crosfield 6–0 6–1
S bt. Mrs M.A. O'Neill 6–0 6–1
F bt. Miss E.M. Ryan 6–0 6–1

Mixed (P.H.M. Albarran)

1 a bye
2 bt. A.J. Gerbault and Mme M. Storms 6–1 6–2
S bt. G. Jung and Miss J. Sanders 6–1 6–1
F lost to M.J.G. Ritchie and Miss E.M. Ryan 1–6 3–4 retd. [12]

Note: [12] Suzanne withdrew – unwell.

Beaulieu (Bristol Hotel), February 23–29

Singles

    1 bt. Mrs Graham 6–0 6–0
    2 bt. Miss H.L. Eddis 6–0 6–0
    S bt. Mrs M.A. O'Neill 6–0 6–0
    F bt. Miss E.M. Ryan 6–2 6–0

Mixed (M.J.G. Ritchie)

    1 bt. 'A.N. Other' and Mrs D. Hutchins 6–1 6–0
    2 bt. M.D. Hick and Miss N. Durlacher 6–1 6–0
    S bt. A.N. Dudley and Mrs W.G. Beamish 6–3 9–7
    F bt. F.G. Lowe and Miss E.M. Ryan 6–4 4–6 6–3

Monte Carlo (Condamine), March 1–7

Singles

    1 bt. Miss H.G. Layton Blunt 6–0 6–0
    2 bt. Mme S. Fick 6–1 6–1
    3 bt. Lady D. Crosfield 6–0 6–0
    S bt. Mrs W.G. Beamish 6–3 6–4
    F bt. Miss E.M. Ryan 6–1 6–2

Doubles (Miss E.M. Ryan)

    1 a bye
    2 bt. Miss Bishell and Miss H.G. Layton Blunt 6–0 6–0
    S bt. Mrs C.E. Hunter and Mrs Perrett 6–0 6–2
    F bt. Mrs W.G. Beamish and Mme S. Fick 6–1 6–2

Mixed (P.H.M. Albarran)

    1 a bye
    2 bt. K. Playfair and Miss A. Harrison 6–0 6–0
    3 bt. E. Chapple and Miss H. Humphreys 6–0 6–0
    S bt. A.L. Resuge and Mme S. Fick w.o.
    F bt. M.J.G. Ritchie and Miss E.M. Ryan 8–6 8–6

Riviera Championships, Menton, March 8–14

Singles

    1 lost to Mrs G. Lowe w.o. [13]

Note: [13] Suzanne withdrew after the draw.

South of France Championships, Nice (Place Mozart), March 15–21

Singles

    1 bt. Miss O. Rimington w.o.
    2 bt. Miss P.L. Howkins 6–1 6–2
    3 bt. Mme M. Gondoin 6–0 6–1
    S bt. Mrs M.A. O'Neill 6–2 6–1
    F lost to Mrs W.G. Beamish w.o. [14]

Mixed (P.H.M. Albarran)

    1 bt. X de Poligny and Mlle S. Voet 6–0 6–0
    2 bt. Marquis L. Tornielli and Miss Setheie w.o.
    3 bt. W.G. Ireland and Mrs P.H. Satterthwaite 6–0 6–2
    S bt. A.C. Hunter and Mrs M.A. O'Neill 6–2 6–2
    F bt. A.N. Dudley and Mrs W.G. Beamish 2–6 6–2 7–5

Cote d'Azur Championships, Cannes (Cannes Club), March 22–28

Singles

    1 bt. Miss 'Blank' w.o.
    2 lost to Miss M. Hunnewell w.o. [15]

Doubles (Miss E.M. Ryan)

    1 a bye
    2 bt. Lady S. Wavertree and Mme M. Storms w.o.
    S bt. Mme S. Fick and Mrs E.B.W. Warburg 6–0 6–0
    F bt. Mrs W.G. Beamish and Mrs P.H. Satterthwaite 6–1 6–1

Mixed (P.H.M. Albarran)

    1 a bye
    2 lost to G. Millard and Miss D.C. Shepherd w.o.

Notes:
    [14] Suzanne indisposed – too tired after playing mixed doubles final.
    [15] Suzanne withdrew after the draw unwell, but able to contest the doubles.

RECORDS – 1920

Cannes (Beau Site Hotel), April 26–30

Singles

    1 bt. Miss D.C. Shepherd w.o.
    2 bt. Miss E. Sanders 6–0 6–0
    S bt. Mlle S. Jung 6–0 6–0
    F bt. Mme S. Fick 6–1 6–1

Mixed (P.H.M. Albarran)

    1 bt. H.E.T. Dawes and Miss Eastwood 6–0 6–0
    S bt. R. Dunkerley and Mlle S. Jung 6–1 6–1
    F bt. B.C. Covell and Mme M. Storms 6–2 6–1

World's Hard Court Championships, Paris (St. Cloud), May 23–30

Singles

    1 lost to Mlle S. Amblard w.o. [16]

French National Championships, Paris (Racing Club de France), June 5–13

Singles

    1 bt. Mlle E. d'Ayen 6–0 6–1
    2 bt. Mme G. Golding 6–2 6–3
    F bt. Mme J. Vaussard 6–1 6–1
   CR bt. Mme M. Billout 6–1 7–5

Doubles (Mlle E. d'Ayen)

    1 bt. Mlle M. Conquet and Mme M. Danet 6–1 8–6
    S bt. Mlle S. Amblard and Mme M. Billout w.o.
    F bt. Mme G. Golding and Mme J. Vaussard 6–1 6–1

Mixed (M.O. Decugis)

   CR bt. M. Dupont and Mlle M. Conquet 6–0 6–3

The Championships, Wimbledon, (Worple Road), June 21–July 3

Singles

   CR bt. Mrs D.K. Chambers 6–3 6–0 (Thu 1/7 CC)

Note: [16] Suzanne withdrew unwell after the singles draw.

Doubles (Miss E.M. Ryan)

    1 bt. Miss D.C. Shepherd and Mrs E.B.W. Warburg 6–0 6–0
    2 bt. Miss E.H. Harvey and Mrs C.E. Hunter 6–1 6–1
    3 bt. Miss K. McKane and Mrs W.A. McNair 6–3 6–3
    S bt. Mrs B.R. Armstrong and Miss O.B. Manser 6–1 6–0
    F bt. Mrs D.K. Chambers and Mrs E.W. Larcombe 6–4 6–0

Mixed (G.L. Patterson)

    1 bt. H.R. Barrett and Miss S. Lance 6–3 6–0
    2 bt. C.S. Garland and Mrs M. Mallory 6–0 6–3
    3 bt. J.M. Hillyard and Mrs P.H. Satterthwaite 6–2 6–1
    4 bt. Z. Shimidzu and Mrs D.K. Chambers 6–2 7–5
    S bt. A.E. Beamish and Mrs W.G. Beamish 6–1 6–4
    F bt. R. Lycett and Miss E.M. Ryan 7–5 6–3

Ostende, August 3–9

Singles

    1 bt. Mlle F. Arendt 6–0 6–0
    2 bt. Mlle Camont 6–0 6–0
    S bt. Mme A. de Borman 6–2 6–1
    F bt. Mrs F.H. Leisk 6–0 6–0

Mixed (R.V. Thomas)

    1 a bye
    2 bt. V. de Laveleye and Mme M. Storms
    S bt. A. Zerlendi and Mme A. de Borman
    F bt. P. de Borman and Mrs F.H. Leisk 6–2 9–7

Knokke-Sur-Mer, August 9–12

Singles

    1 a bye
    2 bt. Mlle Innes 6–0 6–1
    3 bt. Mme Leclerc 6–0 6–0
    4 bt. Mlle Dupich 6–0 6–0
    S bt. Mme S. Washer 6–1 6–1
    F bt. Mme A. de Borman 6–0 6–2

Doubles (Mme A. de Borman)

    S bt. Miss Berseig and Miss Beauchamp 6–1 6–1
    F bt. Mme S. Washer and Mme Leclerc 6–1 6–0

RECORDS – 1920

Mixed (R.V. Thomas)

    S bt. A.Jamar and Mlle H. Van der Kindere 6–0 6–2
    F bt. J. Washer and Mme A. de Borman 6–0 6–3

Olympic Games, Antwerp (Beerschot Tennis Club), August 15–23

Singles

    1 bt. Mme M. Storms 6–0 6–0
    2 bt. Mrs W.A. McNair 6–0 6–0
    3 bt. Mlle L. Stromberg 6–0 6–0
    S bt. Mme S. Fick 6–0 6–1
    F bt. Miss E.D. Holman 6–3 6–0 (Gold Medal)

Doubles (Miss E. d'Ayen)

    1 a bye
    2 bt. Mme S. Fick and Mlle L. Stromberg 6–4 6–3
    S lost to Miss K. McKane and Mrs W.A. McNair 6–2 3–6 6–8

        (Third place: bt. Mlle F. Arendt and Mme M. Storms w.o – Bronze Medal)

Mixed (M.O. Decugis)

    1 bt. T.M. Alonzo and Srta Rozpyde w.o.
    2 bt. A.E. Beamish and Mrs W.G. Beamish 6–2 6–0
    3 bt. E. Lammens and Mme Chaudoir 3–6 6–1 6–1
    S bt. E. Tegner and Mme Hansen 6–0 6–1
    F bt. M. Woosnam and Miss K. McKane 6–4 6–2 (Gold Medal)

Boulogne, August 30–September 5

Singles

    1 bt. Miss Bradshaw 6–0 6–0
    2 bt. Mlle F. Massiet du Biest 6–0 6–0
    S bt. Miss M.A. Wright 6–0 6–0
    F bt. Mrs M.A. O'Neill 6–0 6–0

Doubles (Mrs M.A. O'Neill)

    1 bt. Mrs Houghton and Mlle Gandillot 6–0 6–0
    S bt. Mlle F. Massiet du Brest and Mlle ed Sars Le Comte 6–0 6–0
    F bt. Mrs F.A. Jackson and Miss M.A. Wright 6–2 6–0

Le Touquet, September 6–12

Singles

    S bt. Mrs B.G. Colston 6–0 6–0
    F bt. Mrs M.A. O'Neill 6–0 6–1

Doubles (Mrs M.A. O'Neill)

    S bt. Mlle J. Marion and Mlle Requier 6–0 6–0
    F bt. Mrs F.A. Jackson and Miss M.A. Wright 6–1 6–1

Mixed (C.E.L. Lyle)

    S bt. W.P. Wright and Miss M.A. Wright 6–0 6–0
    F bt. W.H. Laurentz and Mrs B.G. Colston w.o.

1921

Cannes (Beau Site Hotel), New Year Meeting, January 3–10

Singles

    1 bt. Miss N.B. Brown 6–0 6–0
    2 bt. Mrs R.D. Watson 6–0 6–0
    S bt. Miss J. Sanders 6–0 6–0
    F bt. Mrs B.G. Colston 6–0 6–0

Mixed (A.W. Myers)

    1 bt. C.E. Aeschliman and Miss M. Hunnewell 6–2 6–0
    2 bt. Major H.C. Cumberbatch and Mrs E.M. Hobson 6–0 6–0
    S bt. W.H. Grace and Mrs P.G. Hurst 6–0 6–0
    F bt. F.M.B. Fisher and Lady S. Wavertree 6–2 6–2

Cannes (Carlton Club), New Year Meeting, January 10–16

Singles

    1 bt. Mlle A. Visart de Bocarme 6–0 6–0
    2 bt. Miss E. Sanders w.o.
    S bt. Mrs M.A. O'Neill 6–0 6–0
    F bt. Miss E.M. Ryan 6–0 6–1

Mixed (F.M.B. Fisher)

    1 bt. C.E. Aeschliman and Miss S. Jung 6–1 6–3
    2 bt. Col. M.R. Head and Mrs Johnson 6–0 6–0
    3 bt. J.M. Hillyard and Mrs P.H. Satterthwaite 6–1 6–2
    S bt. G. Millard and Mrs B.G. Colson 6–0 6–0
    F bt. F.G. Lowe and Miss E.M. Ryan 6–1 6–1

Nice (Place Mozart), February 7–14

Singles

    1 bt. Mlle L. Sequin 6–0 6–0
    2 bt. Mrs B.G. Colson 6–0 6–0
    S bt. Mrs P.H. Satterthwaite 6–0 6–0
    F bt. Miss E.M. Ryan 6–0 6–2

Mixed (A.R.F. Kingscote)

    1 bt. J. Firks and Miss M. Smailes 6–0 6–1
    2 bt. Joseph and Mme Sequin 6–0 6–1
    S bt. J.M. Hillyard and Mrs P.H. Satterthwaite 7–5 6–2
    F bt. F.G. Lowe and Miss E.M. Ryan 6–2 6–4

Cannes (Carlton Club), February 14–21

Singles

    1 bt. Mrs H. Nickerson 6–0 6–0
    2 bt. Mlle S. Voet 6–0 6–0
    3 bt. Mrs W.G. Beamish 6–1 6–0
    S bt. Mrs P.H. Satterthwaite 6–0 6–0
    F bt. Miss E.M. Ryan 6–0 6–2

Doubles (Miss E.M. Ryan)

    1 a bye
    2 bt. Miss Dallett and Mme Le Grain 6–0 6–0
    S bt. Mrs D.K. Chambers and Mrs P.H. Satterthwaite 6–2 6–0
    F bt. Mrs W.G. Beamish and Miss E.A. Goss 6–0 6–1

Mixed (A.R.F. Kingscote)

    1 a bye
    2 bt. R. Raulent and Miss M. Towler 6–0 6–0
    S bt. J.M. Hillyard and Mrs P.H. Satterthwaite 6–1 8–6
    F bt. F.G. Lowe and Miss E.M. Ryan 6–3 6–2

Beaulieu (Bristol Hotel), February 21–27

Doubles (Miss E.M. Ryan)

    1 bt. Miss P.J. Anderson and Miss B.W. Donaldson 6–1 6–1
    2 bt. Mlle Bower and Mme Le Cherny w.o.
    S bt. Mrs M.A. O'Neill and Mme S. Fick 6–1 6–3
    F bt. Mrs D.K. Chambers and Miss E.A. Goss 6–0 6–0

Mixed (A.R.F. Kingscote)

    1 bt. N. Willford and Mrs Willford 6–0 6–2
    2 bt. J.R. Tunis and Mrs Bethoud 6–1 6–0
    3 bt. Capt. Gracey and Mrs E.M. Gracey 6–1 6–0
    S bt. F.G. Lowe and Miss E.M. Ryan 6–1 8–6
    F bt. J.M. Hillyard and Mrs P.H. Satterthwaite 6–3 6–0

Monte Carlo (La Festa), February 28–March 6

Singles

    1 a bye.
    2 bt. Mme S. Fick 6–2 6–0
    3 bt. Mlle M. Septier 6–0 6–1
    4 bt. Miss M. Towler 6–0 6–0
    S bt. Mrs W.G. Beamish 6–1 6–0
    F bt. Miss E.M. Ryan 6–2 6–0

Doubles (Miss E.M. Ryan)

    1 a bye.
    2 bt. Miss P.J. Anderson and Miss B.W. Donaldson 6–0 6–1
    3 bt. Mrs M.H. Clayton and Miss D.C. Shepherd 6–1 6–0
    S bt. Mrs W.G. Beamish and Miss P.L. Howkins 6–1 6–2
    F bt. Mrs D.K. Chambers and Mrs P.H. Satterthwaite 6–0 6–3

Mixed (A.R.F. Kingscote)

    1 bt. Capt. R.A. Boyd and Mrs R.A. Boyd 6–0 6–1
    2 bt. C. Owen and Miss H.G. Layton Blunt 6–0 6–0
    3 bt. Maj. A.N.W. Dudley and Miss P.L. Howkins 6–1 6–0
    S bt. A.F. Poulin and Mrs W.G. Beamish 6–0 6–0
    F bt. F.G. Lowe and Miss E.M. Ryan 6–1 8–6

Riviera Championships, Menton, March 7–14

Singles

    1 a bye.
    2 lost to Mrs M.H. Clayton w.o. [17]

Doubles (Miss E.M. Ryan)

    1 a bye.
    2 bt. Miss Davies and Miss Fletcher 6–0 6–0
    S bt. Mrs W.G. Beamish and Mrs P.H. Satterthwaite 6–1 6–1
    F bt. Miss P.L. Howkins and Miss D.C. Shepherd 6–0 6–1

Mixed (A.W. Myers)

    1 a bye.
    2 bt. R. Rickets and Sigra P. Bologna w.o.
    3 bt. G. Poulin and Mme S. Fick 6–1 6–0
    S bt. Maj. A.N.W. Dudley and Mrs W.G. Beamish 6–1 6–2
    F lost to F.G. Lowe and Miss E.M. Ryan w.o. [18]

South of France Championships, Nice (Place Mozart), March 14–21

Singles

    1 bt. Miss N.Q. Platt 6–1 6–0
    2 bt. Miss P.L. Howkins 6–2 6–1
    3 bt. Mme S. Fick 6–0 6–0
    S bt. Mrs P.H. Satterthwaite 6–3 6–1
    F bt. Mlle M. Septier 6–1 6–1

Notes:
    [17] Suzanne entered Singles but withdrew after the draw.
    [18] A.W. Myers withdrew – suddenly recalled to London.

Doubles (Miss E.M. Ryan)

    1   bt. Mrs F.A. Jackson amd Miss M.A. Wright 6–1 6–0
    2   bt. Miss A. Rodocanachi and Mrs E.L. Wilkinson 6–1 6–1
    S   bt. Miss P.M. Radcliffe and Miss N.Q. Redcliffe Platt 6–0 6–1
    F   bt. Mrs W.G. Beamish and Mrs P.H. Satterthwaite 6–1 6–2

Mixed (Count M. Soumarokoff)

    1   bt. A.C. McLaughlin and Mlle J. Franke 6–0 6–0
    2   bt. S. Glen Walker and Miss E.L. Wilkinson 6–0 6–1
    3   bt. Col. Elwes and Mlle M. Sichel 6–0 6–0
    S   bt. Count M. Balbi and Miss P.L. Howkins w.o.
    F   bt. J.M. Hillyard and Mrs P.H. Satterthwaite 6–1 6–2

Cote d'Azur Championships, Cannes (Cannes Club), March 21–28

Doubles (Miss E.M. Ryan)

    1   a bye
    2   bt. Mrs D.K. Craddock and Lady S. Wavertree w.o.
    S   bt. Mrs W.G. Beamish and Mrs P.H. Satterthwaite 6–0 6–1
    F   bt. Miss P.L. Howkins and Miss D.C. Shepherd 6–0 6–3

Mixed (Lord Rocksavage) [19]

Cannes (Carlton Club), April 11–18

Singles

    1   bt. Mrs Dermer 6–1 6–1
    2   bt. Mlle A. Visart de Bocorme 6–0 6–0
    3   bt. Mrs D.K.Craddock 6–0 6–0
    S   bt. Mrs A. Edgington 6–0 6–2
    F   bt. Mrs P.H. Satterthwaite 6–1 6–0

Mixed (Lord Rocksavage)

    1   bt. B.A. Gaekwar and Miss Anderson 6–0 6–0
    2   bt. A.C. Hunter and Miss P.L. Howkins 8–6 6–3
    S   bt. G.L.A. Brian and Mrs A. Edgington 6–0 7–5
    F   lost to J.M. Hillyard and Mrs P.H. Satterthwaite w.o. [20]

Notes:

[19] Suzanne and Lord Rocksavage entered the event but withdrew before the draw, owing to Lord Rocksavage suffering from a bout of influenza.

[20] Lord Rocksavage withdrew – left for Paris in his motor, with a view to breaking the time record.

Beausoleil Championships, Monte Carlo (La Festa), April 25–May 1

Singles

    1   bt. Miss Oxlade 6–0 6–0
    S   bt. Miss M. Smailes 6–0 6–0
    F   bt. Mrs P.H. Satterthwaite 6–1 6–0

Mixed (C.F. Aeschliman)

    1   bt. R. Dunkerley and Miss M. Smailes 6–1 6–0
    S   bt. P. Dufan and Mrs Fawcett 6–2 6–2
    F   lost to J.M. Hillyard and Mrs P.H. Satterthwaite 5–7 6–4 2–2 retd.

French National Championships, Paris (Racing Club de France), May 12–22

Singles

    CR   bt. Mme G. Golding w.o.

Doubles (Mme G. Pigueron)

    1   a bye
    S   bt. Mlle M. Conquet and Mme M. Danet 6–1 6–1
    F   bt. Mme M. Billout and Mlle S. Deve 6–2 6–1

Mixed (J. Brugnon)

    1   a bye
    2   bt. L.J. Aslangul and Mme J. Vaussard 6–1 6–2
    S   bt. J. Samazeuith and Mme M. Goudoin 8–6 6–0.
    F   bt. M.O. Decugis and Mme M. Billout 6–4 6–1

World's Hard Court Championships, Paris (St. Cloud), May 28–June 5

Singles

    1   a bye
    2   bt. Mme A. de Borman 6–0 6–0
    3   bt. Mlle S. Deve 6–0 6–0
    S   bt. Mrs I. Peacock 6–1 6–0
    F   bt. Mrs M. Mallory 6–2 6–3

Doubles (Mme G. Golding)

   1 bt. Mrs M. Mallory and Miss E. Sigourney 6–4 6–1
   2 bt. Mme M. Billout and Mlle D. Speranza 6–0 6–1
   S bt. Mlle G. Cousin and Mlle S. Deve 6–1 6–0
   F bt. Miss E.D. Holman and Mrs I. Peacock 6–2 6–2

Mixed (M.O. Decugis)

   1 a bye
   2 bt. A. Lammens and Mme A. de Borman 6–0 6–0
   3 bt. J. Brugnon and Mme M. Billout 6–1 8–6
   S bt. P. Hirsch and Mme G. Pigueron 6–0 6–1
   F bt. W.H. Laurentz and Mme G. Golding 6–3 6–2

The Championships, Wimbledon, (Worple Road), June 20–July 2

Singles

   CR bt. Miss E.M. Ryan 6–2 6–0 (Fri 1/7 CC)

Doubles (Miss E.M. Ryan)

   1 bt. Miss K. McKane and Mrs W.A. McNair w.o.
   2 bt. Miss D. Kemmis Betty and Mrs M.B. Parton 6–0 6–1
   3 bt. Mrs D.K. Chambers amd Mrs E.W. Larcombe 6–2 6–2
   S bt. Miss P.L. Howkins and Miss D.C. Shepherd 6–2 6–0
   F bt. Mrs W.G. Beamish and Mrs I. Peacock 6–1 6–2

Mixed (A.H. Gobert)

   1 bt. G.R. Sherwell and Mrs W.G. Beamish 7–5 7–5
   2 lost to R. Lycett and Miss E.M. Ryan w.o. [21]

United States Women's Championships, Philadelphia, August 15–28

Singles

   1 bt. Miss E.A. Goss w.o.
   2 lost to Mrs M. Mallory 2–6 0–30 retd. [22]

Notes:

   [21] A.H. Gobert withdrew – injured ankle.
   [22] Suzanne withdrew – unwell.

1922

South of France Championships, Nice (Parc Imperial), March 13–19 [23]

Doubles (Miss E.M. Ryan)

    1 bt. Mlle J. Franke and Miss M. Smailes 6–2 6–1
    S bt. Mlle D. Speranza and Miss M. Tripp 6–1 6–1
    F bt. Miss P.M. Ratcliffe and Miss N.Q. Ratcliff-Platt 6–0 6–0

Mixed (Count M. Soumarakoff)

    1 bt. M. Vilgrain and Mme Le Cherpy 6–0 6–1
    2 bt. R. Wilkinson and Miss A. Hulbert 6–0 6–1
    S bt. B.M. Crawford and Mlle D. Speranza 6–0 6–1
    F bt. Lord Rocksavage and Miss E.M. Ryan 6–2 6–2

Cannes (Beau Site Hotel), March 27–April 2

Mixed (J.R. Borotra)

    1 bt. M. D. Hick and Miss P. Dransfield 6–0 6–2
    2 bt. B. Hillyard and Mrs B. Hillyard 6–0 6–0
    3 bt. R. Stock and Miss M. Tripp 6–1 6–0
    S bt. J.M. Hillyard and Mrs P.H. Satterthwaite 6–1 6–2
    F lost to S. Hardy and Mrs D.K. Chambers w.o. [24]

Cannes (Metropole Hotel), April 3–9

Singles

    1 lost to Miss P.L. French w.o. [25]

Mixed (J.R. Borotra)

    1 a bye
    2 w.o.
    S bt. A.C. Hunter and Mlle S. Jung 6–2 6–2
    F bt. J. Nielsen and Mrs M.A. O'Neill 6–1 6–2

Notes:

    [23] Suzanne's first tournament for six months.
    [24] J.R. Borotra withdrew – football match in Paris.
    [25] Suzanne entered singles but withdrew.

Beausoleil Championships, Monte Carlo (La Festa), April 17–23

Singles

    1   bt. Miss M. Smailes 6–0 6–0
    2   bt. Miss G. Bristed 6–0 6–0
    S   bt. Miss M. Tripp 6–0 6–0
    F   bt. Miss E.A. Goss 6–0 6–0

Mixed (A.J.G.M.Gerbault)

    1   bt. Capt. Baille Hamilton and Miss D. Spens 6–0 6–0
    2   bt. R.A. Boyd and Miss M. Tripp 8–6 6–4
    S   bt. G. Manset and Miss E.R. Sears 6–1 6–2
    F   bt. A.H. Chaplin and Mrs M.A. O'Neill 6–1 6–1

World's Hard Court Championships, Brussels (Royal Leopold Club), May 13–21

Singles

    1   a bye
    2   bt. Mlle H. Van der Kindere 6–0 6–0
    3   bt. Mme M. Dupont 6–0 6–0
    4   bt. Mlle P. Alison 6–0 6–0
    S   bt. Miss K. McKane 10–8 6–2
    F   bt. Miss E.M. Ryan 6–3 6–2

Doubles (Miss E.M. Ryan)

    1   a bye
    2   bt. Mme A. de Borman and Mme M. Dupont 6–3 6–1
    S   bt. Mrs I. Peacock and Mrs P.H. Satterthwaite 6–1 6–3
    F   bt. Mrs W.G. Beamish and Miss K. McKane 6–0 6–4

Mixed (H.J. Cochet)

    1   bt. F.G. Lowe and Mrs P.H. Satterthwaite 6–2 6–0
    2   bt. M. Alonso and Miss E.M. Ryan w.o.
    3   bt. S.N. Doust and Miss D. Kemmis Betty 6–1 6–2
    S   bt. H.R. Barrett and Miss K. McKane 6–3 6–1
    F   bt. J.B. Gilbert and Mrs W.G. Beamish 6–4 4–6 6–0

RECORDS – 1922

Bordeaux, May 23–28

Doubles

    1 a bye
    2 lost to Mlle Y. Bourgeois and Mme G. Pigueron w.o. [26]

Mixed (J.R. Borotra)

    1 a bye
    2 bt. R.Rodel and Mlle Gabotti 6–0 6–0
    3 bt. J. de Cloyet and Mme Gallay 6–0 6–1
    S bt. R. Barbas and Mme G. Pigueron 6–2 6–1
    F bt. J. Samazeuith and Mme N. de Besnerais 6–4 6–0

French National Championships, Paris (Racing Club de France), June 3–11

Singles

    CR bt. Mme G. Golding 6–4 6–0

Doubles (Mme G. Pigueron)

    CR bt. Mlle M. Conquet and Mme M. Danet 6–3 6–1

Mixed (J. Brugnon)

    CR bt. J.R. Borotra and Mme G. Golding 6–0 6–0

Lille, (New Lawn Tennis Club), June 15–18

Singles

    1 bt. Mme H. Sartorius 6–0 6–0
    2 bt. Mlle J. Lescornez 6–0 6–0
    3 bt. Mlle M. Greau 6–0 6–0
    S bt. Mme D. Wolfson 6–1 6–0
    F bt. Mme G. Golding 6–0 6–2

Mixed (R.M.R. Danet)

    1 a bye
    2 bt. F. Houtrart and Mlle G. Greau 6–0 6–0
    3 bt. F. Descamps and Mme J. Descamps 6–2 6–0
    S bt. J. Sabes and Mlle A. Fraipont 6–1 6–0
    F bt. J. Thellier de Ponchville and Mme G. Golding 6–0 6–0

Note: [26] Suzanne without a partner withdrew after the draw.

The Championships, Wimbledon, (Church Road), June 26 – July 8

Singles

    1 bt. Mrs M.F. Ellis 6–0 6–0 (Wed 28/6 No. 3)
    2 bt. Miss K. McKane 6–1 7–5 (Fri 30/6 CC)
    3 bt. Miss E.L. Colyer 6–0 6–0 (Mon 3/7 No. 3)
    4 bt. Miss E.M. Ryan 6–1 8–6 (Tue 4/7 CC)
    S bt. Mrs I. Peacock 6–4 6–1 (Fri 7/7 CC)
    F bt. Mrs M. Mallory 6–2 6–0 (Sat 8/7 CC)

Doubles (Miss E.M. Ryan)

    1 bt. Mrs A. Edgington and Miss H. Hogarth 6–0 6–1
    2 bt. Mrs M. Welsh and Mrs H.B. Watson 6–1 6–0
    3 bt. Miss E.F. Rose and Mrs V.E. Youle 7–5 6–2
    S bt. Mrs D. Green and Mrs W.A. McNair 6–0 6–1
    F bt. Miss K. McKane and Mrs M. Stocks 6–0 6–4

Mixed (P.O. Wood)

    1 bt. A.S. Drew and Mrs R.C. Middleton 6–1 6–1
    2 bt. G.R. Sherwell and Miss D. Kemmis Betty 6–2 6–1
    3 bt. D. Mathey and Mrs M. Mallory 6–2 6–4
    4 bt. J. Washer and Mrs E.B.W. Warburg 6–2 6–1
    S bt. C.J.T. Green and Mrs V.E. Youle 6–2 6–2
    F bt. R. Lycett and Miss E.M. Ryan 6–4 6–3

La Bourboule (Parc de Jeux), July 24–30

Singles

    1 bt. Mlle C. Omer Roy 6–0 6–0
    S bt. Mlle M. Contostavlos 6–1 6–0
    F bt. Mlle H. Contostavlos 6–0 6–1

Mixed (R.M.R. Danet)

    1 bt. Herelle and Mlle Gachou 6–0 6–0
    S bt. H. Gouttenoire and Mlle M. Contostavlos 6–1 6–0
    F bt. R. Champin and Mlle H. Contostavlos 6–0 6–2

Deauville (Sporting Club), July 29–August 6

Singles

- 1 bt. Mme Brochet 6–0 6–0
- 2 bt. Mme D. Wolfson 6–0 6–1
- S bt. Mme M. Danet 6–0 6–0
- F bt. Mme M. Billout 6–1 6–1

Doubles (Mme D. Wolfson)

- 1 bt. Ctesse Pastre and Mme Mouton 6–0 6–0
- S bt. Mme Derouen and Mme Gauthier 6–0 6–1
- F bt. Mme M. Billout and Mlle S. Jung 6–2 6–1

Mixed (R.M.R. Danet)

- 1 bt. Lewisohn and Mme Lewisohn 6–0 6–0
- 2 bt. R. Lafaurie and Mlle S. Jung 6–1 6–1
- S bt. J.R. Lacoste and Mme D. Sperenza-Wyns 6–2 6–2
- F bt. P. Hirsch and Mme M. Billout 6–2 4–6 7–5

Pourville, August 10–13

Singles

- 1 a bye
- S bt. Mlle S. Denamur 6–0 6–1
- F v Mme M. Danet – divided [27]

Mixed (R.M.R. Danet)

- S bt. D. Caillard and Mme D. Caillard 6–0 6–0
- F v J. Brugnon and Mme M. Danet – divided [27]

Le Havre (Athletic Club), August 14–20

Doubles (Mme D. Wolfson)

- S bt. Mme M. Danet and Mme de Ranch 6–0 6–3
- F bt. Mlle Y. Bourgeois and Mme G. Pigueron 6–2 6–3

Note: [27] Finals not played due to rain.

Mixed (R.M.R. Danet)

    1 bt. M. Lafon and Mlle G. Taconet 6–0 6–0
    2 bt. Armengualt and Mme Brochet 6–1 6–1
    S bt. J.R. Lacoste and Mlle Y. Bourgeois 6–0 6–0
    F bt. J. Brugnon and Mme M. Danet 6–1 6–0

Etretat, September 1–3

Doubles (Mme M. Danet)

    F bt. Mlle S. Jung and Mme D. Wolfson 6–4 6–1

Mixed (R.M.R. Danet)

    S bt. M. Dandinos and Mme M. Danet 6–1 6–0
    F bt. M Dupont and Mlle Y. Bourgeois 6–2 6–4

Le Touquet, September 4–9

Singles

    1 bt. Mlle G. Fournier 6–0 6–0
    2 bt. Mrs F.A. Jackson w.o.
    3 bt. Miss C.E. Bosworth 6–0 6–1
    S lost to Mrs E.M. Hannam w.o. [28]

Doubles (Miss E.M. Ryan)

    1 bt. Mlle S. Lorthiois and Mlle Maud Six 6–0 6–1
    2 bt. Miss Morrison and Miss N. Heywood 6–0 6–0
    3 bt. Mlle A. Doublet and Mlle G. Doublet 6–0 6–1
    S bt. Mme M. Danet and Mme D. Wolfson 6–1 6–1
    F bt. Mrs B.R. Armstrong and Mrs A. Edgington w.o.

Mixed (R.M.R. Danet)

    1 bt. J. Norris and Miss G.B. Foster 6–0 6–0
    2 bt. N. Macgregor and Miss S. Wombwell 6–3 6–4
    3 bt. M. Piel and and Mme A. Piel 6–1 6–4
    4 bt. W.P. Wright and Miss A. Wright 6–0 6–3
    S bt. H.A. Davis and Mrs B.R. Armstrong 6–0 6–2
    F bt. F.G. Lowe and Miss E.M. Ryan 7–5 6–1

Note: [28] Suzanne indisposed.

Marseille, September 24–30

Singles

    S bt. Mlle A. Cochet 6–0 6–0
    F bt. Mlle H. Contostavlos 6–1 6–0

Doubles (Mlle H. Contastavlos)

    S bt. Mlle M. Contostavlos and Comtesse de Demandolz 6–0 7–5
    F bt. Mme R. Vlasto and Mlle D. Vlasto 6–1 6–0

Mixed (R.M.R. Danet)

    S bt. H.J. Cochet and Mlle A. Cochet 6–2 6–2
    F bt. J.R. Borotra and Mlle H. Contostavlos 6–2 6–4

1923

Cannes (Beau Site Hotel), New Year Meeting, January 1–7

Singles

    1 a bye
    2 bt. Miss Howett 6–1 6–0
    3 bt. Mme A. Floresco 6–0 6–0
    S bt. Mrs M.A. O'Neill 6–0 6–0
    F bt. Mrs P.H. Satterthwaite 6–4 6–2

Mixed (F.M.B. Fisher)

    1 a bye
    2 bt. Prince Radziwill and Mlle de Mainville 6–0 6–0
    3 bt. C.F. Aeschliman and Miss M. Hunnewell 6–0 6–2
    S bt. D.L. Morgan and Mrs M.A. O'Neill 6–0 6–1
    F bt. J.M. Hillyard and Mrs P.H. Satterthwaite 6–1 6–0

Cannes (Carlton Club), New Year Meeting, January 8–14

Doubles (Miss E.M. Ryan)

    F bt. Mrs M.A. O'Neill and Miss M. Tripp 6–3 6–1 (one match only)

Mixed (F.M.B. Fisher)

    1 bt. J.H. van Alen and Miss A.L. Eno 6–1 6–0
    2 bt. J. Crewe Wood and Miss Meakin 6–2 6–1
    3 bt. C.F. Aeschliman and Miss M. Tripp 8–6 6–0
    S bt. A.C. Hunter and Mrs M.A. O'Neill 6–2 6–2
    F bt. J.M. Hillyard and Mrs P.H. Satterthwaite 6–0 6–1

Nice (Parc Imperial), February 5–11

Singles

    1 bt. Miss M. Brock 6–0 6–0
    2 bt. Miss E.H. Harvey 6–0 6–0
    3 bt. Mrs D.K. Craddock 6–2 6–1
    S bt. Miss L. Cadle 6–0 6–0
    F bt. Miss E.M. Ryan w.o. [29]

Doubles (Miss E.M. Ryan)

    1 bt. Mrs Muir and Miss E. Stephenson 6–0 6–1
    2 bt. Miss M. Brock and Miss L. Cadle 6–2 6–1
    S bt. Mrs D.K. Craddock and Lady D. Crosfield 6–0 6–2
    F bt. Mrs M.A. O'Neill and Miss M. Tripp 6–2 6–1

Mixed (H.G. Mayes)

    1 bt. Lord Charles Hope and Miss R.K. Frost 6–0 6–1
    2 bt. W. David and Mme R. Neveu 6–0 6–0
    3 bt. E. Crawshaw Williams and Miss B.W. Donaldson 6–2 6–0
    S bt. Col. A.W.N. Dudley and Mrs D.K. Craddock 6–1 6–1
    F bt. Lord Rocksavage and Miss E.M. Ryan 6–2 6–1

Cannes (Carlton Club), February 12–18

Singles

    1 a bye
    2 bt. Mrs R.A. Boyd 6–0 6–0
    3 bt. Mlle D. Vlasto 6–0 6–0
    4 bt. Mrs M. Kaehler 6–0 6–0
    S bt. Mrs D.K. Craddock 6–1 6–1
    F bt. Miss E.M. Ryan 6–3 6–1

Note: [29] Miss Ryan – ill with sore throat.

RECORDS – 1923   171

Doubles (Miss E.M. Ryan)

   1 bt. Mrs Alison and Miss Gibbs 6–0 6–0
   2 bt. Mrs Howard and Miss Kavanagh 6–0 6–2
   3 bt. Mrs D.K. Craddock and Lady S. Wavertree w.o.
   S bt. Mrs M.A. O'Neill and Miss M. Tripp w.o.
   F bt. Mrs D.K. Chambers and Miss K. McKane 6–0 6–1

Mixed (H.L. de Morpurgo)

   1 a bye
   2 bt. J.T. Philipson and Mrs Wray 6–0 6–0
   3 bt. A.C. Hunter and Lady D. Linlithgow 6–2 6–0
   4 bt. H.P. Guinness and Miss L. Cadle 6–3 6–2
   S bt. Col. A.W.N. Dudley and Mrs W.G. Beamish 6–1 6–3
   F bt. Lord Rocksavage and Miss E.M. Ryan 7–5 6–4

Beaulieu (Bristol Hotel), February 19–25

Doubles (Invitation) (Miss E.M. Ryan)

   1 bt. Mrs D.K. Craddock and Mrs M.A. O'Neill 6–1 6–0
   F bt. Mrs W.G. Beamish and Mrs P.H. Satterthwaite 6–2 7–5

Monte Carlo Championships, Monte Carlo (La Festa), February 26–March 3

Doubles (Miss E.M. Ryan)

   1 bt. Miss May Green and Mrs Paul Young 6–1 6–0
   2 bt. Mrs E.B.W. Warburg and Lady S. Wavertree w.o.
   3 bt. Miss V.M. Howett and Mrs M. Mallory 6–0 6–1
   S bt. Mrs W.G. Beamish and Mrs P.H. Satterthwaite 6–3 6–4
   F bt. Mrs D.K. Chambers and Miss K. McKane 6–1 3–6 6–4 [30]

Riviera Championships, Menton, March 5–11

Singles

   1 a bye
   2 bt. Miss P. Woodhouse 6–0 6–0
   3 bt. Miss E. Stephenson 6–0 6–0
   4 bt. Miss L. Cadle 6–0 6–1
   S bt. Mrs P.H. Satterthwaite 6–0 6–0
   F bt. Miss K. McKane 6–2 7–5

Note: [30] The only occasion Suzanne and Miss Ryan lost a set in competition.

Doubles (Miss E.M. Ryan)

    1 a bye
    2 bt. Mrs Harrison and Mrs C.P. Michell 6–0 6–0
    3 bt. Miss Chinnery and Miss Gordon w.o.
    4 bt. Miss L. Cadle and Miss E.H. Harvey 6–0 6–2
    S bt. Miss K. McKane and Mrs E.B.W. Warburg 6–2 6–2
    F bt. Mrs W.G. Beamish and Mrs P.H. Satterthwaite 6–2 6–1

South of France Championships, Nice (Parc Imperial), March 12–18

Singles

    1 bt. Miss M.Tobin w.o.
    2 bt. Miss E.H. Harvey 6–0 6–3
    3 bt. Mlle D. Vlasto 6–1 6–1
    S bt. Mrs M. Mallory 6–0 6–0
    F bt. Miss E.M. Ryan 6–1 6–0

Doubles (Miss E.M. Ryan)

    1 bt. Miss M. Tobin and Miss Welch 6–0 6–0
    2 bt. Miss M. Brock and Miss E. Stevenson 6–1 6–0
    S bt. Srta E. Alvarez and Mlle D. Vlasto 6–3 6–0.
    F bt. Mrs D.K. Chambers and Miss K. McKane 6–4 6–2

Mixed (Count M. Soumarokoff)

    1 bt. R. Dunkerley and Mme M. Ellissen 6–0 6–2
    2 bt. J.S. Morpurgo and Srta E. Alvarez 6–0 6–1
    3 bt. Lord Charles Hope and Lady Ward 6–0 6–0
    S lost to R. Lycett and Miss E.M. Ryan 3–6 5–7 [31]

Cote d'Azur Championships, Cannes (Cannes Club), March 19–25

Doubles (Miss E.M. Ryan)

    1 a bye
    2 bt. Mrs C.H. Fenwick and Miss E. Jones 6–0 6–0
    3 bt. Mrs M.M. Bostock and Mrs P. Harrison 6–1 6–1
    4 bt. Sig.na Maud Maquay and Sig.na Margery Maquay 6–0 6–0
    S bt. Mlle N. Descleres and Mme D. Wolfson 6–2 6–1
    F bt. Mrs D.K. Chambers and Miss K. McKane 6–3 6–3

Note: [31] Suzanne's only loss in any match, played to a finish, since the Olympic Games in Antwerp, August 1920.

RECORDS – 1923

Mixed (H.L. de Morpurgo)

1. a bye
2. bt. Capt. Gunning and Miss Spooner 6–0 6–0
3. bt. Col. W.H. Hamilton and Mrs E.B.W. Warburg 6–1 6–1
4. bt. C.F. Aeschliman and Mrs D.K. Chambers 6–3 6–2
5. bt. J.M. Hillyard and Mrs P.H. Satterthwaite 6–3 6–4
F. bt. H.G. Mayes and Miss E.M. Ryan 6–3 6–2

Cannes Championships, Cannes (Beau Site Hotel), March 26–April 1

Mixed (C.F. Aeschliman)

1. a bye
2. bt. W.F. Martin and Mrs Sanderson 6–1 6–3
3. bt. Col. W.H. Hamilton and Miss M. Smailes 6–0 6–0
4. bt. R. de Graffenried and Mrs W.G. Beamish 6–3 6–1
S. bt. H.G. Mayes and Lady D. Crosfield 6–1 6–0
F. bt. J.M. Hillyard and Mrs P.H. Satterthwaite 6–0 6–3

World's Hard Court Championships, Paris (Stade Francais), May 19–27

Singles

1. a bye
2. bt. Frau Redlich w.o.
3. bt. Sig.na G. Perelli 6–0 6–0
4. bt. Mlle M. Conquet 6–1 6–1
S. bt. Mrs W.G. Beamish 6–1 6–2
F. bt. Miss K. McKane 6–3 6–3

Doubles (Mme G. Golding)

1. bt. Mlle K. Bouman and Mlle L'Hoest 6–1 6–1
2. bt. Mme N. Le Besnerais and Mlle D. Vlasto 6–2 6–2
S. bt. Miss L. Bancroft and Miss E.A. Goss 6–3 6–1
F. lost to Mrs W.G. Beamish and Miss K. McKane 2–6 3–6

Mixed (H.J. Cochet)

1. bt. Clifton Herd and Miss L. Bancroft 6–1 6–3
2. bt. H.L. de Morpurgo and Mme J. Vaussard 6–4 6–0
3. bt. C. van Lennep and Mlle K. Bouman 6–1 6–2
S. bt. R.M.R. Danet and Mlle D. Vlasto 6–1 6–1
F. bt. J.B. Gilbert and Miss K. McKane 6–2 10–8

French National Championships, Paris (Racing Club de France), June 9–17

Singles

    1 a bye
    2 bt. Mlle H. Contostavlos 6–2 6–0
    S bt. Mme J. Vaussard 6–0 6–0
    F bt. Mme G. Golding 6–1 6–4

Doubles (Mlle D. Vlasto)

    1 a bye
    S bt. Mme N. Le Besnerais and Mme G. Le Conte 6–2 6–0
    F bt. Mme H. Contostavlos and Mme D. Speranza Wyns 6–1 6–0

Mixed (J. Brugnon)

    1 bt. E. Micard and Mme D. Speranza Wyns w.o.
    2 bt. J. Samazeuilh and Miss D. Vlasto 6–1 6–2
    S bt. M. Cousin and Mme M. Cousin 6–0 6–2
    F bt. H.J. Cochet and Mlle Y. Bourgeois 6–1 7–5

The Championships, Wimbledon, (Church Road), June 25–July 7

Singles

    1 a bye
    2 bt. Miss P.Ingram 6–0 6–0 (Wed 27/6 CC)
    3 bt. Mrs P.L. Covell 6–0 6–3 (Thu 28/6 No. 2)
    4 bt. Mlle D. Vlasto 6–1 6–0 (Sat 30/6 CC)
    5 bt. Mrs M. Hazel 6–2 6–1 (Mon 2/7 No. 2)
    S bt. Mrs W.G. Beamish 6–0 6–0 (Wed 4/7 CC)
    F bt. Miss K. McKane 6–2 6–2 (Fri 6/7 CC)

Doubles (Miss E.M. Ryan)

    1 a bye
    2 bt. Mrs J.B. Perrett and Miss C. Rimington 6–0 6–0
    3 bt. Miss P.M. Radcliffe and Miss N.Q. Radcliffe Platt 6–0 6–1
    4 bt. Mrs W.G. Beamish and Mrs W.A. McNair 6–1 6–2
    S bt. Mrs D.K. Chambers and Miss K. McKane 6–1 6–2
    F bt. Miss J.W. Austin and Miss E.L. Colyer 6–3 6–1

Mixed (J. Washer)

- 1 bt. A.W. Asthalter and Mrs A. Edgington 6–3 6–1
- 2 bt. H.R. Price and Miss J.M. Coote 6–4 6–4
- 3 bt. J.B. Gilbert and Miss E.A. Goss 6–2 6–2
- 4 bt. J. Brugnon and Mrs E. Macready 6–3 6–2
- S lost to R. Lycett and Miss E.M. Ryan 5–7 3–6

Deauville (Sporting Club), July 30 – August 5

Singles

- 1 a bye
- 2 bt. Mme de Andrea 6–0 6–0
- 3 bt. Mlle Y. Huchez 6–0 6–0
- S bt. Mlle G. Cousin 6–0 6–0
- F bt. Mme S. Lafaurie 6–1 6–0

Mixed (R.M.R. Danet)

- 1 bt. Pan and Mme Reith 6–1 6–0
- 2 bt. Le Blant and Mlle L. Huchez 6–0 6–1
- S bt. M. Lafaurie and Mme S. Lafaurie 6–1 6–0
- F bt. J.R. Borotra and Mme M. Danet 6–1 6–0

Pourville, August 11–13

Singles

- 1 bt. Mlle Bovet 6–0 6–0
- 2 bt. Mme Caron 6–0 6–0
- S bt. Mme Canivet 6–0 6–0
- F bt. Mme N. Le Besnerais 6–0 6–0

Mixed (J.R. Borotra)

- 1 a bye
- 2 bt. Evans and Mme Evans 6–2 6–0
- 3 bt. de Rauch and Mme J.M. Barbas 6–0 6–2
- S bt. P. Canivet and Mme Canivet 6–3 6–0
- F bt. R. Barbas and Mme N. Le Besnerais 6–0 6–4

Cabourg, (Garden Tennis Club), August 13–18

Singles

1 a bye
2 bt. Mlle Berthier 6–0 6–0
3 bt. Mlle Colombi 6–0 6–2
4 bt. Miss K. Arnfield 6–0 6–0
S bt. Mlle Rumeau 6–1 6–1
F bt. Mme D. Speranza-Wyns w.o.

Doubles (Mme D. Speranza-Wyns)

1 a bye
2 bt. Miss K. Arnfield and Mlle Hofman 6–0 6–0
3 bt. Mlle Faul and Mlle Lefebure-Dibon 6–0 6–0
S bt. Mlle Fender and Mlle Rottenbourg 6–0 6–0
F bt. Mlle H. Huchez and Mme L. Huchez 6–2 6–0

Mixed (P. Feret)

1 bt. Morizot and Mlle Brayer 6–0 6–0
2 bt. J. Prioux and Mlle Lafoy 6–1 6–0
3 bt. Chain and Mme Faul 6–0 6–4
S bt. Vanson and Mlle Huchez 6–3 6–2
F bt. P.H. Lefebure and Mme D. Speranza-Wyns 6–1 7–5

Chateau d'Ardennes, August 27–September 2

Singles

1 bt. Mme Prion 6–0 6–0
2 bt. Mlle Goetsbloets 6–0 6–0
3 bt. Mlle H. Van der Kindere 6–0 6–0
S bt. Mme P. Mechelynch 6–0 6–0
F bt. Mme M. Dupont 6–1 6–0

Doubles (Mme A. de Borman)

1 bt. Mlle S. Hubert and Mme M. Isaac
S bt. Mme M. Storms and Mme P. Mechelynck 6–1 6–3
F bt. Mme M. Dupont and Mlle L'hoest 6–3 6–1

RECORDS – 1923   177

Mixed (J. Washer)

    1   bt. E. Regout and partner w.o.
    2   bt. A. Laloux and Mme L'hoest 6–2 6–0
    3   bt. J. Relecom and Mlle H. Van der Kindere 6–0 6–0
    S   bt. R. Laloux and Mme M. Dupont 6–1 6–3
    F   bt. G. Watson and Mme M. Storms 6–1 6–1

International Championships of Spain, San Sebastian, (Recreation Club), September 3–10

Singles

    1   a bye
    2   bt. Mlle E. Raoul-Duval 6–1 6–0
    3   bt. Srta M. Satrustegui 6–0 6–0
    S   bt. Srta J. de Gomar 6–1 6–0
    F   bt. Mme N. Le Besnerais 6–0 6–1
  CR   bt. Mme G. Le Conte 6–1 6–0

Doubles (Mme N. Le Besnerais)

    1   bt. Srta M. Muguiro and Srta C. Satrustegui 6–0 6–0
    2   bt. Duguesa de Santona and Sra Barcenas w.o.
    S   bt. Mlle E. Raoul-Duval and Mlle Beauge 6–0 6–0
    F   bt. Srta J. de Gomar and Sra I. de Fleichner 6–1 6–1

Mixed (E. Flaquer)

    1   bt. J.C. Giiell and Srta M. Manguiro 6–0 6–0
    2   bt. J.G. Elorrio and Srta Amat 6–0 6–0
    3   bt. E. Borotra and Mlle E. Raoul-Duval 6–1 6–0
    S   bt. J. Le Besnerais and Mme N. Le Besnerais 6–2 6–1
    F   bt. Conde de Gomar and Mme G. Le Conte 6–0 7–5

Biarritz (Park des Sports d'Aquilea), September 10–17

Singles

    1   bt. Mlle Beauge 6–0 6–0
    2   bt. Mlle E. Raoul-Duval 6–0 6–0
    S   bt. Mme N. Le Besnerais 6–0 6–0
    F   bt. Mme G. Le Conte w.o.

Mixed (E. Flaquer)

    1 a bye
    2 bt. de Luze and Mlle de Amezago 6–0 6–0
    3 bt. Hunt and Mme de las Barcenas 6–0 6–0
    S bt. R. Beauge and Mlle Beauge 6–1 6–0
    F bt. P. Blanchy and Mme N. Le Besnerais w.o.

Portugese International Championships, Lisbon (Club de Cascais), September 24–October 1

Singles

    1 bt. Mrs Ryder 6–0 6–0
    S bt. Sra A. Plantier 6–0 6–0
    F bt. Miss M. Graham 6–0 6–0

Mixed (E. Flaquer)

    1 bt. H. Ryder and Mrs Ryder 6–0 6–1
    F bt. J. Verda and Sra A. Plantier 6–3 6–0

International Championships, Barcelona (Club de Turo), October 6–14

Singles

    1 bt. Srta Tarruella 6–0 6–0
    S bt. Srta R. Torras 6–1 6–0
    F bt. Srta M.L. Marnet 6–0 6–0

Mixed (E. Flaquer)

    1 a bye
    2 bt. J.M. Tarruella and Srta C. Luria 6–1 6–3
    S bt. M. Cousin and Srta R. Torras 6–3 6–4
    F bt. Conde de Gomar and Srta M.L. Marnet 6–1 6–2

1924

Cannes (Beau Site Hotel), New Year Meeting, December 31–January 6

Singles

    1 lost to Mlle A. Visart de Bocarme w.o. [32]

Note: [32] Suzanne entered event but withdrew.

RECORDS – 1924

Mixed (C.F. Aeschliman)

  1 a bye
  2 bt. P. Joseph and Mrs R.A. Boyd 6–0 6–0
  3 bt. A.C. Hunter and Miss M. Tripp 6–2 6–2
  S bt. C.J. Brierley and Mrs M.A. O'Neill 6–0 6–1
  F bt. J.M. Hillyard and Mrs P.H. Satterthwaite 10–8 3–6 6–0

Cannes (Gallia Club), January 21–27

Doubles (Miss E.M. Ryan)

  1 bt. Mrs F.J. Gould and Mlle A. Mallet 6–0 6–0
  2 bt. Mlle P. du Cros and Mrs M.A. O'Neill w.o.
  S bt. Miss M.C. Hervey and Mrs H. Musker 6–0 6–1
  F bt. Mrs D.C. Barron and Mrs P.L. Covell 6–3 6–4

Mixed (H.G. Mayes)

  1 a bye
  2 bt. I.S. White and Miss E. Petchell 6–2 6–1
  3 bt. H. Iwasaki and Mrs Howard 6–1 6–3
  S bt. A.W. Myers and Mrs D.C. Barron 6–2 6–1
  F bt. C.F. Aeschliman and Miss E.M. Ryan 6–4 1–6 15–13 [33]

Nice (Parc Imperial), February (4–10)

Singles

  1 bt. Mme Trussy 6–0 6–0
  2 bt. Miss M. Ashby 6–0 6–0
  3 bt. Miss M. Smailes 6–0 6–0
  S bt. Mrs P.H. Satterthwaite 6–3 6–1
  F bt. Mrs D.C. Barron 6–0 6–1

Doubles (Miss E.M. Ryan)

  1 bt. Mlle de Villemain and Miss B. Stephenson 6–0 6–1
  2 bt. Miss E.M. Green and Miss Young 6–0 6–0
  S lost to Miss M. Ashby and Mrs H. Fleming w.o. [34]

Notes:
  [33] The most games played by Suzanne in a set – 28.
  [34] Miss E.M. Ryan ill – influenza.

Mixed (C.F. Aeschliman)

    1 bt. A. Ter. Hurst and Mme M. Landru 6–1 6–1
    2 bt. I.S. White and Mlle P. du Cros 6–1 6–1
    3 bt. H.G. Mayes and Lady D. Crosfield 6–1 6–2
    S bt. E.T. Lamb and Mrs D.K. Chambers 6–2 6–1
    F bt. J.M. Hillyard and MrsP.H. Satterthwaite w.o.

Cannes (Carlton Club), February 11–17

Doubles (Miss E.M. Ryan)

    1 a bye
    2 w.o.
    3 bt. Miss Kavanagh and Mrs Howard 6–2 6–1
    S bt. Miss E.H. Harvey and Mrs D.K. Chambers 6–1 6–0
    F bt. Mrs D.C. Barron and Mrs P.L. Covell 6–3 7–5

Mixed (C.F. Aeschliman)

    1 bt. A.D. Forster and Miss V.M. Richardson 6–0 6–2
    2 bt. E.T. Wickham and Mrs Muir 6–0 6–0
    3 bt. A.C. Hunter and Miss M. Tripp w.o.
    4 bt. H.G. Mayes and Lady D. Crosfield 6–0 6–3
    S bt. H.L. de Morpurgo and Mlle D. Vlasto 6–0 6–0
    F bt. I.J. Aslangul and Miss E.M. Ryan 6–4 9–7

Riviera Championships, Menton, March 3–9

Singles

    1 a bye
    2 w.o.
    3 bt. Miss F. Dalton 6–1 6–0
    4 bt. Mrs D.C. Barron 6–4 6–0
    S bt. Mrs P.L. Covell 6–2 6–1
    F bt. Miss E.M. Ryan 7–5 6–1

Doubles (Miss E.M. Ryan)

    1 a bye
    2 bt. Miss V. Johnson and Miss H. Jones 6–0 6–0
    3 bt. Miss V. Nichols and Miss Juxon Jones 6–0 6–0
    4 bt. Mrs B. Hillyard and Mrs Holtby 6–1 6–1
    S bt. Miss E.H. Harvey and Mrs P.H. Satterthwaite 6–2 6–2
    F bt. Mrs D.C. Barron and Mrs P.L. Covell 6–1 6–1

Mixed (International) (H.J. Cochet)

    1 bt. F.G. Lowe and Mrs P.L. Covell 6–2 7–5
    F bt. J.M. Hillyard and Mrs P.H. Satterthwaite 6–0 6–3

South of France Championships, Nice (Parc Imperial), March 10–16

  Singles

    1 bt. Mme Lochowska 6–0 6–0
    2 bt. Mme M. Redlich 6–1 6–1
    3 bt. Mlle N. Descleres 6–0 6–0
    4 bt. Mrs M.F. Ellis 6–0 6–0
    S bt. Mrs D.C. Barron 6–2 6–0
    F bt. Mrs P.L. Covell 6–2 6–1

  Doubles (Miss E.M. Ryan)

    1 bt. Miss M. Weatherall and Miss N. Weatherall 6–0 6–0
    2 bt. Lady Denham and Mrs Sanderson 6–0 6–1
    3 bt. Miss E.M. Green and Mrs Young 6–0 6–1
    S bt. Mrs D.K. Chambers and Mrs P.H. Satterthwaite 6–2 6–0
    F bt. Mrs D.C. Barron and Mrs P.L. Covell 6–1 6–4

  Mixed (H.J. Cochet)

    1 bt. Lord Charles Hope and Mrs H. Fleming 6–0 6–2
    2 w.o.
    3 bt. N.E. Brookes and Mlle N. Descleres 6–3 6–0
    4 bt. J.R. Lacoste and Mlle Y. Bourgeois 6–1 6–4
    S bt. H.L. de Morpurgo and Mrs D.C. Barron 6–0 6–4
    F bt. J. Washer and Miss E.M. Ryan 4–6 6–1 7–5

Cote d'Azur Championships, Cannes (Cannes Club), March 17–23

  Doubles (Miss E.M. Ryan)

    1 a bye
    2 bt. Miss Ashlin and Mrs Glascock 6–0 6–0
    3 bt. Miss M.C. Hervey and Mrs H. Musker w.o.
    4 bt. Srta E. de Alvarez and Mlle H. Contostavlos 6–1 6–2
    S bt. Mlle Y. Bourgeois and Mme G. Pigueron w.o.
    F bt. Mrs D.K. Chambers and Mrs P.H. Satterthwaite w.o. [35]

Note: [35] Opponents withdrew – exhausted from semi-final.

Mixed (N.E. Brookes)

    1 a bye
    2 bt. R. Lafaurie and Mme S. Lafaurie 6–0 6–0
    3 lost to Baron de Graffenreid and Mrs E.B.W. Warburg w.o. [36]

Cannes Championship, Cannes (Beau Site Hotel), March 24–30

Doubles (Miss E.M. Ryan)

    1 a bye
    2 bt. Mrs B. Hillyard and Mlle A. Visart de Bocarme w.o.
    3 bt. Miss M.C. Hervey and Mme S. Lafaurie 6–0 6–1
    S bt. Mrs D.C. Barron and Mrs H. Fleming 6–2 6–2
    F bt. Mlle H. Contostavlos and Mlle D. Vlasto 6–1 6–1

Mixed (H.J. Cochet)

    1 a bye
    2 bt. Baron de Banfield and Miss M.C. Hervey 6–0 6–0
    3 bt. Baron de Graffenried and Mme G. Pigueron 6–0 6–1
    4 bt. H.L. de Morpurgo and Miss D. Vlasto 6–3 6–2
    S bt. S. Malmstrom and Mrs D.K. Chambers 6–2 6–0
    F bt. N.E. Brookes and Miss E.M. Ryan 6–1 6–4

Cannes (Metropole Hotel), March 31–April 6

Doubles (Miss E.M. Ryan)

    1 bt. Miss M. B. Brown and Miss F.M. Holland w.o.
    2 bt. Mlle N. Desclercs and Miss M.C. Hervey 6–1 6–2
    S bt. Mlle C. St. Omer Roy and Mlle A. Visart de Bocarme 6–1 6–0
    F bt. Mrs P.L. Covell and Mrs P.H. Satterthwaite 6–1 6–1

Mixed (Invitation) (N.E. Brookes)

    bt. C.F. Aeschliman and Miss E.M. Ryan 6–2 6–3
    bt. J.M. Hillyard and Mrs P.H. Satterthwaite 6–2 6–1
    bt. L.J. Aslangul and Srta E. de Alvarez 6–0 6–1
    bt. H.L. de Morpurgo and Mlle D. Vlasto 6–4 6–4
    bt. J. M. Van Alen and Mrs P.L. Covell 6–3 6–1
    (round-robin – Winners – 5 matches)

Note: [36] N.E. Brookes ill – influenza.

Juan-les-Pins, April 14–20

Doubles (Mrs F. Gould)

    1 bt. Mme A. Floresco and Mlle A. Mallet 6–1 6–0
    S bt. Mrs Musker and Mrs Polley 6–0 6–2
    F bt. Mlle J. Franke and Mlle P. du Cros 6–1 6–1

International Championships, Barcelona (Club de Turo), April 19–27

Singles

    1 bt. Srta J. de Vizacaya 6–0 6–0
    S bt. Miss E.A. Goss 6–0 6–0
    F bt. Srta M.L. Marnet 6–1 6–1

Doubles (Miss E.A. Goss)

    F bt. Srta R. Torras and Srta M.L. Marnet 6–3 7–5 (one match only)

Mixed (E. Flaquer)

    1 bt. C.F. Aeschliman and Miss E.A. Goss 6–2 6–2
    F bt. J.R. Borotra and Sra B. Pons 6–4 6–0

The Championships, Wimbledon, (Church Road), June 23–July 5

Singles

    1 bt. Miss S.C. Lumley Ellis 6–0 6–0 (Tue 24/6 No. 1)
    2 bt. Miss E.R. Clarke 6–0 6–0 (Wed 25/6 No. 1)
    3 bt. Mrs H. Wightman 6–0 6–0 (Fri 27/6 CC)
    4 bt. Miss E.M. Ryan 6–2 6–8 6–4 (Mon 30/6 CC)
    S lost to Miss K. McKane w.o. [37]

Doubles (Miss E.M. Ryan)

    1 a bye
    2 bt. Miss E.M. Head and Miss E.R. Clarke 6–0 6–3
    3 bt. Mrs H.B. Weston and Miss J. Reid-Thomas 6–3 6–1
    4 lost to Mrs H. Wightman and Miss H.N. Wills w.o. [37]

Mixed (J.R. Borotra)

    1 bt. C.S. Fletcher and Miss O.M. Walker 6–0 6–1
    2 bt. J.J. Lezard and Mrs J.B. Barrett 6–0 6–1
    3 bt. R.D. Poland and Miss C. Tyrrell 6–2 6–3
    4 lost to M. Woosnam and Mrs P.L. Covell w.o. [37]

Note: [37] Suzanne withdrew – unwell.

1925

Cannes (Beau Site Hotel), New Year Meeting, December 29–January 4 [38]

Doubles (Miss E.M. Ryan)

1 bt. Miss L. Hall and Mrs Wentworth Smith 6–0 6–2
2 bt. Mlle C. St. Omer Roy and Mrs B. Hillyard 6–0 6–0
S bt. Miss E.V. Bennett and Miss P.L. French 6–0 6–0
F bt. Mrs P.H. Satterthwaite and Mrs C. Neville Smith 6–0 6–2

Cannes (Carlton Club), New Year Meeting, January 5–11

Doubles (Miss E.M. Ryan)

1 bt. Miss S. Roderick and Miss K.M. Scott 6–0 6–0
2 bt. Mlle A. Mallet and Mme Taunay 6–0 6–0
S bt. Miss M. Ashby and Mrs M.A. O'Neill 6–1 6–0
F bt. Mrs P.H. Satterthwaite and Mrs C. Neville Smith 6–0 6–1

Mixed (H.G. Mayes)

1 bt. P.R.R. Harditch and Miss P.L. French 6–1 6–2
2 bt. B. Hillyard and Mrs B. Hillyard 6–0 6–0
3 bt. F.A. Ward and Mrs C.W. Grogan 6–2 6–0
S bt. C.F. Aeschliman and Miss M. Tripp 6–3 6–2
F bt. H.K. Lester and Miss E.M. Ryan 4–6 6–2 6–0

Cannes (Gallia Club), January 19–25

Doubles (Miss E.M. Ryan)

1 Mrs L. Aeschliman and Miss P.L. French 6–1 6–0
2 bt. Mrs C.W. Grogan and Partner w.o.
S bt. Miss E.V. Bennett and Mrs C. Neville Smith 6–0 6–1
F lost to Mrs W.G. Beamish and Mrs P.H. Satterthwaite w.o. [39]

Notes:
[38] Suzanne's first tournament since Wimbledon 1924.
[39] Suzanne – indisposed.

Nice (Parc Imperial), February 2–8

Singles
- 1 bt. Mrs Bramley Moore 6–0 6–0
- 2 bt. Miss N.Q. Ratcliffe Platt 6–0 6–0
- 3 bt. Mlle J. Franke 6–1 6–0
- S bt. Miss E.V. Bennett 6–0 6–0
- F bt. Miss M. Tripp 6–0 6–1

Doubles (Mlle D.Vlasto)
- 1 bt. Mme de Junca and Mrs Bramley Moore 6–0 6–0
- 2 bt. Miss P.M. Ratcliffe and Miss N.Q. Ratcliffe Platt 6–0 6–2
- 3 bt. Miss E.V. Bennett and Mrs D.K. Chambers 6–3 6–0
- F bt. Mrs W.G. Beamish and Mrs P.H. Satterthwaite 6–3 6–1

Mixed (H.L. Morpurgo)
- 1 bt. "Perier" and Mlle P. Joyeux 6–0 6–1
- 2 bt. M. Germot and Mme de Junca 6–3 6–1
- 3 bt. F.R. Scovell and Miss E.V. Bennett 6–0 6–3
- S bt. R.L. James and Miss C. Hardie 6–1 6–0
- F bt. E.T. Lamb and Mrs D.K. Chambers 6–1 6–0

Cannes (Carlton Club), February 9–15

Doubles (Miss E.M. Ryan)
- 1 a bye
- 2 bt. Mrs W. H. Day and Miss V.M. Richardson 6–0 6–0
- 3 bt. Mrs C.W. Grogan and Mrs M.A. O'Neill 6–0 6–0
- S bt. Mrs A.A. Hall and Miss M. Tripp 6–0 6–0
- F bt. Mrs D.K. Chambers and Miss E.H. Harvey 6–0 6–2

Beaulieu (Bristol Hotel), February 16–22

Doubles (Miss E.M. Ryan)
- 1 bt. Miss P. Bainbridge and Miss S. Curtis 6–0 6–0
- 2 bt. Miss M. Towler and Miss M.A. Wright 6–1 6–0
- 3 bt. Miss E.M. Green and Miss M.C. Marshall 6–2 6–0
- S bt. Miss E.V. Bennett and Mrs J.W. Lycett 6–1 6–0
- F bt. Mrs D.K. Chambers and Miss E.H. Harvey 6–1 6–1

Monte Carlo Championships, Monte Carlo (La Festa), February 23–29

Doubles (Mrs D.K. Chambers)

1 bt. Miss M. Lees and Miss M.C. Marshall 6–0 6–0
2 bt. Miss E. Connell and Miss M. Rosenbaum 6–0 6–0
3 bt. Mrs Fernan and Miss K. Still w.o.
S v Miss M. Blake and Miss C. Hardie or Miss E.V. Bennett and Lady D. Crosfield (Event abandoned – rain)

Riviera Championships, Menton, March 2–8

Doubles (Miss E.M. Ryan)

1 a bye
2 bt. Miss V. Hoyle and Miss K. Vereker 6–0 6–0
3 bt. Miss K. Houghton and Miss V.B. Southam 6–0 6–1
4 bt. Mrs J.W. Lycett and Miss J.C. Ridley 6–0 6–1
S bt. Mrs D.K. Chambers and Miss E.H. Harvey 6–0 6–1
F bt. Mrs W.G. Beamish and Mrs P.H. Satterthwaite 6–0 6–1

Mixed (International) (J.R. Lacoste)

1 bt. H.S. Utz and Mrs H.S. Utz 6–0 6–1
S bt. R. Lycett and Mrs J.W. Lycett 6–2 6–2
F bt. F.R. Scovel and Miss E.M. Ryan 6–3 6–3

South of France Championships, Nice (Parc Imperial), March 9–15

Singles

1 a bye
2 bt. Miss I. Maltby 6–1 6–0
3 bt. Miss C. Hardie 6–1 6–2
4 bt. Miss H. Woolrych 1–0 retd.
S bt. Mlle D. Vlasto 6–2 6–0
F bt. Miss E.H. Harvey w.o. [40]

Doubles (Miss E.M. Ryan)

1 bt. Miss Higinbotham and Miss de Jongh 6–0 6–0
2 bt. Mlle G. de Nicot and Miss Somerfelt 6–0 6–0
S bt. Miss E.H. Harvey and Mrs J.W. Lycett w.o.
F bt. Mrs W.G. Beamish and Mlle D. Vlasto 6–1 6–2

Note: [40] Miss Harvey withdrew – ill with chill.

Mixed (C.F. Aeschliman)

    1 bt. N. Mikhailof and Mlle J. Franke 6–0 6–1
    2 bt. P. Dufau and Mlle P. Joyeux 6–1 6–3
    3 bt. H.S. Utz and Mrs H.S. Utz 6–2 6–1
    S bt. H.L. Morpurgo and Mlle D. Vlasto 6–1 5–7 6–1
    F bt. R. Lycett and Miss E.M. Ryan 6–1 6–3

Cote d'Azur Championships, Cannes (Cannes Club), March 16–22

Doubles (Miss E.M. Ryan)

    1 bt. Miss D. Cowan and Mlle C. de Fonvillars 6–2 6–0
    2 bt. Lady D. Crosfield and Miss C. Hardie 6–3 6–1
    3 bt. Mrs H.S. Utz and Mrs A. Slazenger 6–0 6–2
    S bt. Mrs E.B. Morris and Mrs D. Coleman 6–0 6–1
    F bt. Mrs W.G. Beamish and Mrs P.H. Satterthwaite 6–1 7–5

Mixed (C.F. Aeschliman)

    1 a bye
    2 bt. M.D. Hick and Miss V.B. Southam 6–3 6–4
    3 bt. D. Stralem and Mlle J. Franke 6–1 6–2
    4 bt. F.R. Scovel and Mrs W.G. Beamish 6–1 6–3
    S bt. G.R. Sherwell and Mrs P.H. Satterthwaite 6–0 6–4
    F lost to H.L. de Morpurgo and Miss E.M. Ryan 3–6 3–6 [41]

Cannes Championships, Cannes (Beau Site Hotel), March 23–29

Doubles (Miss E.M. Ryan)

(Entered event but tournament abandoned due to bad weather)

Beausoleil Championships, Monte Carlo (La Festa), April 6–12

Doubles (Mrs P.H. Satterthwaite)

    1 bt. Miss N. Gilchrist and Miss V. Grabham 6–0 6–1
    2 bt. Mrs Auberton and Miss Brackenbury w.o.
    S bt. Miss M.C. Marshall and Mrs Hocker 6–0 6–0
    F bt. Mlle C. St. Omer Roy and Miss M.A. Wright 6–0 6–1

Note: [41] Suzanne's first loss in any event since Mixed Doubles at Wimbledon, 1923.

Mixed (Lord Cholmondeley)

    1 bt. Count M. Balbi and Sig.ra D. Petrocochino 6–2 6–1
    2 bt. Maj. H. Smithson and Miss G.M. Thomas 6–2 6–0
    3 bt. F.T. McKeon and Miss E.M. Green 6–1 6–0
    S bt. B. Marion Crawford and Srta L. de Alvarez 6–3 6–2
    F bt. C.F. Aeschliman and Mrs P.H. Satterthwaite 6–2 6–2

French Championships, Paris (St. Cloud), May 27–June 7

Singles

    1 a bye
    2 bt. Mlle S. des Landes de Danot 6–0 6–0
    3 bt. Mrs E. Macready 6–0 6–0
    4 bt. Miss E.L. Colyer 6–0 6–2
    S bt. Mlle H. Contostavlos 6–2 6–0
    F bt. Miss K. McKane 6–1 6–2

Doubles (Mlle D. Vlasto)

    1 a bye
    2 bt. Mlle G. Charnelet and Mlle G. Glasset 6–2 6–1
    S bt. Miss E.H. Harvey and Mrs C.G. McIlquham 6–1 6–3
    F bt. Miss E.L. Colyer and Miss K. McKane 6–1 9–11 6–2

Mixed (J. Brugnon)

    1 a bye
    2 bt. Das de Kapurthala and Mme J. Vaussard w.o.
    3 bt. G.R. Crole Rees and Miss E. H. Harvey 6–0 6–3
    S bt. P.D.B. Spence and Miss E.L. Colyer 6–4 6–2
    F bt. H.J. Cochet and Mlle D. Vlasto 6–2 6–2

The Championships, Wimbledon, (Church Road), June 22–July 4

Singles

    1 bt. Mrs A. Edgington w.o.
    2 bt. Miss E.M. Ryan 6–2 6–0 (Thu 25/6 CC)
    3 bt. Miss E.A. Goldsack 6–1 6–0 (Fri 26/6 No. 1)
    4 bt. Mrs W.G. Beamish 6–0 6–0 (Sat 27/6 CC)
    S bt. Miss K. McKane 6–0 6–0 (Wed 1/7 CC)
    F bt. Miss J. Fry 6–2 6–0 (Fri 3/7 CC)

RECORDS – 1925

Doubles (Miss E.M. Ryan)

   1 bt. Miss E.L. Colyer and Mrs J.W. Lycett 6–0 6–4
   2 bt. Mrs J.L. Colgate and Miss C. Tyrrell 6–0 6–2
   3 bt. Miss P. Dransfield and Miss H. Hogarth 6–0 6–2
   4 bt. Miss E. Boyd and Mrs H.S. Utz 6–0 6–2
   S bt. Mrs W.G. Beamish and Miss E.R. Clarke 6–0 6–2
   F bt. Mrs A.V. Bridge and Mrs C.G. McIlquham 6–2 6–2

Mixed (J.R. Borotra)

   1 bt. R.D.N. Pryee-Jones and Miss E.M. Head 6–2 6–1
   2 bt. H. Timmer and Miss K. Bouman 6–3 6–0
   3 bt. R.D. Poland and Miss C. Tyrrell 6–1 6–1
   4 bt. J.B. Gilbert and Miss K. McKane 6–1 6–2
   S bt. R. Lycett and Mrs J.W. Lycett 6–4 5–7 6–3
   F bt. H.L. de Morpurgo and Miss E.M.Ryan 6–3 6–3

Pourville, July 17–30

Singles

   1 bt. Mlle Denamur 6–0 6–0
   2 bt. Mlle P. Holzchurch 6–1 6–0
   3 bt. Mme A. Quennouelle w.o.
   S bt. Mlle N. Descleres w.o.
   F bt. Mlle Y. Bourgeois 6–0 6–0

Mixed (R.M.R. Danet)

   1 a bye
   2 bt. Le Blant and Mlle P. Holzchurch 6–2 6–3
   S bt. R. Barbar and Mlle N. Descleres 6–2 6–2
   F bt. A. Aron and Mme M. Danet 6–2 6–0

Deauville (Sporting Club), August 23–30 [42]

Singles

   1 bt. Miss Fender 6–0 6–0
   2 bt. Mlle L. Huchez 6–0 6–0
   S bt. Miss F. St. George 6–0 6–0
   F bt. Miss D.J. Akhurst 6–2 6–2

Note: [42] During this tournament, an International match between France and Australia took place – Suzanne bt. Mrs L.A. Harper 6–0 6–4, and Miss E. Boyd 7–5 6–1 and with Miss D. Vlasto bt. Miss E. Boyd and Miss F. St. George 6–3 3–6 6–3.

Doubles (Mlle Y. Bourgeois)

    S bt. Mme M. Danet and Mme K, Fenwick 6–0 6–1
    F bt. Miss D.J. Akhurst and Miss F. St. George 7–5 6–3

Mixed (Count L. Salm)

    3 bt. P. Laurent and Mlle Deroven 6–4 6–0
    S lost to J. Arago and Mlle Y. Huchez 3–6 8–6 retd. [43]

Chateau d'Ardenne, August 31– September 6

Singles

    1 bt. Mme P. Burnay 6–0 6–0
    2 bt. Mlle G. de Borman 6–1 6–0
    S bt. Mme M. Dupont 6–1 6–1
    F bt. Mme S. Washer 6–0 6–0

Mixed (J. Washer)

    1 bt. J. Laloux and Mme De Fraipont 6–0 6–0
    2 bt. R. Laloux and Mme M. Dupont 6–1 6–2
    S bt. L. de Borman and Mlle G. de Borman 6–1 6–2
    F bt. W. Van den Bemden and Mme M. Levy-Ittner 6–0 6–0

Biarritz (Park des Sports d'Aquilia), September 7–13

Singles

    1 bt. Mlle E. Raoul-Duval 6–0 6–0
    2 bt. Mlle A. de Langourian 6–0 6–0
    3 bt. Mme N. Le Besnerais 6–1 6–0
    S bt. Mlle G. Cousin 6–0 6–2
    F bt. Mme M. Billout 6–0 6–0

Doubles (Mme G. Pigueron)

    S lost to Mlle G. Cousin and Mlle J. Cantenat w.o.

Mixed (Count L. Salm)

    3 bt. F. Restrepo and Mme M. Danet 6–0 6–0
    S bt. J. Le Besnerais and Mme M. Billout 6–4 6–2
    F bt. P. Blanchy and Mlle G. Cousin 6–4 6–4

Note: [43] Count Salm – injured wrist.

Cromer (Covered Courts), October 26–31 [44]

Doubles (Mrs D.K. Chambers)

    1 bt. Miss W.L. Prior and Mrs S. Wellesley 6–0 6–0
    S bt. Miss N. Fox and Miss Wentworth Reeve 6–1 6–1
    F bt. Miss E.V. Bennett and Miss E.H. Harvey w.o. [45]

Mixed (J. Brugnon)

    1 bt. D.A. Hodges and Mrs G.G. Morse w.o.
    2 bt. C.H.L. Cazalet and Mrs Cazalet 6–1 6–1
    3 bt. A.H. Bloomer and Mrs E.M. Haylock 6–1 6–0
    S bt. G.W. Hillyard and Mrs D.K. Chambers 6–2 6–3
    F bt. C.H. Kingsley and Miss E.V. Bennett 6–1 6–2

1926

Monaco Championships, Monte Carlo (La Festa), December 14–20

Doubles (Mrs P.H. Satterthwaite)

    1 bt. Mrs E. Noble and Mrs C. Pittman 6–0 6–0
    2 bt. Mlle P. du Cros and Mlle J. Franke 6–0 6–0
    F bt. Mrs E. Macready and Mrs M.A. O'Neill 6–0 6–1

Mixed (J. Brugnon)

    1 bt. M. Smithson and Miss Thomas 6–0 6–0
    2 bt. R. Bocelardo and Mlle P. du Cros 6–1 6–0
    S bt. D.N. Bralle and Mrs C. Pittman 6–3 6–0
    F bt. F.M.B. Fisher and Mrs P.H. Satterthwaite 6–0 6–2

Cannes (Beau Site Hotel), New Year Meeting, December 28–January 4

Doubles (Mrs P.H. Satterthwaite)

    1 bt. Miss K.A. Frischer and Mlle A. Mallet 6–0 6–0
    2 bt. Mrs M.A. O'Neill and Mme Taunay 6–0 6–0
    S lost to Mme S. Lafaurie and Mrs M. Morris w.o. [46]

Notes:

    [44] The only tournament Suzanne ever played in England other than Wimbledon.
    [45] Miss Harvey withdrew – following extremely hard match in final of singles.
    [46] Suzanne indisposed – chill.

Mixed (F.M.B. Fisher)

    1 a bye
    2 bt. Dr. A. Warden and Mrs E.H. Keays 6–1 6–1
    3 bt. R. Lafaurie and Mme S. Lafaurie 6–0 6–3
    S bt. C.F. Aeschliman and Mlle C. St. Omer Roy 6–4 7–5
    F lost to D.M. Greig and Mrs P.H. Satterthwaire w.o. [47]

Cannes (New Courts Club), January 11–18

Doubles (Mrs P.H. Satterthwaite)

    1 a bye
    2 bt. Mrs E.M. Haylock and Mrs Bramley Moore 6–0 6–0
    3 bt. Lady G. Roundway and Mrs M. Morris w.o.
    S bt. Mrs E.H. Keays and Miss L. Cadle 6–0 6–0
    F bt. Mrs D. Coleman and Miss E. Petchell 6–1 6–1

Mixed (H.J. Cochet)

    1 a bye
    2 bt. H. Czetwertynski and Miss Hunter 6–0 6–0
    3 bt. Lord Charles Hope and Miss E. Petchell 6–0 6–0
    S bt. H.G. Mayes and Lady D. Crosfield 6–0 6–1
    F bt. J. Brugnon and Mrs P.H. Satterthwaite 6–0 6–4

Cannes (Metropole Hotel), January 18–24

Doubles (Mlle D. Vlasto)

    1 bt. Miss M.B. Brown and Miss K.M. Scott 6–0 6–1
    2 bt. Lady D. Crosfield and Mrs M. Morris 6–2 6–0
    S bt. Miss M. Tripp and Miss L. Cadle 6–3 6–0
    F bt. Mlle H. Contostavlos and Mrs P.H. Satterthwaite 6–3 6–2

Mixed (J. Brugnon)

    1 bt. A.D. Vickers and Mrs G. Calder 6–2 6–2
    2 bt. W.P. Pinckney and Mrs M.A. O'Neill 6–0 6–2
    3 bt. F.R. Scovel and Miss E.V. Bennett 6–1 6–2
    S bt. C.F. Aeschliman and Miss E. Petchell 6–1 6–0
    F bt. F.M.B. Fisher and Mlle H. Contostavlos 6–0 6–1

Note: [47] Suzanne indisposed – chill.

Nice (Parc Imperial), February 1–7

Singles

- 1   bt. Mlle S. Haefferty 6–0 6–0
- 2   bt. Mlle Marjollet 6–0 6–0
- 3   bt. Mrs L. Aeschliman 6–0 6–0
- S   bt. Mrs E.M. Haylock 6–0 6–0
- F   bt. Miss M.A. Wright 6–0 6–0

Doubles (Mrs P.H. Satterthwaite)

- 1   bt. Mlle Bourdineau and Mlle P. Joyeux 6–0 6–0
- 2   lost to Mrs Bramley Moore and Mlle Crimon w.o. [48]

Mixed (H.L. Morpurgo)

- 1   bt. Jaureguiberry and Miss M.C. Marshall 6–0 6–0
- 2   bt. N.S. Hopkins and Miss E. Fargus w.o.
- 3   bt. V. Landau and Sig.ra D. Petrocochino 6–0 6–1
- S   bt. R. Gallepe and Miss E. Petchell 6–1 6–1
- F   bt. C.F. Aeschliman and Miss H.N. Wills 6–1 6–2

Cannes (Carlton Club), February 8–16)

Singles

- 1   a bye
- 2   bt. Miss M.C. Bower 6–0 6–0
- 3   bt. Miss M. Cambridge 6–0 6–0
- 4   bt. Lady G. Roundway 6–0 6–0
- S   bt. Mlle H. Contostavlos 6–0 6–2
- F   bt. Miss H.N. Wills 6–3 8–6

Doubles (Mlle D. Vlasto)

- 1   bt. Miss B. Gould and Mrs L. Hall 6–0 6–1
- 2   bt. Miss M.A. Dallett and Mrs S. Westcott 6–0 6–0
- 3   bt. Lady D. Crosfield and Mme Papalex w.o.
- S   bt. Miss P.M. Radcliffe and Miss N.Q. Radcliffe Platt 6–0 6–0
- F   bt. Mlle H. Contostavlos and Miss H.N. Wills 6–4 8–6

Note: [48] Mrs Satterthwaite withdrew – accident.

Mixed (F.M.B. Fisher)

  1 a bye
  2 lost to H.A. Milne and Miss A. Redmayne w.o. [49]

Beaulieu (Bristol Hotel), February 15–21

Doubles (Mrs P.H. Satterthwaite)

  1 a bye
  2 bt. Mrs E. Noble and Mrs C. Pitman 6–0 6–0
  S lost to Mrs Creasy and Miss H. Woolrych w.o. [50]

Monte Carlo Championships, Monte Carlo (La Festa), February 22–28

Doubles (Beumont Cup) (Mlle D. Vlasto)

  1 bt. Mme Taunay and Mme Westselaar w.o.
  S bt. Miss P.M. Radcliffe and Miss N.Q. Radcliffe Platt 6–3 6–0
  F bt. Mrs P.H. Satterthwaite and Miss E.V. Bennett 6–4 8–6

Cannes (Carlton Club), March 29–April 4

Doubles (Mrs P.H. Satterthwaite)

  1 a bye
  2 bt. Mrs Holman and Miss Weiwers 6–0 6–0
  3 bt. Mrs E.H. Keays and Mme Taunay 6–0 6–0
  S bt. Mrs D. Coleman and Miss E. Petchell 6–2 6–0
  F bt. Srta E. de Alvarez and Mrs D.C. Barron 6–0 6–1

Beausoleil Championships, Monte Carlo (La Festa), April 5–11

Doubles (Mrs P.H. Satterthwaite)

  1 a bye
  2 bt. Lady Bird and Miss Bird 6–0 6–0
  S bt. Miss Adams and Mrs Arthur 6–0 6–0
  F bt. Srta E. de Alvarez and Mrs D.C. Barron 6–4 6–4

Notes:
    [49] Suzanne withdrew.
    [50] Suzanne indisposed.

Rome Championships, Rome, April 26–May 1

Singles

- 1 bt. Sig.na Miclavez 6–0 6–0
- 2 bt. Mlle P. du Cros 6–0 6–0
- S bt. Sig.na A. Macchi di Cellere 6–0 6–0
- F bt. Sig.na M. Rosenbaum 6–0 6–0

Doubles (Mlle P. du Cros)

- 1 bt. Sig.na Carpegna and Sig.na L. Rosaspina 6–0 6–0
- S bt. Sig.na Pollio and Miss Ramsey 6–0 6–0
- F bt. Sig.na Miclavez and Sig.na M. Rosenbaum 6–0 6–0

Mixed (J. Brugnon)

- 1 bt. Olivares and Sig.na Carpegna 6–0 6–1
- S bt. C. d'Avalos and Sig.na L. Rosaspina 6–0 6–0
- F bt. G. de Stefani and Sig.na A. Macchi di Cellere 6–1 6–1

French Championships, Paris (Racing Club de France), June 2–14

Singles

- 1 bt. Mme I. Peteri 6–0 6–0
- 2 bt. Mrs D.C. Barron 6–0 6–0
- 3 bt. Mme S. Mathieu 6–0 6–0
- S bt. Miss J. Fry 6–2 6–1
- F bt. Miss M.K. Browne 6–1 6–0

Doubles (Mlle D. Vlasto)

- 1 a bye
- 2 bt. Mme A. de Borman and Mlle G. de Borman 6–0 6–0
- 3 bt. Mme S. Mathieu and Mlle G. Grasset 6–3 6–2
- S bt. Mrs D.C. Barron and Miss J. Fry 6–2 6–1
- F bt. Mrs K. Godfree and Miss E.L. Colyer 6–1 6–1

Mixed (J. Brugnon)

- 1 a bye
- 2 bt. H. Timmer and Miss K. Bouman 6–2 6–2
- 3 bt. J. C. Gregory and Mrs D.C. Barron 6–2 6–4
- 4 bt. B. de Kehrling and Miss M.K. Browne 4–6 6–4 6–1
- S bt. L.A. Godfree and Mrs K. Godfree 6–2 6–1
- F bt. J.R. Borotra and Mme N. Le Besnerais 6–4 6–3

The Championships, Wimbledon, (Church Road), June 21–July 3

Singles

    1 bt. Miss M. K. Browne 6–2 6–3 (Tue 22/6 CC).
    2 bt. Mrs M.E.R. Dewhurst 6–2 6–2 (Fri 27/6 No. 1).
    3 lost to Miss C. Beckingham w.o. [51].

Doubles (Miss D. Vlasto)

    1 a bye
    2 lost to Miss M.K. Browne and Miss E.M. Ryan 6–3 7–9 2–6.

Mixed (J.R. Borotra)

    1 bt. H.I.P. Aitken and Miss B.C. Brown 6–3 6–0.
    2 lost to H.O. Kinsey and Miss M.K. Browne w.o. [51].

Note: (51) Suzanne withdrew – injured arm – last time she played as an amateur.

Exhibition Matches

Over the years Suzanne played numerous exhibition matches, many associated with her tournament appearances. Unfortunately, complete match details were frequently not reported, while others have been lost through the passage of time.

1915

Cannes (Beau Site Hotel), April 27–29

War charity matches in aid of the South African Ambulance Hospital in Cannes. G.M. Simond and Suzanne bt. T. Burke and Roman Najuch 6–3 7–5 and 6–2 6–1.

Monte Carlo (La Festa), August/September

War charity matches. Suzanne played for Nice in a match against Monte Carlo, paired with H.Winthrop. Also took part in other matches – (no details available).

1916

Cannes (Cannes Club), March

War charity matches in aid of Tom Burke. Suzanne (owe 30) bt. C.P. Hatch (owe 3) in final of a mixed singles handicap, 6–2 6–1.

Round robin doubles: Suzanne and Col. Puckle bt. G.M. Simond and Mme S.A. Puget; lost to R. Dunkerley and C.H. Ridding; lost to C.P. Hatch and T. Burke.

Suzanne and G.M. Simond lost to T. Burke and C.H. Ridding 7–9 6–2 4–6.

Cannes (Beau Site Hotel), April 26–30

War charity matches in aid of the South African Ambulance Hospital in Cannes. Suzanne lost to C.H. Ridding 4–6 3–6 ret'd (hot day); bt. B. Marion Crawford 6–0 6–1; bt.G.M. Simond 6–2 6–4; lost to T. Burke 7–5 0–3 ret'd.(all level).

1917

Cannes (Beau Site Hotel), April

War charity matches in aid of the Russian Hospital in Cannes. Suzanne won a level mixed singles from an entry of 28. She bt. L. Relecom in semi-final w.o. and B. Marion Crawford in final w.o. (injured hand). Also played a mixed event with B. Marion Crawford. In the semi-final bt. L. Relecom and H. Netts 6–0 6–1 and in final bt. T. Burke and C.P. Hatch 6–2 7–5.

1918

Cannes (Beau Site Hotel), May

Suzanne played with A.H. Gobert and others. In practice bt. Gobert 6–1 6–1 (No other details available).

1919

Cannes (Beau Site Hotel), March 31

M.O. Decugis and Suzanne lost to P.H.M. Albarran and A.H. Gobert 1–6. Albarran and Suzanne lost to Decugis and Gobert 1–6. Gobert and Suzanne lost to Albarran and Decugis 3–6 (all one set matches).

Cannes (Beau Site Hotel), May 5

Invitation doubles. Paired with C.P. Hatch, Suzanne played three matches. In the final they bt. W.H. Grace and B.I. Williams 6–3 6–1.

Paris (Racing Club de France), May 23

M. O. Decugis and Suzanne bt W. H. Laurentz and Mme J. Vaussard 6–2 6–2.

Paris (Racing Club de France), May 25

M. O. Decugis v Suzanne 7–5 2–6.

Paris (Racing Club de France), June 1

Inter-Allied Championships. W. H. Laurentz and Suzanne bt. J. Kozeluh and K. Kozeluh, 6–2 6–3.

Deauville, August 26

A.R.F. Kingscote and Suzanne v P.H.M. Albarran and P.M. Davson (one set – no details available).

1920

Cannes (Beau Site Hotel), January 3

R. Storms and Suzanne bt. P.H.M. Albarran and R. Dunkerley, 7–5 in the third set.

Cannes (Beau Site Hotel), April 26–30

King Gustav of Sweden and Suzanne bt. P.H.M. Albarran and Mme S. Fick 6–4 6–2.

Cannes (Beau Site Hotel), March 29

Suzanne and Miss E.M. Ryan bt. Mrs M. A. O'Neill and Mme S. Fick 6–0 6–0.

London, Sussex Lodge, Regent's Park, July 4

Lady Wavertree's charity matches. Eight top class pairs competed in a mixed doubles event, with each team playing each other in the best of nine games match. G.L. Patterson and Suzanne were runners-up with 31 games.

Eastbourne, Davis Cup, France v USA, July 9–10

M.O. Decugis and Suzanne bt. R.N. Williams and Mrs W.A. McNair 7–5 6–2. G.L. Patterson and Suzanne bt. M.O. Decugis and Mrs W.A. McNair (no details available).

Trianon – Palace Versaille, early September

P.H.M. Albarran and Suzanne played a match (no details available).

Marseille, September 26

A.L. Resuge and Suzanne bt. S. Vidal and H-J. Phalhe 6–3 5–7 6–3 and L.H. Nouveau and H-J. Phalhe 7–5 6–0 and 6–3 6–3.

1921

Monte Carlo. Opening of new La Festa courts, January 28

F. Gordon Lowe and Suzanne bt. A.J.G.M. Gerbault and A. Wallis Myers 6–3 6–1. Also doubles with three men.

Cannes (Beau Site Hotel), March 28

King Manuel of Portugal and Suzanne bt. King Gustav of Sweden and Mrs W.G. Beamish 6–2 6–2. King Gustav of Sweden and Suzanne bt. King Manuel of Portugal and Mrs W.G. Beamish 6–3 3–6 6–0.

Nice, February 7

Played doubles matches with three men. (no details available).

Monte Carlo, February 28

Played doubles matches with three men. (no details available).

Paris (St. Cloud). During Hard Court Championships, May 28–June 5

W.T. Tilden bt. Suzanne 6–0 (level terms).

London, Sussex Lodge, Regent's Park, July 4

Lady Wavertree's charity matches in aide of the Invalid Children's Aid Association. Suzanne and Miss K.McKane bt. Mrs E.W. Larcombe and Miss E.M. Ryan 9–7 7–5.

USA, New Jersey, South Orange Country Club, September 10

Mrs D. Mills and Suzanne bt. Miss L. Bancroft and Miss M.Bayard 7–5 9–7.

USA, Bay Ridge, Crescent Athletic Club, September 11

W.M. Hall and Suzanne lost to H. Throckmorton and Miss L. Bancroft 6–8 ret'd.

1922

Cannes (Cannes Club), March 25

Suzanne and Miss E.M. Ryan v Mrs D.K. Chambers and Mrs P.H.Satterthwaite (no details available).

Cannes (Beau Site Hotel), March 27–April 1

King Gustav of Sweden and Suzanne v Lord Balfour and Mrs W.G. Beamish. (no details available).

Cannes (Carlton Club), April 10–17

A.J. Gerbault and Suzanne bt. B.Hillyard and J. Nielsen 6–2 6–2.

London, Roehampton, June 24

J.R. Borotra and Suzanne bt. W.C. Crawley and Miss K. McKane 6–1 6–3.

London, Sussex Lodge, Regent's Park, July 9

Lady Wavertree's charity matches, in aid of the Invalid Children's Aid Association. J.R.Borotra and Suzanne bt. H.J. Cochet and Miss K.McKane, 2 sets to 1.

Wimbledon, All England Lawn Tennis Club, July 14

Charity matches between British Isles and France in aid of rebuilding of Verdun. J.R. Borotra and Suzanne bt. W.C. Crawley and Miss K. McKane 6–4 4–6 6–1.

Le Havre, August 14–20

J. Brugnon and Suzanne bt. R.M.R. Danet and M. Dupont 6–4 6–4.
R.M.R. Danet and Suzanne bt. P. Du Pasquier and J. Roederer 6–3 6–3.

Boulogne, August 28–September 3

R.M.R. Danet and Suzanne bt. R. Sabes and G. Manset 6–2 6–1.

Le Havre, September 17

P. Hirsch and Suzanne bt. M. Dupont and J. Roederer 7–5 6–1.

Paris (Auteuil), Covered Courts Meeting, December

J. Brugnon and Suzanne played a match (no details available).

1923

Cannes (Beau Site Hotel), January 8

H.G. Mayes bt. Suzanne 6–1 5–0 retired (level terms).

Cannes (Gallia Club), January 9

Opening of new courts. F.B.M. Fisher and Suzanne bt. J.M. Hillyard and Lord Rocksavage 6–4 6–2 6–3.

Toulon, Municipal Stadium, April

H.G. Mayes and Suzanne bt. C.F. Aeschliman and Mlle Graffenried 6–2 6–3 7–5.

Algiers, April 10–15

Suzanne bt. Mlle Damin 6–0 6–0 and Mme Giroud 6–0 6–0.

London, Sussex Lodge, Regent's Park, July 9

Lady Wavertree's charity matches in aid of Invalid Children's Aid Association. W.M. Johnson and Suzanne bt. R. Lycett and Miss E.M. Ryan 6–4 6–4.

Eastbourne, Davis Cup, Holland v Spain, July 10

E. Flaquer and Suzanne bt. Count de Gomer and C. van Lennep 6–2 7–5.

Strasbourg, July 14

Charity match in aid of Pasteur Laboratories in Strasbourg. J. Samazeuilh and Suzanne v A. Gentien and Le Blant (no details available).

Etretat, August 20

Suzanne played a match (no details available).

San Sebastian, September 3

E. Flaquer and Suzanne v. C. Satrustegui and Count de Gomer – one set all.

Bilbao, Club Nautico de Los Arenas, September 21–23

Suzanne played two matches (no details available).

Huelva, Recreative Club, October 2–4

E. Flaquer and Suzanne v Count de Gomar and R. Morales. Lost 8–6 3–6 1–6, won 2–6 6–2 6–1, won 7–5 6–3.

Barcelona, Club de Turo, October 6–7

During Spain v France International: G. Gouttenoire and H. Gouttenoire bt. M. Cousin and Suzanne, 2 sets to 1.

Zaragosa, Sociedad Athletica, October 17–18

E. Flaquer and Suzanne bt. R. Morales and J.M. Tarruella 6–1 6–4 6–2 and 6–4 6–2 6–3.

1924

London, Gipsy LTC, Stamford Hill, June 20

Charity matches in aid of Prince of Wales Hospital, Tottenham. S.N. Doust and Suzanne bt. D.M. Greig and Mrs D.K. Chambers 9–7 6–3.

1925

Beaulieu, Opening of new En-tout Cas Courts at Bristol Hotel, February 2

C.F. Aeschliman and Suzanne bt. H.G. Mayes and Lord Cholmondeley 6–1 6–2 and 5 all.

Juan-Les-Pins, March 30

Suzanne played a match (no details available).

London, Gipsy LTC, Stamford Hill, June 19

Charity matches in aid of Prince of Wales Hospital, Tottenham. J.R. Lacoste and Suzanne bt. E.T. Lamb and A. Wallis Myers 6–1 10–8.

London, Roehampton Club, June 21

International Club Overseas Reception. Suzanne played a match (no details available).

Dieppe, August 3

Suzanne played a match with J.R. Lacoste (no details available).

Villa d'Este Tennis Club, Lake Como, September 18

Count L. Salm and Suzanne bt. C. Colombo and Signa T.G. Perelli (no details available).

Milan, Tennis Club, September

Suzanne played a match v Sig.na G. Perelli (no details available).

Vienna, Vienna Athletic Club, October 9–11

Suzanne bt. Frau E. Redich 6–0 6–0; bt. Frau N. Neppach 6–1 6–1; bt. Frau M. Redlich 6–0 6–1. Count L. Salm and Suzanne lost to K. Kozeluh and Frau Neppach 3–6 4–6; lost to P. Brick and F.Glanz 5–7 1–3 retd; bt Brick and Frau Neppach 6–3 (one set) Kozeluh and Suzanne bt. Salm and Frau Neppach 6–0 (one set); bt. Salm and Frau Neppach 6–3 (one set).

Brno, Lazanky Park, October 15

Suzanne bt. Frau E. Redlich 6–2 (one set). Count L. Salm and Suzanne bt. F.and Mrs G. Rohrer 6–1 7–5.

Prague, Prague LTC, October 16–19

Suzanne bt. Mrs M. Sindelarova 6–0 6–0; bt. Miss A. Janotova 6–1 6–1 Count L. Salm and Suzanne bt. J.Kozeluh and Miss R. Zahnova 6–2 6–2; bt. Kozeluh and Miss Janotova 6–4 6–3.

Cromer, Covered Courts, October 28

J. Brugnon and Suzanne v. H.G. Mayes and C.H. Kingsley 6–8 6–2.

London, Royal Botanic Society, October 30

J. Brugnon and Suzanne bt. H.G. Mayes and N. Mishu (no details available).

1926

Villa d'Este Tennis Club, Lake Como, March

P. Gaslini and Suzanne bt. Count M. Balbi and Mrs P.H. Satterthwaite (no details available).

Milan Tennis Club, March

Suzanne played matches (no details available).

Turin Tennis Club, March

J. Brugnon and Suzanne played Count Bonacossa and P. Gaslini and Count Bonacossa and Sig.na P. Bologna (no details available).

Genoa, March

Suzanne played matches (no details available).

Villa d'Este Tennis Club, Lake Como, April 16

Suzanne played matches (no details available).

Rome, May 2

Suzanne and P. Gaslini bt. G. de Stefani and C. d'Avalos 6–0 6–4.

London, Roehampton Club, June 20

International Club Overseas Reception. Suzanne played a match (no details available).

Wimbledon, June 21

Suzanne and Miss E.M. Ryan lost to Miss K. Bouman and Mrs K. Godfree 6–8 (one set).

Nice L.T.C. Championships (Members Only)

1913   January 27 – 30   Ladies' Singles. Suzanne lost to Miss E. M. Ryan in semi-final w.o.
Won handicap Singles – bt. Miss A Hulbert in final 6–3 6–3.

1914   January 26 – 29   Ladies' Singles. Suzanne bt. Mme Gondoin in final.
Also won the mixed doubles with W. Caudery and the handicap mixed doubles with Prince Bahram de Perse.

1920   January 26 – 29   Ladies' Singles. Suzanne bt. Mlle Beale in final 6–0 6–0.
Also won mixed doubles with P. H. M. Albarran.

1921   January 24 – 27   Ladies' Singles. Suzanne bt. Mlle M. Septier in final 6–0 6–0.
Also won mixed doubles with Count M. Soumarokoff.

1922   Did not enter.

1923   January 22 – 28   Ladies' Singles. Suzanne bt. Miss M. Tripp in final 6–0 6–0.
Also won mixed doubles with A. J. G. M. Gerbault.

1924   January 14 – 20   Ladies' Singles. Suzanne won title.
Also won doubles with Mlle Haefferley and mixed doubles with M. Stocq.

1925   January 12 – 18   Ladies' Singles. Suzanne won title.
Also won doubles with Mlle P. du Cros.

1926   January 4 – 10   Ladies' Singles. Suzanne bt. Mlle J. Franke in final.
Also won doubles with Mlle P. du Cros and mixed doubles with J. Brugnon

North American Professional Tour 1926 – 1927

The players – Miss M.K. Browne, Mlle S.R.F. Lenglen, P. Feret, H.O. Kinsey, V. Richards, H.B. Snodgrass and substitutes W. Wesbrook and C.M. Wood.

1	Saturday 9 October (8.30pm) 13,000	NEW YORK New York, USA (Madison Square Garden)	Richards bt Feret 6–3 6–4 Lenglen bt Browne 6–1 6–1 Richards and Snodgrass bt Feret and Kinsey 6–2 Richards and Lenglen bt Kinsey and Browne 6–2
2	Sunday 10 October (8.30pm) 5,000	NEW YORK New York, USA (Madison Square Garden)	Richards bt Snodgrass 6–4 4–1adv, ret'd (unwell) Lenglen bt Browne 6–2 6–1 Kinsey and Snodgrass bt Feret and Richards 6–2 Richards and Lenglen bt Snodgrass and Browne 6–2
3	Tuesday 12 October (8.30pm) 6,000	TORONTO Ontario, Canada (The Arena)	Richards bt Kinsey 6–1 6–3 Lenglen bt Browne 6–0 6–2 Kinsey and Richards bt Feret and Snodgrass 6–4 Snodgrass and Browne bt Feret and Lenglen 6–3
4	Thursday 14 October (8.30pm) 5,000	BALTIMORE Maryland, USA (5th Regiment Armory)	Richards bt Snodgrass 6–3 6–4 Lenglen bt Browne 6–0 6–0 Kinsey and Richards bt Feret and Snodgrass 6–2 6–2 Feret and Kinsey bt Richards and Lenglen 6–1 (Browne too fatigued to play mixed doubles)
5	Saturday 16 October (8.15pm) 8,000	BOSTON Massachusetts, USA (Boston Arena)	Richards bt Snodgrass 6–2 6–2 Lenglen bt Browne 6–2 6–1 Kinsey and Richards bt Feret and Snodgrass 6–1 7–5 Feret and Lenglen bt Kinsey and Browne 6–4
6	Tuesday 19 October 3,000	PHILADELPHIA Pennsylvania, USA (Sesqui Auditorium)	Richards bt Feret 2–6 6–3 6–2 Lenglen bt Browne 6–2 6–2 Kinsey and Snodgrass drew with Feret and Richards 2–6 6–3 Feret and Lenglen bt Snodgrass and Browne 6–3
7	Saturday 23 October (8.30pm) 8,500	MONTREAL Quebec, Canada (The Forum)	Richards bt Kinsey 6–1 6–2 Lenglen bt Browne 6–1 6–1 Richards and Snodgrass drew with Feret and Kinsey 6–3 1–6 Richards and Browne bt Feret and Lenglen 8–6

8	Tuesday 26 October 2,000	BUFFALO New York, USA (Broadway Auditorium)	Richards bt Feret 6–4 6–3 Lenglen bt Browne 6–2 6–2 Feret and Snodgrass bt Kinsey and Richards 12–10 Richards and Lenglen bt Snodgrass and Browne 6–3
9	Thursday 28 October (8.30pm) 10,000	CLEVELAND Ohio, USA (Public Auditorium)	Richards bt Snodgrass 2–6 6–4 6–4 Lenglen bt Browne 6–0 6–2 Feret and Richards bt Kinsey and Snodgrass 6–4 Feret and Lenglen bt Kinsey and Browne 6–4
10	Tuesday 2 November (8.30pm) 6,000	PITTSBURG Pennsylvania, USA (Motor Square Garden)	Kinsey bt Richards 7–5 6–4 Lenglen bt Browne 6–3 6–0 Richards and Snodgrass drew with Feret and Kinsey 6–3 4–6 Feret and Lenglen bt Snodgrass and Browne 7–5
11	Thursday 4 November 3,000	COLUMBUS Ohio, USA (State Fairgrounds Coliseum)	Richards bt Feret 6–1 6–3 Lenglen bt Browne 6–2 6–2 Kinsey and Richards bt Feret and Snodgrass 6–3 6–2 Snodgrass and Lenglen bt Feret and Browne 6–3
12	Tuesday 9 November 5,000	DETROIT Michigan, USA (State Fair Coliseum)	Richards bt Snodgrass 8–6 6–0 Lenglen bt Browne 6–3 6–2 Kinsey and Snodgrass bt Feret and Richards 6–3 Feret and Lenglen bt Kinsey and Browne 7–5
13	Thursday 11 November 1,500	CINCINNATI Ohio, USA (Freeman Avenue Armory)	Richards bt Kinsey 2–6 6–4 6–4 Lenglen bt Browne 6–1 6–1 Richards and Snodgrass bt Feret and Kinsey 7–5 Feret and Lenglen bt Snodgrass and Browne 6–4
14	Tuesday 16 November	MINNEAPOLIS Minnesota, USA (Minneapolis Arena)	Richards bt Feret 6–4 6–2 Lenglen bt Browne 6–4 6–1 Feret and Snodgrass bt Kinsey and Richards 6–4 Snodgrass and Lenglen bt Kinsey and Browne 6–2
15	Thursday 18 November 7,100	CHICAGO Illinois, USA (Coliseum)	Richards bt Snodgrass 6–4 6–2 Lenglen bt Browne 7–5 6–1 Feret and Richards bt Kinsey and Snodgrass 6–3 Richards and Lenglen bt Snodgrass and Browne 7–5

16	Saturday 20 November (8.30pm) 2,000	ST. LOUIS Missouri, USA (Coliseum)	Richards bt Kinsey 7–5 7–5 Lenglen bt Browne 6–3 6–1 Richards and Snodgrass bt Feret and Kinsey 6–3 7–5 Feret and Lenglen bt Kinsey and Browne 9–7
17	Tuesday 23 November 2,000	KANSAS CITY Kansas, USA (American Royal Pavilion)	Richards bt Feret 12–10 6–3 Lenglen bt Browne 6–1 6–3 Kinsey and Richards bt Feret and Snodgrass 6–3 Feret and Lenglen bt Snodgrass and Browne 6–4
18	Wednesday 24 November (8.30pm) 500	WICHITA Kansas, USA (The Forum)	Richards bt Snodgrass 7–5 8–6 Lenglen bt Browne 6–2 7–5 Feret and Richards drew with Kinsey and Snodgrass 6–4 3–6 Kinsey and Browne drew with Feret and Lenglen
19	Saturday 27 November (8.30pm) 1,700	DENVER Colorado, USA (Stockyards Stadium)	Richards bt Kinsey 6–1 6–2 Lenglen bt Browne 6–1 6–2 Richards and Snodgrass bt Feret and Kinsey 6–3 6–2 Feret and Lenglen bt Snodgrass and Browne 6–4
20	Wednesday 1 December (8.30pm)	VICTORIA British Columbia, Canada (Willows Arena)	Feret bt Richards 7–5 6–2 Lenglen bt Browne 6–1 (One set match) Feret and Snodgrass bt Kinsey and Richards 6–0 Snodgrass and Lenglen bt Kinsey and Browne 7–5
21	Thursday 2 December (8.30pm) 2,800	VANCOUVER British Columbia, Canada (The Arena)	Richards bt Snodgrass 10–8 6–4 Lenglen bt Browne 6–2 6–2 Feret and Richards bt Kinsey and Snodgrass 12–10 Kinsey and Browne bt Feret and Lenglen 6–2
22	Friday 3 December (8.00pm) 1,500	SEATTLE Washington, USA (National Guard Armory)	Richards bt Kinsey 6–4 6–1 Lenglen bt Browne 6–2 6–0 Richards and Snodgrass bt Feret and Kinsey 6–2 Snodgrass and Browne bt Feret and Lenglen 6–4
23	Saturday 4 December	PORTLAND Oregon, USA (Coliseum)	Richards bt Feret 6–1 6–4 Lenglen bt Browne 11–9 (Only one set played) Kinsey and Richards bt Feret and Snodgrass 6–3 6–4 (Mixed doubles cancelled – Lenglen exhausted)

24	Tuesday 7 December (8.30pm) 6,000	SAN FRANCISCO California, USA (Civic Auditorium)	Richards bt Kinsey 2–6 6–0 9–7 Lenglen bt Browne 8–6 6–2 Feret and Richards bt Kinsey and Snodgrass 6–2 Richards and Lenglen bt Snodgrass and Browne 6–2
25	Thursday 9 December (8.30pm) 3,000	OAKLAND California, USA (Oakland Auditorium)	Richards bt Snodgrass 6–4 5–7 7–5 Lenglen bt Browne 6–2 7–5 Feret and Snodgrass bt Kinsey and Richards 6–3 Snodgrass and Lenglen bt Kinsey and Browne 6–4
26	Tuesday 28 December (8.00pm) 9,000	LOS ANGELES California, USA (Olympic Auditorium)	Richards bt Snodgrass 6–4 6–4 Lenglen bt Browne 6–0 6–1 Snodgrass and Wesbrook bt Kinsey and Richards 6–4 6–4 Snodgrass and Browne bt Feret and Lenglen 3–6 6–3 6–3
27	Sunday 2 January (8.00pm) 1,000	SAN ANTONIO Texas, USA (Municipal Auditorium)	Richards bt Feret 6–4 6–4 Lenglen bt Browne 6–3 6–1 Feret and Kinsey bt Richards and Snodgrass 6–4 Kinsey and Browne bt Snodgrass and Lenglen 7–5
28	Tuesday 4 January (8.00pm) 1,000	DALLAS Texas, USA (Gardner Park)	Richards bt Kinsey 7–5 6–1 Lenglen bt Browne 6–2 6–1 Kinsey and Snodgrass bt Feret and Richards 6–4 Snodgrass and Browne bt Feret and Lenglen 6–2
29	Thursday 6 January (8.30pm)	HOUSTON Texas, USA (City Auditorium)	Richards bt Feret 6–0 6–4 Lenglen bt Browne 6–1 8–6 Kinsey and Richards bt Feret and Snodgrass 6–4 6–3 (Mixed doubles cancelled – Lenglen injured)
30	Sunday 9 January 4,000	NEW ORLEANS Louisiana, USA (Jai alai Fronton)	Richards bt Snodgrass 6–4 6–0 Lenglen bt Browne 6–2 6–2 Richards and Snodgrass bt Feret and Kinsey 6–3 Kinsey and Browne bt Feret and Lenglen 6–4
31	Tuesday 11 January (8.30pm)	BIRMINGHAM Alabama, USA (Municipal Auditorium)	Kinsey bt Feret 9–7 4–6 6–4 Lenglen bt Browne 6–1 6–2 Kinsey and Lenglen bt Snodgrass and Browne 6–1 (Only three matches played – Richards ill)

32	Saturday 15 January (8.30pm) 2,000	ATLANTA Georgia, USA (City Auditorium)	Snodgrass bt Feret 6–2 6–0 Lenglen bt Browne 6–4 6–2 Kinsey and Lenglen bt Snodgrass and Browne 4–6 6–2 6–2 (Only three matches played – Richards ill)
33	Wednesday 19 January (8.30pm) 1,800	TAMPA Florida, USA (Davis Island Coliseum)	Snodgrass bt Kinsey 4–6 6–3 6–4 Lenglen bt Browne 6–0 2–6 6–1 Kinsey and Lenglen bt Feret and Browne 6–4 (Only three matches played – Richards ill)
34	Sunday 23 January (8.30pm) 5,000	MIAMI Florida, USA (Biscayne Jai alai Fronton)	Kinsey bt Feret 6–3 6–2 Lenglen bt Browne 6–1 6–1 Kinsey and Lenglen bt Snodgrass and Browne 6–4 6–4 (Only three matches played – Richards ill)
35	Wednesday 26 January (9.00pm)	HAVANA Cuba (Jai alai Fronton)	Snodgrass bt Feret 6–3 1–6 6–3 Lenglen bt Browne 6–2 6–0 Kinsey and Lenglen bt Snodgrass and Browne 10–8 (Only three matches played – Richards ill)
36	Wednesday 9 February (8.30pm) 2,000	HARTFORD Connecticut, USA (State Armory)	Feret bt Kinsey 6–4 4–6 6–3 Browne bt Lenglen 6–3 (One set match) Kinsey and Snodgrass bt Feret and Richards 6–2 3–6 6–3 (Mixed doubles cancelled – Lenglen unwell)
37	Thursday 10 February (8.30pm) 4,000	NEWARK New Jersey, USA (113th Regiment Armory)	Feret bt Snodgrass 6–4 6–3 Richards and Lenglen bt Kinsey and Browne 6–3 6–4 Feret and Richards bt Kinsey and Snodgrass 6–3 6–3 (Lenglen did not play singles – unwell)
38	Friday 11 February (8.30pm) 2,000	NEW HAVEN Connecticut, USA (The Arena)	Kinsey bt Snodgrass 3–6 7–5 10–8 Richards and Lenglen bt Snodgrass and Browne 6–3 6–4 Kinsey and Snodgrass bt Richards and Wood 6–3 (Lenglen did not play singles – unwell)

39	Saturday 12 February (8.30pm) 2,000	BROOKLYN New York, New York (23rd Regiment Armory)	Kinsey bt Richards 8–6 6–4 Snodgrass and Browne bt Kinsey and Lenglen 6–8 6–2–6–0 Richards and Wood bt Kinsey and Snodgrass 9–7 6–3 (Lenglen did not play singles – unwell)
40	Monday 14 February (8.15pm) 2,500	PROVIDENCE Rhode Island, USA (Rhode Island Auditorium)	Snodgrass bt Kinsey 6–4 6–1 Kinsey and Snodgrass bt Richards and Lenglen 6–4 Kinsey and Snodgrass bt Richards and Wood 6–3 6–1 (Lenglen did not play singles – unwell)

British Professional Tour, 1927

The players – Mrs M. E. R. Dewhurst, Frl D. Koring, Mlle S. R. F. Lenglen, H. O. Kinsey and K. Kozeluh and reserve Miss V. M. Glasspool.

1	Wednesday 29 June	HENLEY England (Phyllis Court Club)	Rained off
2	Saturday 2 July (5.00pm)	HENLEY England (Phyllis Court Club)	Kozeluh bt Kinsey 6–1 6–2 Lenglen bt Koring 6–1 6–2 Kinsey and Lenglen bt Kozeluh and Dewhurst 6–1 6–2
3	Tuesday 5 July (8.30pm) 5,000	LONDON England (Holland Park Hall – Rink)	Kozeluh bt Kinsey 7–5 7–5 Lenglen bt Koring 6–3 6–0 Kozeluh and Lenglen bt Kinsey and Dewhurst 8–6 3–6 8–6
4	Wednesday 6 July (8.30pm)	LONDON England (Holland Park Hall – Rink)	Kinsey v Kozeluh Lenglen bt. Dewhurst 6–2 6–2 Kinsey and Lenglen v Kozeluh and Dewhurst

5	Friday 8 July (8.30pm)	LONDON England (Holland Park Hall – Rink)	Kozeluh bt Kinsey 8–6 4–6 6–2 Lenglen bt Dewhurst 6–0 6–1 Kinsey and Lenglen bt Kozeluh and Dewhurst 9–7 6–4
6	Tuesday 12 July (6.30pm) 8,000	GLASGOW Scotland (Queen's Park Football Club)	Kinsey bt Kozeluh 4–6 7–5 6–2 Lenglen bt Dewhurst 6–2 6–0 Kozeluh and Lenglen bt Kinsey and Dewhurst 6–4 3–6 6–1
7	Friday 15 July (3.00pm) 7,000	BLACKPOOL England (Blackpool Football Club)	Kinsey bt Kozeluh 6–4 6–3 Lenglen bt Dewhurst 6–1 6–4 Kinsey and Lenglen bt Kozeluh and Dewhurst 6–1 6–4
8	Saturday 16 July (2.00pm) 15,000	MANCHESTER England (Manchester United Football Club)	Kozeluh bt Kinsey 7–5 4–6 6–2 Lenglen bt Dewhurst 6–0 6–2 Kinsey and Lenglen bt Kozeluh and Dewhurst 6–2 6–2

Index

Aeschliman, Charles (SUI) 59, 66, 76, 78, 82
Aeschliman (Bancroft), Mrs Leslie (USA) 84
Aitken, Harold (RSA) 89
Akhurst, Miss Daphne (AUS) 70
Albarran, Pierre (FRA) 13, 23, 26, 103
Altcock, Nick (USA) 97, 99
Amblard, Mlle Blanche (FRA) 8, 10
Amblard, Mlle Suzanne (FRA) 8, 10
Arendt, Mlle Fernande (FRA) 29
Aussem, Frl. Cilly (GER) 110
Austin, Henry (Bunny) (GBR) 119
Austin, Miss Joan (GBR) 54
Ayres, Dr Horace (USA) 96

Balbi di Robecco, Count Mimo (ITA) 84
Baldwin, Mrs Anita (USA) 117
Baldwin, Baldwin (USA) 103, 110, 111, 114, 117, 118, 123
Baldwin, Elias Jackson (USA) 103
Baldwin, (Wilson), Nell Maxime, Mrs (USA) 117, 118, 123
Bancroft, Miss Leslie (USA) 39, 84
Barger-Wallach, Mrs Maud (USA) 4
Barron, Mrs Dorothy (GBR) 59, 85
Bayard, Miss Martha (USA) 39
Beamish, Alfred (GBR) 27
Beamish, Mrs Geraldine (GBR) 23, 27, 31–33, 52–54, 68
Beckett, Mrs D G (GBR) 6
Beckingham, Miss Clair (GBR) 90
Beekman, Leonard (USA) 38
Bennett, Miss Eileen (GBR) 65, 73, 84
Billout (Broquedis), Mme Marguerite (FRA) 26, 47, 70
Bocciardo, Roberto (ITA) 84

Bologna, Sig.na Paolo (ITA) 84
Bonacossa, Count Alberto (ITA) 70, 84
Borotra, Jean (FRA) 41, 44, 45, 47, 61–63, 70, 71, 73, 75, 89, 90, 122, 124
Bouman, Miss Kornelia (Kea) (HOL) 87
Bourgeois, Mlle Yvonne (FRA) 70
Boussus, Christian (FRA) 124
Boyd, Miss Esna (AUS) 70
Brick, Paul (AUT) 71
Bridge, Mrs Kathleen (GBR) 69
Brookes, Norman (AUS) 60, 61
Broquedis, Mlle Marguerite (FRA) 8, 26
Brown, Miss Beatrice (GBR) 89
Browne, Miss Mary (USA) 86, 88, 89, 94, 103, 105, 107–110
Brugnon, Jacques (FRA) 32, 44, 54, 66, 73, 84, 86, 88, 91, 124
Bundy, Miss May (USA) 39
Burke, Albert (GBR) 122
Burrow, Francis (Frank) (GBR) 88
Butler, Miss Bertice (GBR) 6, 10

Cadle, Miss Lesley (GBR) 52
Carpentier, Georges (FRA) 95
Cazalet, Clement (GBR) 78
Chambers, Mrs Dorothea (GBR) 8, 16, 17, 21, 26, 27, 51, 73, 91
Cizelly, Dr (FRA) 3
Clarke, Miss Edith (GBR) 62
Cobb, Mrs Annis (GBR) 14
Cochet, Henri (FRA) 44, 53, 63
Cochran, Charles (GBR) 110, 112, 113
Colston, Mrs Gladys (GBR) 6, 7
Colyer, Miss Evelyn (GBR) 45, 54, 66
Connaught, Duke of (GBR) 78

Connolly, Maureen (USA) 126
Conquet, Mlle Marie (FRA) 8
Contostavlos, Mlle Helene (FRA) 47, 49, 53, 54, 66, 76, 77, 82
Court, Mrs Margaret (AUS) 126
Courtneidge, Cicely (GBR) 120
Cousin, Maurice (FRA) 57
Covell, Mrs Phyllis (GBR) 54, 59, 60
Craddock, Mrs Doris (GBR) 16
Crawford, Jack (AUS) 119
Crawley, William (GBR) 45, 47
Crose, Ben (USA) 102
Cyr, Lt. St. (FRA) 60

d'Ayen, Mlle Elisabeth (FRA) 26, 29, 66
d'Hainault, Mlle Berthe (FRA) 1
d'Hainault, Mlle Eloide (FRA) 1
d'Hainault, Louis (FRA) 1
d'Hainault, Mlle Rachel (FRA) 1
Danet, Mme Marie (FRA) 49
Danet, Roger (FRA) 49, 103
Dale, Miss (GBR) 6
Damin, Mlle S (FRA) 52
Davis, Willie (USA) 39
de Alvarez, Srta Elia (Lili) (ESP) 91
de Borman, Mme Anne (BEL) 10, 29
de Bourbel, Count (FRA) 78
de Bourbon, Prince P (FRA) 13
de Gomar, Count Manuel (ESP) 55–57
de Graffenried, Baron (SUI) 78
de Joannis, Albert (FRA) 33, 36
de Morpurgo, Baron Hubert (ITA) 66, 76
de Rivas, Mlle Elena (FRA) 95
des Landes de Danoet, Mlle Simone (FRA) 66
du Cros, Mlle Pat (FRA) 84
du Pasquier, Pierre (FRA) 52

Decugis, Max (FRA) 8, 13, 14, 26, 29, 32, 73
Dempsey, Jack (USA) 95
Destremau, Bernard (FRA) 124
Dewhurst, Mrs Evelyn (GBR) 88, 89, 111–114
Doust, Stanley (AUS) 27
Dunlop, Alfred (NZL) 8
Dunkerley, R (GBR) 78
Dupont, Marcel (FRA) 52
Dupont, Mme Marthe (FRA) 70

Edgington, Mrs Aorea (GBR) 26, 78
Elizabeth, Queen (BEL) 44
Ellis, Mrs M F (GBR) 45

Feret, Paul (FRA) 95–98, 100, 101, 105, 107, 108, 110, 119
Fick, Mrs Sigrid (SWE) 26, 29
Fisher, Francis (NZL) 78
Flaquer, Eduardo (ESP) 55–57, 61, 103
Fry, Miss Joan (GBR) 69, 86

Gagliardi, Sig.na Rosetta (ITA) 84
Garland, Charles (USA) 27
Gaslini, Placido (ITA) 84, 103
Gault, Georges (FRA) 10, 60
George, Prince (GRE) 78
George V, King (GBR) 16, 45, 86–88
Gerbault, Alain (FRA) 41, 61
Germot, Maurice (FRA) 52
Gillou, Pierre (FRA) 75, 124
Giroud, Mme (FRA) 52
Glanz, Franz (AUT) 71
Glasspool, Miss Vivien (IRL) 111
Gobert, Andre (FRA) 14, 33
Godfree (McKane), Mrs Kathleen (GBR) 87, 91, 111
Golding, Mme Germaine (FRA) 8, 10, 26, 32, 44, 53, 85
Goldsack, Miss Elsie (GBR) 68
Goss, Miss Eleanor (USA) 35, 38, 41, 61
Gould, Mrs Florence (FRA) 61
Gouttenoire, George (FRA) 57
Gouttenoire, Henri (FRA) 57
Graff, Miss Steffi (GER) 125
Gustav V, King (SWE) 26

Hall, Walter Merrill (USA) 39
Hardy, Samuel (USA) 35, 38
Harper, Mrs Sylvia (AUS) 70

Harvey, Miss Ermyntrude (GBR) 65, 73
Hayward, William (USA) 93
Hazel, Mrs Marie (GBR) 54
Hillyard, Cmdr George (GBR) 78, 82, 88
Hirset, Pierre (FRA) 52
Holman, Mrs Dorothy (GBR) 29
Hope, Lord Charles (GBR) 78, 82
Hulbert, Miss A (GBR) 6

Ingram, Miss Margaret (GBR) 54
Ingram, William (GBR) 27

Jacobs, Miss Helen (USA) 118, 119, 122
Janotova, Miss Anna (TCH) 72
Jennings, Joseph (USA) 36
Jessop, Mrs Marian (USA) 35
Johnston, Bill (USA) 95

King, Mrs Billie Jean (USA) 125
Kingsley, Charles (GBR) 73
Kinsey, Howard (USA) 95–99, 102, 103, 105, 107–110, 112–115
Koring, Frl Dorothea (Dora) (GER) 111–113
Kozeluh, Jan (TCH) 72
Kozeluh, Karel (TCH) 71, 72, 110, 112–114, 118

Lacoste, Rene (FRA) 63, 73
Larcombe, Dudley (GBR) 90
Larcombe, Mrs Ethel (GBR) 15, 21, 27
Laurentz, William (FRA) 21
Le Besnerais, Mme Nanette (FRA) 56
Le Conte, Mme Germaine (FRA) 56
Leisk, Mrs Helen (GBR) 29
Lenglen, Eugene (FRA) 1
Lenglen (d'Hainault), Mme Anaise (FRA) 1, 21
Lenglen, Charles (FRA) 1, 3, 10, 118
Lenglen, Phillipe (FRA) 1
Levi (Rosenbaum), Baroness Maud (USA) 84
Locker-Lampson, Cmdr Oliver (GBR) 73
Lumley-Ellis, Miss Sylvia (GBR) 61
Lycett, Randolph (GBR) 27, 52, 55

Macready (d'Ayen), Mrs Elisabeth (GBR) 66
Mallory, Mrs Anna (Molla) (USA) 27, 32, 35–39, 46, 51, 52, 54, 91, 94, 107
Manuel, King (POR) 78
Maria, Queen (ROM) 101
Marcot, Mlle L (FRA) 6
Marnet, Srta Maria Luisa (ESP) 57, 61
Mary, Princess (GBR) 16
Mary, Queen (GBR) 16, 86–89
Mathey, Dean (USA) 38
Mathieu, Mme Simone (FRA) 86
Matthey, Mlle Jeanne (FRA) 46
Mayes, Col Henry (CAN) 59, 73, 85
McKane, Miss Kathleen (GBR) 16, 27, 29, 32, 44–47, 51–54, 63, 66, 68, 87
McNair, Mrs Winifred (GBR) 29
McIlquham, Mrs Mary (GBR) 70
Michael, Grand Duke (RUS) 78
Mills, Mrs David (USA) 39
Mishu, Nicholas (ROM) 73
Moody (Wills), Mrs Helen (USA) 118
Morales, Raimundo (ESP) 57
Morgan, Miss Anne (USA) 33
Morris, Miss Margaret (GBR) 122, 123
Myers, Wallis (GBR) 66

Najuch, Roman (POL) 78, 118
Navratilova, Miss Martina (USA) 125
Neppach, Frau Nelly (GER) 71
Nice Lawn Tennis Club 2–3, 10, 21, 39, 41, 49, 76, 124
Norton, Brian (RSA) 27
Nuthall, Miss Betty (GBR) 110, 111

O'Brien, Bill (USA) 98
O'Neill, Mrs Madelaine (GBR) 23

Parton, Mrs Mabel (GBR) 27
Patou, Jean (FRA) 26
Patterson, Gerald (AUS) 27, 29, 33
Peacock, Mrs Irene (RSA) 32, 33, 45
Peteri, Mrs Ilona (HUN) 85
Pickens, William (USA) 93, 94, 110
Pigueron, Mme Germaine (FRA) 32, 44
Plaa, Martin (FRA) 119

INDEX

Plantier, Sra Angelica (POR) 56
Professional Tour of Great Britain
   Blackpool 113
   Glasgow 113
   Henley 112
   Kensington, London 112
   Manchester 114
Professional Tour of North America
   Atlanta 107
   Baltimore 98
   Birmingham 105
   Boston 98
   Brooklyn 108, 109
   Buffalo 98
   Chicago 100
   Cincinnati 100
   Cleveland 98
   Columbus 100
   Dallas 105
   Denver 101
   Detroit 100
   Hartford 108
   Havana 107
   Houston 105
   Kansas City 100
   Los Angeles 103
   Miami 107
   Minneapolis 100
   Montreal 98
   Newark 108
   New Haven 109
   New Orleans 105
   New York 96
   Oakland 102
   Philadelphia 98
   Pittsburg 99
   Portland 102
   Providence 109
   San Antonio 103
   San Francisco 102
   Seattle 102
   St Louis 100
   Tampa 107
   Toronto 98
   Vancouver 101
   Victoria 101
   Wichita 101
Pudakota, Rajah of (IND) 78
Puget, Mme S A (FRA) 6
Pyle, Charles (USA) 93–96, 98, 99, 102, 110

Ranson, Miss O (GBR) 6
Read, Charles (GBR) 112
Records 131

Redlich, Frau Erna (AUT) 7, 72
Redlich, Frau Maria (AUT) 71
Renshaw, Ernest (GBR) 4
Renshaw, William (GBR) 4
Richards, Mrs Claremont (USA) 95, 103
Richards, Vincent (USA) 39, 95–103, 105, 107–110
Ritchie, Major (GBR) 23
Rodel, Raymond (FRA) 122
Rohrer, Friedrich (TCH) 72
Rohrer, Mrs Gretal (TCH) 72
Rosenbaum, Sig.na Maud (ITA) 84
Royal, Princess (GBR) 47
Runyon, Damon (USA) 93
Ryan, Miss Alice (USA) 6
Ryan, Miss Elizabeth (USA) 6, 8, 10, 16, 23, 26, 27, 31–33, 41, 44–46, 51, 52, 54, 55, 59, 61–63, 65, 66, 68, 69, 76, 86–89, 91

St. George, Miss Floris (AUS) 70
Sabelli, Humbert (GBR) 124
Salm, Count Ludwig (AUT) 10, 70–72
Satterthwaite, Mrs Phyllis (GBR) 10, 16, 31, 32, 51, 52, 76, 84
Schardt, Al (USA) 97, 99
Selfridges Ltd 119, 120
Septier, Mlle M (FRA) 31
Serpieri, Jean (Johnny) (GRE) 110
Simond, George (GBR) 66, 78
Sindelarova, Mrs Maria (TCH) 72
Snodgrass, Harvey (USA) 95, 96, 100–103, 105, 107–110
Soumarokoff, Count Mikhail (RUS) 31, 41, 52
Stocks, Mrs Margaret (GBR) 46
Storms, Mme Marie (BEL) 29
Stromberg von Essen, Miss Lily (SWE) 29
Stuart, Miss M E (GBR) 6

Tarruella, Jose Marie (ESP) 57
Throckmorton, Harold (USA) 39
Tilden, William (Bill) (USA) 27, 32, 33, 95, 96
Tolley, Cyril (GBR) 78, 82
Torras, Srta Rosa (ESP) 57
Tournaments
   Amiens 10
   Antwerp
      Olympic Games 29

Barcelona
   International Championships 57, 61
Beaulieu 23, 59, 64
Biarritz 56, 70
Bordeaux 44
Boulogne 29, 49
Brussels
   World Hard Court Championships 44
Cabourg 21, 55
Cannes
   Beau Site Hotel
      Cannes Championships 13, 52, 64
      April meetings 26, 41
      New Year meetings 7, 23, 31, 51, 65, 76
   Cannes Club
      Cote d'Azur Championships 26, 44, 52, 60, 66, 84
   Carlton Club
      April meetings 8, 31, 84
      February meetings 13, 31, 51, 59, 76
      New Year meetings 7, 23, 31
   Gallia Club 59, 76
   Metropole Hotel 8, 41, 60, 75, 76
   New Courts Club 76
Chantilly 6
Chateau D'Ardennes 55, 70
Compiegne 4, 6, 10
Cromer 73
Deauville 21, 47, 55, 70
Dublin
   Irish Championships 91
Edgbaston 91
Etretat 10, 49
Juan-les-Pins 61
Knokke-sur-Mer 29
La Bourboule 47
Le Havre 49
Le Touquet 6, 7, 21, 29, 49
Lille 6, 10, 44
Lisbon
   Portuguese Championships 56
Marseille 49
Menton
   Riviera Championships 13, 52, 59, 84

Monte Carlo
  Monaco Championships
    (La Festa) 75
  Beau Soleil 31, 41, 84
  Condamine 6, 7, 23
  La Festa 13, 31, 51, 59, 65, 84
New York
  United States Womens
    Championship 34
Nice
  Country Club 8
  February meetings 31, 51, 59,
    65, 76
  New Year meetings 6
  Parc Imperial
    South of France
      Championships 41, 52,
      60, 65, 84
  Place Mozart
    South of France
      Championships 4, 6, 8,
      13, 23, 31
Ostend 29
Paris
  Racing Club de France 13
  French Championships 8, 26,
    32, 44, 53, 66
  Olympic Games 63
  World Hard Court
    Championships 10, 26,
    32, 52

Pourville
  Picardie Championships 6
  other meetings 49, 55, 70
Rome
  Rome Championships 84
San Sebastian 56
Wimbledon
  Worple Road
    The Championships 10,
    14, 26, 32
  Church Road
    The Championships 45,
    54, 61, 68, 86
Wimereux 6

Towle, Sir Francis (GBR) 78
Tripp, Miss M (GBR) 65

van Lennep, Christiaan (HOL) 55
Vaussard, Mme Jeanne (FRA) 26,
    53
Vines, Ellsworth (USA) 119
Vlasto, Mlle Julie (Diddie) (FRA)
    54, 61, 65, 66, 70, 76, 78,
    82, 84, 86–89, 110
Von Krohn, Frl Dagmar (GER) 6
Vienne, Mlle (FRA) 10

Wales, Prince of (GBR) 88
Ward, Miss M (GBR) 7
Washer, Jean (BEL) 51, 54

Washer, Mme Simone (BEL) 70
Wavertree, Lady Sophie (GBR) 27,
    33, 46, 55, 63, 84, 118,
    119
Wesbrook, Walter (USA) 103
Westminster, Duke of (GBR) 78
Wibaux, Mme Leon (FRA) 6
Wightman, Mrs Hazel (USA) 33, 62
Wilding, Anthony (NZL) 7, 60
Wills, Miss Helen (USA) 63,
    75–77, 79, 80, 82, 84, 85,
    93, 94, 102, 118, 126
Wilson, Margaret (USA) 123
Wilson, Rowena Schneider (USA)
    123
Wimborne, Lord (GBR) 21
Winch, Mrs Ruth (GBR) 7
Wolfson, Mme Doris (FRA) 13, 44
Wood, Charles (USA) 109
Wood, Pat O'Hara (AUS) 46
Woosnam, Max (GBR) 29

Zahnova, Miss Renata (TCH) 72
Zay, M (FRA) 124